WARLORDS
OF CRIME

Also by Gerald Posner:

MENGELE: THE COMPLETE STORY

WARLORDS OF CRIME

Chinese Secret Societies— The New Mafia

GERALD L. POSNER

McGraw-Hill Book Company
New York   St. Louis   San Francisco
Hamburg   Mexico   Toronto

1 2 3 4 5 6 7 8 9 DOC DOC 8 9 2 1 0 9 8

ISBN 0-07-050600-0

Library of Congress Cataloging-in-Publication Data

Posner, Gerald L.
   Warlords of crime: Chinese secret societies—the new Mafia /
Gerald L. Posner.
     p. cm.
   Includes index.
   ISBN 0-07-050600-0
   1. Organized crime—Hong King. 2. Organized crime—United States.
3. Drug traffic—Asia, Southeastern. 4. Asian American criminals—
United States. I. Title. II. Title: Chinese secret societies.
HV6453.H75P67 1988
364.1'06'051--dc19
                                   88-9667
                                      CIP

Book design by Kathryn Parise

For my mother and
in memory of my father

Contents

Acknowledgments   ix

Preface   xv

1   Enter the Dragon   1

2   China White   12

3   The Triads   27

4   The Red Pole   44

5   The Politics of Heroin   61

6   Princes of Darkness   78

7   "The Town That Dope Built"   98

8   Too Few Good Men   110

9   The Incorruptible Cop   131

10   "White Powder Ma"   150

11   The Five Dragons   169

Contents

12 The Unicorn   183

13 The Invasion   202

14 The Chinese Laundry   221

15 The Dragon Heads   236

16 The Challenge   248

Bibliography   263

Index   277

Acknowledgments

Writing a book about underworld empires involving tens of billions of dollars in annual profits is a difficult task. Resolved to escape detection and arrest, criminals utilize increasingly sophisticated methods to conceal their identities and their illicit networks. Police are reluctant to supply information that could compromise multiyear investigations if prematurely disclosed in a book. Eventually persistence does pay off, and in this case two years of research yielded results far beyond my original expectations.

During that time I have conducted research in nineteen countries on five continents. I spent months in Europe and Asia, including the heroin-producing Golden Triangle, tracking down leads in the criminal underworld. More than 200 hours of conversations with criminals, money launderers, addicts, and law-enforcement officials were recorded, yielding more than 9,000 pages of transcripts. I reviewed more than 30,000 pages of documents, including nearly 3,000 just declassified by the United States government. I also had access to confidential files of the Royal Hong Kong Police. In addition to Hong Kong, I had full cooperation from the police of the Netherlands, Thailand, and the local police in a number of major U.S. cities, as well as the Drug Enforcement Administration.

I am satisfied I have conducted a diligent and thorough investigation. I take full responsibility for the accuracy of the facts and the validity of the judgments presented. Much of my research would not have been possible without the assistance of many people and organizations. They made the research gratifying and the book possible. Before thanking them I must first pay tribute to my wife, Trisha, and not merely because she suffered in patience while I toiled on this book. She was my fearless, indomitable, and resourceful partner, accompanying me on most of my journeys, even to countries where the work was uncomfortable and dangerous. Often dealing with faceless, unprincipled, desperate people who necessarily inhabit the criminal and narcotics underworld, her unerring judgment and commonsense approach proved invaluable in sustaining my own equilibrium and preventing me from falling into the pitfalls that dot the road of such research. At various times she has played the roles of researcher, secretary, interviewer, organizer, and unofficial editor. There would be no book without her.

Before listing those who aided me in this project in alphabetical order (and omitting some who requested anonymity), I take pleasure in separately mentioning the following friends, colleagues, and experts whose guidance and assistance proved indispensable.

Helping through a myriad of difficulties in Southeast Asia were Michael O'Neil, editor in chief, and Teresa Gibbs, research editor, and Leticia S. Cortan, archive director, of *Asiaweek,* Hong Kong; Alan Farrelly, editor in chief, and Judy Young, archive director, and May Chau, deputy librarian, *The South China Morning Post,* Hong Kong; Derek Davies, editor in chief, and Jan Bradley, archive director, and Emily Lau, reporter, *Far Eastern Economic Review,* Hong Kong; Theh Chongkhadikij, editor in chief, and Arunie Anne Ieamsuri, editorial director, *Bangkok Post,* went out of their way to open doors that would otherwise have remained closed. All of these individuals not only provided unrestricted access to the confidential files of their publications but they also led to unexpected and crucial sources of information.

Tony Paul, the editor of *Asian Reader's Digest,* has developed excellent contacts throughout Asia during his twenty years of investigative field reporting. He was unselfish in allowing me to meet his private sources, people who were critical to the accuracy of the final product.

Members of the Hong Kong police assisted my research in many ways during all hours of the day and night. Without their help much of the information on Triads would have remained hidden. Special thanks must go to Police Commissioner R. H. Anning, who initially set the tone for the full and complete cooperation that greeted me in Hong Kong. Also special acknowledgments to K. L. Mak, Chief of the Customs Investigation Bureau; David Hodson, Senior Superintendent; Sidney Chau and David Thain of the Interpol Bureau, Hong Kong police branch; Gordon Mortimer, Police Commissioner for Narcotics; Brian Webster, Deputy Director of Crime; Brian Merritt, Chief Staff Officer, Serious Crime; John Bagley, Chief Staff Officer, Narcotics; A. P. Lee, Detective Superintendent, Criminal Intelligence Bureau; and T. R. Coombs, Commissioner's Office.

David F. Lee and Benny Kwong used their substantial business contacts in the Far East to assist the research past many difficult stages. Their help went beyond the call of friendship.

In Thailand extensive government files and sources were made available through the persistent efforts of General Chavolit Yodmanee, Director of the Office of Narcotics Control Bureau; Colonel Viraj Juttimita, Chief of the Narcotics Suppression Office; Major Bancherd Pongsiriwan, Commander of the Border Patrol Police, Chiang Mai; and Captain Wipon, Chiang Mai.

Research in the Netherlands would have been stymied without the unselfish assistance of Inspector Richard Weijenburg, National Criminal Intelligence Service, The Hague; and Inspector Arie Bax, Amsterdam police. They spent night and day with me to ensure that I had access to important information.

Without the help of several people in the United States, the story would have been incomplete. John McKenna, former Chief of the San Francisco Police Gang Task Force, is one of the most knowledgeable law-enforcement officers on Triads and Chinese organized crime. He always responded to the smallest requests. Mike Yamaguchi, Assistant United States Attorney, San Francisco, helped the project from its inception. Edith Mirante, director of Project Maje, a New Jersey-based effort to publicize Shan rights, was very helpful regarding the sometimes deadly effects of the U.S.-sponsored herbicide spraying program in the Golden Triangle. She has excellent access to Burmese insurgency groups, and her perspective helped avoid stumbling blocks.

I received substantial assistance from the Drug Enforcement

Administration. Without the concerted help of many agents, much of the information in this book would have been unavailable. Some of the agents cannot be acknowledged because they are currently involved in undercover operations. But to those who can be publicly thanked, I cannot overestimate their importance to this book. They include Stephen Tse, San Francisco; Greg N. Korniloff, Kahn Dougherty, Don Ferrarone, and Morton Goren, Washington, D.C.; Robert Stuttman and Robert Strang, New York; William Wolff, The Hague; Mike Campbell, London; Jim Kennedy and Rolland Hughes, Bangkok; Ben Yarbrough, Mike Bansmere, and Stephen Worobec, Chiang Mai; and Jim Harris and George Harkin, Hong Kong.

With apologies to those I may have inadvertently omitted, I list the following who were most instrumental in bringing this project to fruition:

Jeff Acerson, Orem, Utah; Vera Ajjimanont, Bangkok; Alexander Anolik, Esq., San Francisco; Ron Bass, California Attorney General's Office, San Francisco; Mark Boyd, Hong Kong Information Bureau, New York; Fenton Bresler, London; J. C., Bangkok; Detective Joseph Carone, Chicago; Phisakdi Chakkaphak, San Francisco; Jean Chan, Narcotics Division, Hong Kong; Paul Chang, Dominican Republic; Cynthia Christfield, United States Senate Permanent Subcommittee for Investigations, Washington, D.C.; Robert W. Collins, Monterey Park Police, Monterey Park, California; Tony Crittendon, Bureau of Organized Crime and Criminal Intelligence, Terrorism Section, Sacramento, California; Barbara Crossette, *The New York Times*, Bangkok; Steve Czulegar, United States Attorney's Office, Los Angeles; Michael Di Feo, U.S. Department of Justice, Washington, D.C.; Thomas Donnelly, Police Research, Hong Kong; V. E., Bangkok; Denis Gray, Associated Press, Bangkok; Richard Haynes, Department of the Treasury, Washington, D.C.; Richard W. Held, FBI, San Francisco; Alvin Hickson, State Department, Washington, D.C.; Cat Hon, *The South China Morning Post*, Hong Kong; E. D. Howard, Washington, D.C.; E. K., Bangkok; Joseph G. Ferrara, Esq., New York; Lillian Fong, Los Angeles; Robert B. Kaiman, Federal Reserve System, Washington, D.C.; Akber Khan, Hong Kong; David E. Kaplan, Center for Investigative Reporting, San Francisco; A. E. L., Rangoon; B. L., Hong Kong; Bob Labi, Micro-Rent, London; Malcolm Levene, London; David

Llewellyn, Hong Kong; Chip Lowenstein, United States Attorney's Office, New York; Anne Lugthart, *Panorama Magazine*, Haarlem, Netherlands; S. S. Lung, Hong Kong; Richard Mangan, Drug Enforcement Administration, San Francisco; Dick Mann, Highland Development Project, Chiang Mai; David Marwell, Washington, D.C.; Alice T. McGillion, New York Police Department, New York; Sergeant James McVeety, New York Police Department, New York; A. N., Panama City, Panama; Michael Nearny, United States Attorney's Office, San Francisco; Christopher Nedeau, District Attorney's Office, San Francisco; Commander Benny Ng, Royal Hong Kong Police, Kowloon; Jeanette Oberle, University Microfilms, Ann Arbor, Michigan; Lieutenant Peter Otten, San Francisco Police Department, San Francisco; Nigel Parker, Chiang Mai; Anne C. Paul, Hong Kong; Gloria Posner, San Francisco; Norachai Prasertmanukitch, Chiang Mai; R. T. R., Taipei, Taiwan; Lieutenant Frank Rahill, Police Gang Task Force Commanding Officer, New York; S. Jeffrey Ross, Department of Justice, Washington, D.C.; Joseph Russoniello, United States Attorney, San Francisco; Nancy Ryan, District Attorney's Office, New York; T. D. S., Singapore; Detective James Sakoda, Los Angeles Police Department, Washington, D.C.; Ann Skillian, New York Public Library, New York; David Smith, *Asiaweek,* Hong Kong; Ian Lacy Smith, Deputy Commander, Royal Hong Kong Police, Kowloon; Lionel Stewart, Drug Enforcement Administration, Washington, D.C.; Lee Strickland, Central Intelligence Agency, Washington, D.C.; Sangworn Suntisuk, Chiang Mai; Surapol Tourn-ngern, *Bangkok Post,* Bangkok; Lieutenant Colonel Sawanit Trikityanukul, Bangkok; Sven Van De Kampner, London; Anne Vitale, United States Attorney's Office, New York; Y. W., Penang; Robert Walsh, FBI, Chicago; Michael Wilson, FBI, Chicago; Sylvia Woo, Hong Kong; Lui Yi, VCT, New York; Jim Young, Chiang Rai, Thailand; Y. Y., Bangkok.

Researching a book that requires months of traveling worldwide cannot be successfully undertaken without enormous cost. This project was assisted by the donation of corporate products and/or services. Special acknowledgment is due Zenith Data Systems of America, Olympus Optical Company, Wordperfect Corporation, Silver Reed Corporation of America, Sheraton Hotels (Bangkok), Hyatt Regency (Hong Kong), and Meridien Hotels (Bangkok).

Mere words are but empty expressions in thanking Gladys Justin Carr, vice president and publisher at McGraw-Hill, Peter C. Grenquist, general manager, and Tom Quinn, senior editor. They needed vision to contract for this book and always provided as much cooperation as an author can expect from his publisher. Tom Quinn also shaped the manuscript from early drafts into its final form, and his input and comments were insightful and indispensable to the final product. He stimulated my writing and expedited the completion of this book. As always, I was supported by my friend and agent, Pam Bernstein. Without her impeccable business sense, this project would never have gotten off the ground.

Although this book would not have been possible without the help of everyone listed above, in the end, for whatever was done or was left undone, I accept sole responsibility.

Preface

The concept for this book originated during 1984, when I spent several months in South America researching my last book, a co-authored biography of Nazi fugitive Dr. Josef Mengele. During the course of my Paraguayan investigations, I met neo-Nazis who were business partners with a Corsican heroin trafficker. The Corsican was Auguste Joseph Ricord, the mastermind of the French connection, the Turkey-to-Marseilles-to-New York pipeline that had supplied most of America's heroin through the mid-1970s. While the Nazi sympathizers were reluctant to talk about Mengele, they spoke openly about an issue they thought was safe since I was not writing about it—the heroin trade.

At the time I had a misconception shared by many people. I believed heroin addiction had declined during the past twenty years, and that the big money in the narcotics trade was earned by the Latin American cocaine cowboys. The Nazis and the Corsicans showed me I was wrong. I learned that the number of heroin addicts had doubled within the past decade. It is a growth business, expanding rapidly and turning more than $200 billion annually in illegal profits. And although I determined there was significant heroin cash in South America, I discovered the most powerful heroin and crime empires were in the Orient.

Although I was intrigued by my discussions in Paraguay, it was more than a year, late 1985, before I could devote my full energies to determining whether a story might be developed—a story that broke new ground by pinpointing the dimensions of the problem and highlighting the key players in the trade. What had started as interesting weekend stories in Paraguay developed into a multiyear investigation to uncover the modern heroin trade and the imposing threat of Chinese organized crime.

During the course of my investigations I discovered that the story was not merely the staggering size of the heroin business, or that most of it comes from Southeast Asia, or that it was overlooked by many law-enforcement agencies worldwide. The real story was that heroin served as the backbone of Chinese secret societies called Triads, based in Hong Kong. These criminal syndicates, with branches spread around the world, are the Asian equivalents of the Sicilian Mafia. Since Hong Kong returns to the control of mainland China in 1997, these secret societies are looking to emigrate. The United States is high on their list. I discovered that the Triads control the heroin trade in the United States, and that they are slowly challenging traditional organized crime for dominance of the underworld in both Europe and America. Law-enforcement efforts are sporadic and ineffective.

This book is based upon personal observation as well as research in public and private archives of different nations. Some of the incidents described during the investigations are unique. Among them are visits to an opium den in Hong Kong and a shooting gallery of heroin addicts in New York City; a meeting with a senior Triad officer in a Hong Kong discotheque; an illegal crossing into Burma, accompanied by two young heroin traffickers, to see the remains of a jungle heroin laboratory; a visit to a child whorehouse on the edge of the Golden Triangle; an armed tour with Hong Kong police through a lawless hovel called the Walled City, and all-night surveillance missions with Drug Enforcement agents. I was fortunate to witness these and other incidents. They add a dimension to my understanding, and I hope to the reader's, that could not be garnered from mere library research or interviews.

One final point must be borne in mind. In the following pages a group of criminals are exposed for their systematic and vicious control of large, illicit empires. All of these kingpins are Chinese. During the course of my research I have read many books about Chinese culture and history. I have met many Chinese people. I have great respect for the hardworking, honest nature of the vast majority of Chinese. They are members of a race and culture at the forefront since the inception of written history.

When Moses led the Israelites through the wilderness, Chinese laws and religious knowledge exceeded those of Egypt. They had the wheelbarrow a thousand years before one appeared in the West. Seismographs and compasses were invented in China before the birth of Christ. Hundreds of years before musical compositions were made in the West, the Chinese composed classics which are still played today. While Homer was singing *The Iliad,* Chinese minstrels were celebrating ancient heroes who had already been with them for thirteen centuries. When the inhabitants of the British Isles were still painting their bodies in blue paint and fishing from willow canoes, the Chinese dressed in fine silk robes and had one of the most sophisticated imperial courts the world has known. By the time England was invaded by Norman conquerors, China already had a fully developed literature. The Great Wall was built 220 years before Christ and contained enough material to build a six-foot wall around the globe. The Chinese invented firearms, the art of printing, paper, gunpowder, suspension bridges, and sulfur matches, among a myriad of contributions. In astronomy they sighted the first nova and in medicine compiled a comprehensive pharmacopoeia nearly 2,000 years before Christ.

In America, Chinese immigrants built most of the railroads. Although they were treated worse than any other ethnic minority, legally barred from becoming American citizens until World War II, they have excelled in the United States. The Chinese have demonstrated their talents from computer giants like Wang to one of the world's most profitable banks, the Hong Kong-Shanghai. The Chinese have developed a thumbnail portion of Asia, Hong Kong, into the world's third-largest financial center, right after New York and London.

The same ingenuity and dedication of purpose that allowed the Chinese to develop a culture before the pharaohs and to make Hong Kong a commercial paradise are some of the same traits that have been applied by Chinese criminals, through the secret societies, to create massive underworld empires. Just as legitimate Chinese efforts have produced high yields, the same is true in the criminal world. Although only a small percentage of Chinese may be involved in illegal activities, their impact in crime is disproportionate to their numbers.

As a result of my research I am absolutely convinced that Chinese Triads are the most powerful criminal syndicates in existence and that they pose the most serious and growing threat confronting law enforcement. The gravity of the situation became apparent in a recent arrest by U.S. drug agents. Kon "Johnny" Yu-leung was arrested in New York in March 1988. According to the Drug Enforcement Administration, Johnny Kon's syndicate was responsible for importing nearly one-half ton of pure heroin, worth more than $1 billion, into the United States. The government moved to confiscate $20 million of Kon's property located in San Francisco and New York. But Kon is just one of the new Chinese crime and drug kingpins. Despite his arrest, his syndicate remained largely intact. His arrest was merely the first salvo in a war in which law enforcement is far behind. The problem in the United States and Europe will only worsen as crime bosses like Johnny Kon flee Hong Kong before the colony is returned to the Communists in 1997.

This exposé of the Triads is intended in no way to denigrate the achievement of millions of honest and industrious Chinese. This book focuses only on an unfortunate segment of the Chinese race. Although it does not address the advances of honest Chinese around the globe, it is not intended to slight those advances. But there can be no denial that the Chinese virtually invented organized crime with the Triads, that they exist today, and that together with Asia's heroin syndicates, they are more powerful than ever before. That is the focus of this book.

1

Enter the Dragon

It was Friday evening at 7 p.m., a busy time in the heart of Kowloon's ritziest tourist mecca, Tsimhatshui. Dozens of foreigners and local Hong Kong residents strolled the crowded sidewalks just in front of the large, brightly lit plate glass windows of one of Kowloon's many jewelry salons. Five neatly dressed Chinese men in their late twenties entered the store and spread out before the various showcases crammed with precious stones and elaborate gold and platinum trinkets. Suddenly one of the five strolled behind a security guard who was cradling a shotgun. The young man whipped out a .357 Magnum pistol from under his sports jacket and pressed the steel barrel into the base of the guard's neck. I could not hear what he said, but he screamed something. As the guard let the shotgun drop to the floor and raised his hands, the other four drew .357 Magnums from under their jackets and started screaming and running around, waving their weapons and shoving the terrified customers and employees flat on the floor in the middle of the store.

Two of the gunmen guarded the half dozen people lying on their stomachs, their arms crossed behind the backs of their heads. Inside the store the other gunmen ran around smashing the glass display cases and stuffing the jewelry into sacks they had pulled out of the backs of their trousers. For the shocked pedestrians on the street, the large illuminated windows gave an unobstructed view of the deadly events inside. But someone on the street had enough presence of mind to find some police, as two uniformed foot patrolmen came running around the corner at full speed. They slowed as they approached the scene of the crime and drew .38-caliber revolvers from their leather holsters. I looked at the five gunmen inside the store, frantically trying to finish scooping the jewelry into the canvas sacks. They had no idea that two armed police were only feet away. The police got on their hands and knees and crawled behind the protection of a small slab of marble that served as the base for the store's windows, still out of sight of the gunmen. Unknown to the policemen, the gunmen had finished their jewelry heist and were gathering near the front of the shop to exit in a group.

As the gunmen shuffled close to the front door, the two policemen sprung to their feet, jumped into the doorway, and pointed their guns directly at the burglars. Before the police could even demand that they surrender, the two closest gunmen, their weapons already raised, started blazing their small hand cannons at the two uniformed figures in the doorway. A .357 bullet has enough force to stop a charging 600-pound grizzly bear. Fired at point-blank range, it strikes its target with tremendous force.

The smallest of the police, the one who was almost a step into the shop, had the first bullet hit him in the nape of the neck. It almost decapitated him, a gush of blood shooting back over his shoulder, splattering across the chest of his stunned partner. Another bullet struck him near the thigh, his holster belt splitting in two and flying away. A small stream of blood oozed from his leg as his body spun back and smashed against the side of the store's display window. The glass exploded with a thousand shimmering splinters flying into the street as the uniformed body crashed halfway into the case, the policeman's legs still hanging in the doorway while his torso and almost severed head slammed grotesquely on top of the empty jewelry displays in the front window.

The other policeman got off two wild shots that struck the back wall of the store before the first Magnum hit him square in the stomach, splitting his gut and folding him in two and staggering him backward onto the sidewalk. Passersby were frozen in terror, and I could see some of them screaming although I could not hear any sound from their mouths. The young policeman had started to turn, and I could see his face. I will never forget his look of horror and pain. One of the gunmen came out of the front door and raised his pistol in front of the reeling cop and he pressed the trigger again, this time shattering the policeman's right wrist, making his pistol fly near the curb. The policeman dropped to his knees, bleeding heavily but still trying to contort his body backward to reach his revolver with his still usable hand. The gunman stepped closer and raised his gun. He paused for a moment, and the store's lights reflected off the chrome-plated barrel. Then he executed the young cop in front of a dozen witnesses. He pulled the trigger twice and I could see flashes from the end of the barrel. The bullets struck the cop in the chest, and the uniformed body momentarily lifted off the ground, jerked forward, and settled on the now-crushed rib cage.

Another gunman ran out of the store and joined the executioner. Their adrenaline and emotions at a frenzied peak from the gun battle, they ran up and down the sidewalk screaming things I could not hear and wildly waving their guns. The remaining pedestrians fled in horror, ducking low and hoping that any bullets that were fired would miss them. None were shot. When the street was clear, not sure if more police were waiting around the corner, the two gunmen rejoined their three comrades inside the jewelry shop. Even though the noise from the gun battle had been heard for several city blocks, they stayed inside, apparently arguing frantically over what they should do.

It was a gruesome scene. Five young Chinese men in sports jackets, open shirts, and neat trousers standing in the middle of the store carrying on an animated argument, each holding identical Magnum pistols. Near their feet half a dozen petrified hostages lay trembling on the floor. Between the store's entrance and the front display window a policeman was sprawled out, an ever-increasing pool of blood highlighted by the bright lights. In front of the store lay the crumpled body of another cop, a darkening circle of blood also spreading out into the curb.

Suddenly the group had made up its mind, for again it approached the front door and this time one of the gunmen jumped outside brandishing the security guard's shotgun, waving it up one side of the street and then whirling around and pointing it down the other side. When no one appeared to challenge him, the others assumed the scene was clear. They came out of the store in a tight circle. With their weapons pointed outward and high, they took off in a sprint around the corner into an alley-way. Unknown to them, two more police, this time undercover detectives, had arrived at the scene and were running up the al-ley to reach the store just as the group of gunmen appeared at the other end of the alley. The two police dived for cover be-hind the front of a parked van, while the gunmen stayed in a tight circle, partially hidden by a group of garbage cans.

For the next minute a fierce gun battle erupted. The police reloaded their weapons twice, and the five burglars had their Magnums blazing almost in unison, chipping away small portions of the front of the van. No one was hit by the dozens of shots but the police were clearly at the disadvantage, outnumbered and with much less firepower. Suddenly the gang made a break from their end of the alley and ran toward the van, all the while shoot-ing wildly toward where the police were cowering for cover. The barrage of bullets was so great that while the criminals ran to-ward the van, the police were not able to get off a single shot. The gang made it safely to the side of the parked van and pulled the sliding doors open and jumped inside. When the police heard the doors of the van opening and felt the vehicle shake as peo-ple jumped inside, they realized they had inadvertently chosen the getaway car as their cover in the gun battle.

One of the police raised his pistol to the side window on the passenger side and started shooting wildly inside. As the glass shattered I could see patches of the front seat's upholstery flying into the back of the van, but incredibly not one of the gunmen was hit. When the undercover cop drew his pistol back to reload, one of the gang members lurched over to the smashed side win-dow, shoved his Magnum out of the van, and started emptying it at the crouching policeman. Chips of sidewalk flew up into the air as the bullets slammed into the ground around the cop. Be-fore he was hit he stood up and ran away down the alley as fast as possible, leaving his partner on his own with the five gang members.

The last cop had been crouching on one knee near the front bumper. He jumped up and pointed his gun at the front wind-shield, but before he could get off his first shot, the glass burst from the inside. One of the gunmen had started blazing away at the solitary figure in front of the getaway vehicle. Splinters of flying glass cut into the undercover agent's face. The bullet that broke the windshield found its target, ripping into the policeman's foot and severing his toes. The cop fell into a ball on the floor of the alley, directly in front of the van. Knowing he was crippled, one of the gunman ran to the front, pointed his gun at the policeman's skull, and pulled the trigger. Nothing happened. As that cop would later recount, the gun jammed. The gang member screamed for another weapon, but the van's engine kicked on and the would-be executioner was pulled inside while the driver gunned the van over the prone policeman, hoping they would kill him by running him over. Expecting this assault, the cop lay as flat as possible, bleeding profusely from his ragged shoe. As the van sped away its steel underbelly passed within inches of his bloody face.

"That is still confidential," said the police superintendent as he flicked off the video machine and turned the lights up. I was sitting in a restricted section of the intelligence branch of the Royal Hong Kong Police headquarters. "You're the first person outside of the department to see that film. Two police dead, another disabled for life, and they got away. It took us another seven months to find them."

I was on a trip through Southeast Asia, a journey that would put me on the trail of Chinese secret criminal societies and the largest heroin traffickers in the world. My first stop was Hong Kong.

Those five murderers belonged to one of the largest criminal societies in the British colony. They were foot soldiers for the 14K Triad, a secret society that Hong Kong police intelligence estimates has about 30,000 members. And there are at least fifty secret Triad societies like that in Hong Kong.

"I wanted you to see that film because you are embarking on this research, and it's best you know what you're dealing with," the superintendent continued as he brought me a cup of tea. "The Chinese invented organized crime. And they are the best at it. They have made it into big business and they are absolutely ruthless. I have been in this job for more than twenty-five years and I have a lot of friends in law enforcement in the United States, and I can assure you that these criminal Triads based out of Hong Kong make the Mafia look like child's play. No one else comes close—not the Sicilians, not the Corsicans, not the Colombians, no one."

The Triad societies have existed for hundreds of years. Although headquartered in Hong Kong, they have tentacles spread around the globe, bound together by elaborate ritual, kinship, and the desire to make money. They operate an underground banking system that moves billions of dollars a year without leaving a trace of paper. "And if you are white, you can't get inside," the police superintendent told me as we walked back to his office. "It is a totally closed group of criminal societies. It's taken us here in Hong Kong years to try to understand the background of these criminal groups and to try to develop some methods of fighting them. In Canada and the United States and in Europe, law enforcement is at least thirty years behind us. They are totally perplexed by the Chinese Triads. They hear the unusual names and the strange language and they don't understand any of it, so they leave them alone and hope it all goes away."

The failure of Western law enforcement to cope with the Triad societies is critical as the clock ticks down on a time bomb set to detonate in 1997. That is the year when Hong Kong reverts to mainland China. Hong Kong police intelligence has compiled extensive evidence that the large criminal societies have already prepared to flee to other countries. The underworld syndicates fear they will not be able to work under the Communists, so they will pack up their operations and move to another democracy where they have all the privileges that such systems afford criminals. Where will they go? "Your guess is as good as mine," said the superintendent as he thought for a moment while sipping his tea. "But I am sure the United States is near the top of the list for some of them. That's not to say they aren't already there, but I can assure you that if you get an invasion of criminals in 1997, U.S. law enforcement will be totally unprepared for it and these Triads will have a picnic.

"Look, as well as we know these groups, they can still confound us. The video you just saw is a good example. We had a tip that there was going to be a robbery of that jewelry store. We had set cameras across the street from the shop and on each of the streets from which the criminals could escape. We wanted to record the robbery and the getaway so we could get to their base of oper-

ations. We felt that this group had been responsible for quite a
few armed robberies, and we wanted to get back to their headquarters and smash the syndicate. If we arrested them at the
store, they would just have been replaced with five new gunmen
the next day. The two uniformed police officers who came onto
the scene were not supposed to be there. They did not know that
we were there filming the robbery. But when we saw them come
onto the street there was nothing we could do. If we tried to warn
them, the gang would have seen us and more police might have
gotten shot. It was one of the worst things I ever had to endure,
to watch these murderers kill two policemen, to watch fellow officers walk right into a certain death. That's when it was decided
to arrest them at the scene. So the two undercover officers went
to the street to try to hold them until backup units arrived. Well,
it just wasn't our night because, as you saw, they had the bad
luck of choosing the getaway car for their cover spot in the gun
battle. Those two detectives are lucky to be alive. The one who
was run over would have been dead for sure if the Triad's gun
had not jammed."

"And why did it take another seven months to arrest the gang
members?"

"Ah, that is the key question. Even though we had the van and
the license on film, we couldn't track down the Triad gang. The
van was stolen, and we couldn't even find it. We recovered some
fingerprints from the jewelry shop, but they were inconclusive.
You probably don't realize it in the States, but the Chinese criminal societies establish an enormous infrastructure wherever they
go, and that is true whether they are in Hong Kong or New
York's Chinatown. All Chinese are barred by a wall of silence
when it comes to talking about Triad activities. They could have
stayed underground for a very long time. Eventually we got them
because senior officers in the Triad society decided to slip us the
information on their identities and whereabouts in order to take
the heat off the entire syndicate. We were pressing pretty hard
because there were two dead police.

"And when we found them, we picked them up at an apartment with two kilos of pure heroin. And this brings me to the
last point I want to make to you. You have to concentrate on the
heroin end of the story if you want to do a complete job."

The Chinese criminal syndicates make billions of dollars a year

WARLORDS OF CRIME

8

from all of the regular businesses of organized crime—gambling, prostitution, extortion, loan sharking, protection rackets, murder for hire, and political and civic corruption. But there is one thing that makes them unique. Heroin. They have control over most of the world's heroin supply from the Golden Triangle, a mountainous patch of land covering parts of Thailand, Laos, and Burma that produces more than 70 percent of the world's opium and heroin. It gives them an advantage that other criminal syndicates do not have. It generates staggering profits for the Chinese syndicates, and it is their mainstay. Without heroin they are just another group of criminals. With heroin they have a potential for profit unmatched in the annals of organized crime. The story of the Chinese criminal Triads cannot be told without telling the story of heroin in Southeast Asia.

On that muggy spring day in Hong Kong I had my first glimpse of Chinese gangsters. Eventually, police in Hong Kong, Thailand, the United States, and Europe introduced me to criminals who gave me an unprecedented view of the otherwise impenetrable Chinese drug and crime world. It is a view that few if any journalists have ever seen before.

During my investigations I visited heroin refineries in the jungle, saw caches of heroin hidden in mountain caves, observed dens of addicts in Hong Kong and New York, met key players in the narcotics and crime underworld, and watched firsthand the efforts of law enforcement to slow the unparalleled growth of the illegal syndicates. I went on all-night surveillance missions with U.S. Drug Enforcement agents in the opium-filled hills of northern Thailand. I met Chinese crime bosses in Hong Kong discotheques and Amsterdam restaurants. I saw money-laundering centers clear the illegal profits in places as diverse as a storefront bank in the Bahamas, a casino in the Dominican Republic, and the business nerve center of Hong Kong.

The heroin and crime trail in Southeast Asia involves tens of billions of illegal dollars, insurgent armies commanded by narcotics warlords, exiled Chinese generals directing thousands of troops, Communist guerrillas, Corsican gangsters left over from the Saigon days, and Chinese secret criminal societies, Triads, spread across the globe. It involves corruption at the highest levels of government and police, portions of the private international banking system that have become an integral part of a highly sophisticated network that launders heroin profits into legitimate businesses. It involves the tacit support of the heroin trade not only from some governments but also from a number of national intelligence organizations, including the CIA.

The heroin tail of the Chinese crime dragon can be found in the hills of the Golden Triangle. Originating with nearly 1,500 tons of opium harvested annually from poppies by hill tribes indigenous to the Golden Triangle, the opium is bought by private armies who employ skilled Chinese chemists to convert it to heroin in jungle laboratories before transporting it by mule and horseback to the borders of several Asian countries. From there, by truck, air, and ship, more than 100 tons of heroin are sent to Chinese criminal societies on five continents for distribution to addicts. The heroin leaving Southeast Asia each year has a street value in the United States of more than $150 billion. Law-enforcement agencies around the world, mostly well-intentioned, have little understanding of either the origins of Southeast Asian heroin or the global network of highly sophisticated Chinese criminals that is the backbone of the business. More than two tons of virtually pure Southeast Asian heroin is seized each year by police in dozens of countries, but that is less than 3 percent of the heroin flood.

The annual profits earned by the heroin armies in Asia and the Chinese secret societies around the globe are larger than the gross national products of all but a dozen of the industrialized nations. More money is earned in one year than the entire value of U.S. currency in circulation. The illegal narco-dollars stashed in countries competing for the business earn millions of dollars in interest every day.

And while law-enforcement officials in the United States focused on traditional sources of organized crime, primarily the Italian Mafia, and while antidrug efforts concentrated on cocaine abuse, Chinese Triad societies, with their natural control over much of the world's heroin supply, have built a virtually untouchable business in providing a daily fix to most of the United States' 750,000 heroin addicts.

Chinese heroin is flooding the United States and Europe and law enforcement is only starting to acknowledge it. American narcotics officials have felt that Southeast Asian heroin accounted historically for less than 20 percent of the United States market.

This estimate was based on a testing program developed by the Drug Enforcement Administration and conducted on samples of seized heroin. However, in two 1985 raids on heroin labs, Hong Kong officials were shocked to discover detailed directions so the chemist could make "China White" look as if it was processed in Lebanon or Mexico or another high-priority target on the DEA list. By the addition or deletion of a few chemicals, the top Chinese chemists have disguised their heroin so the DEA lab in Washington will continuously fail to identify the source. DEA agents working on the Chinese syndicates believe that the Chinese have captured more than half of the U.S. heroin market. Classified CIA documents conclude that the traditional view of American narcotics officials that Southeast Asian heroin accounts for only 18 to 20 percent of the United States market is "dated." The CIA-prepared report concludes that Southeast Asian heroin "probably constitutes one-half of the street-level heroin consumed in the United States" and an even "higher percentage in Europe."

In 1986, for the first time, the FBI listed Chinese trafficking groups as a priority target. In a front-page story in 1987, *The New York Times* stated that "Chinese criminals have taken over the dominant role in New York City's heroin industry" and "that Chinese organized crime is on the rise around the country." By 1988 the Drug Enforcement Administration conceded that 70 percent of the heroin arriving in New York was controlled by Chinese syndicates. U.S. law enforcement, understanding neither the language nor the customs of the group it is trying to fight, is at the same stage it was with the Italian mob at the turn of the century. The difference this time is that the Chinese Triads are more sophisticated and armed with much more money than the Italian Mafia. According to a senior officer in the Drug Enforcement Administration, the Chinese criminal groups, together with the heroin syndicates out of Asia, are "the most formidable foe we have ever faced. Period."

As the police superintendent had told me in Hong Kong, although heroin may be the largest money-maker for the Chinese secret societies, in each country where they have settled they are also heavily involved in the traditional businesses of organized crime. Without dealing in a single gram of heroin they would still reap billions of dollars each year from their other illegal ventures. Because they have grown unchallenged in the West, they pose a fundamental problem for law enforcement. To understand how it has been possible for Chinese Triads to develop into some of the most powerful international criminal organizations, and to further understand how heroin has become an ingrained part of political and criminal life in Southeast Asia, it is necessary to examine the historical background of both the Triads and the heroin problem in Asia.

2

China White

Opium poppies were originally discovered growing wild near the eastern Mediterranean, between 5000 to 7000 B.C. Ancient medical journals show that early physicians, including Hippocrates, valued opium as a wonder drug, "a gift from the gods." Although modern doctors know little more about the drug's mysterious soothing properties than did the ancients, there has never been any doubt that it was a revolutionary pain-relieving discovery. Over the centuries opium drew the admiration of the medical community, and in nineteenth-century England the most widely used medicines for ailments ranging from fevers to headaches to the common cold were opium-based compounds like codeine.

While opium was used for thousands of years by physicians, it was not until 1805 that medical science finally extracted pure morphine from pure opium. Considerably more potent than opium and injected directly into the bloodstream for fast relief, morphine was hailed as a modern-day "wonder drug." It became widely used as an anesthetic and a general medication, but an almost blind reliance by doctors on morphine and opium-based prescriptions soon created a serious drug addiction problem.

In 1874, in the midst of a growing boom in the number of opiate-based addicts, an English researcher, C. R. Wright, chemically bonded morphine and a common industrial acid and unexpectedly synthesized a new drug. The acidic bond fortified the morphine and made the new discovery ten times more powerful than pure morphine. Unknown to Wright, the chemical bond also greatly strengthened the addictive characteristics of morphine. The new drug was given the medical name "diacetylmorphine." It took twenty years before German scientists conducting tests with diacetylmorphine would conclude erroneously that the drug cured bronchitis and tuberculosis. Since morphine and codeine users were willing to abandon their habits for the new drug, the German researchers also mistakenly assumed it was a cure for opiate addiction. The Bayer company of Germany, founders of Bayer Aspirin, decided to mass-market the newest wonder drug under the trademarked name Heroin. By 1898, Bayer was having great success in marketing heroin in a dozen countries.

The international medical community hailed heroin as a miracle drug, and most doctors considered it a revolutionary breakthrough for medical science. Within a few years it became one of the most widely prescribed drugs in the world. With millions of people using heroin for treating everything from coughs to toothaches, massive addiction could not be far behind. By 1906 the American Medical Association (AMA) approved heroin for general use in the United States. Unrestricted use by doctors and pharmacists accelerated an already booming drug addiction problem.

In the United States alone there were almost a quarter million heroin addicts by the early 1920s, and in New York City almost 95 percent of all crimes were committed by addicts. By 1924, Congress realized the darker lining to heroin far outweighed the benefits. The drug was banned, but the damage had been done.* A sizable number of Americans had experienced the deep euphoric state induced by heroin, ensuring that a steady stream of customers would be available for opiates. Although the supplier would change from legal pharmacies to an assortment of criminal syndicates, one constant remained—the slavish addiction of the opiate user. Even today the plight of the addict remains much the same as it was hundreds of years ago. During my investigations I twice witnessed dens of addicts in their drug-induced stu-

*Since medical science has never been able to develop an effective substitute for codeine, raw opium is still classified as a vital commodity by the United States and a large cache of the narcotic has been maintained in the U.S. Strategic Materials Stockpile since the end of World War II.

pefied splendor. Those two occasions allowed me to see addiction in such a direct and blunt way that there could be no doubt about the horror of the drug.

In Hong Kong, a city filled with colorful side streets and menacing back alleys, Ladder Street is one of the most unusual. Nestled in central Hong Kong, in the middle of the densest urban population in the world, Ladder Street is two hundred feet of uneven stone steps that zigzag precariously down a very steep incline. It was chiseled into existence in the 1800s so that sedan-chair bearers could more easily carry their human cargo to the wealthy residential enclave of Caine Road. Some of those ornate houses are still jammed along Ladder Street, next to and on top of dozens of minuscule stores hawking fake and real antiques and open-air stalls chocked with rattan, blackwood tables and chests, snuff bottles, and a seemingly infinite variety of porcelains.

Ladder Street is almost always a scene of intense excitement. Packed with traders and workers carrying goods for sale, children scurrying about, and a mixture of tentative but curious tourists, it could be Hong Kong in the early 1900s if not for the occasional gaudy neon sign jutting over the steps.

I was taken there by Benny, a confidential informant to the Royal Hong Kong Police, after being introduced by a senior superintendent in the narcotics division. Benny had a criminal record for gang activities since the age of thirteen. Now twenty-six, he manages a small jade store in Kowloon and claims that although his friends are still involved in the gang business, he is completely legitimate. However, his cover story did not stop him from promising to take me to one of the few remaining underground opium dens, their popularity having dropped because of the increasing use of heroin.

"Only the old-timers smoke opium," said Benny. "If the old ones didn't have a place to smoke, some of them would die. Some of them, they've been chasing the dragon [street slang for smoking opium or heroin] for fifty or sixty years. If they don't get the stuff to smoke, their bodies will not be able to take the change. They'll die and the police know it. So they allow a couple of dens to exist, and as long as they don't get too noisy or large and no other dope is sold there, the police will 'forget' the den is there. Everyone in the neighborhood knows it's there, they can smell it—but no one will complain about a few old guys getting together to smoke a little opium."

On the day I met Benny to go to the den there was a steady drizzle. It was quite warm and humid for an early spring day in Hong Kong. Benny was one of the truly fat Chinese I met. He looked as if he was ready to go on a gambling junket to Las Vegas, dressed in a pair of black crocodile loafers with white socks, gray trousers, a black silk shirt, and an astoundingly bright and shiny blue silk blazer with an extra-large black paisley pattern embroidered on it. The cheeks of his Buddha-like face moved like jelly as he walked about, an engraved ivory toothpick always dangling from very yellow teeth. A mild case of asthma made his breathing labored.

"I'm taking you to a place where some of my friends provide the protection. [I would later learn it was Benny's former gang.] I've told them I met you when I was in the States last year and that you are a writer, so it's okay to look nosy. I've told them you are okay, no pictures, no names, no talking to the police, just in case. Anyway, they think you're pretty strange to want to see a smoking den—it's not going to be much. I'm sure you'll be disappointed."

Benny underestimated the impact of an opium den on a Westerner who is totally uninitiated in the Asian drug world. As I would soon see, it is a quick glimpse at hell. It is man in a state where he has sunk so low, it is embarrassing to be part of the species.

So it was my journey with Benny that took me to Ladder Street. And close to Hollywood Road, near the Thieves Market, we walked into an ancient house with a wooden balcony and elaborate carvings around the door, past an open-air fresh-orange-juice stand, and up two flights of stairs to a small landing. In a dimly lit hallway a young Chinese boy, sixteen at most, his head almost completely shaven, putting on a great air of "toughness," sat on a wooden box in front of a closed door. Benny spoke to him in Cantonese. The boy vaguely seemed to acknowledge Benny, and after a momentary hesitation he opened the door and let us enter.

I walked into a dimly lit room, maybe ten by fifteen feet, with dark green curtains pulled low over the only windows at the far end. There was one weak, naked light bulb hanging at the end of a group of exposed wires dangling from the center of the ceiling. Several opium lamps on the floor added a soft eerie glow. The walls and the floor were filthy, from what I could see, black from years of neglect and smoke. The air was oppressive, filled with a pungent and thick smoke.

Eight wooden platforms with soiled matting were lined up in the room. Only four Chinese were inside. Three appeared to be in their sixties. One seemed much younger, although in the darkness it was difficult to determine age very precisely. Three of the Chinese lay curled up on the beds, in different stages of the opium dream state. Their faces were gaunt, their skin chapped and cast in almost a greenish tint, their eye sockets were deeply sunken. They could have been Chinese or white or black—their drug addiction mattered more than their race. They had the universal look of a junkie, a nationality all its own.

Benny and I stood near the doorway and watched the youngest man, who seemed to have recently arrived, as he devoted his full concentration to the ritual of smoking opium. A small lamp was on the floor in front of him, and a pipe with a long stem and a bowl were next to him on the bed. With a thin metal rod he speared a ball of opium the size of a large pebble, and then held the opium over the lamp's flame. When it was on fire he jammed the burning opium into his pipe bowl, and then he put his pipe bowl over the lamp. As the opium fried he inhaled deeply on the long stem. He cooked the lumps of opium repeatedly, packing them deeply into the pipe and trying to keep the valued smoke from wasting out the side of the lamp.

After maybe ten minutes he dropped the pipe from his hand and leaned back against the wall. There was a glaze over his eyes, which were almost closed—he had entered the opium dream state. I realized that during the entire time Benny and I had been in that hovel, no one had spoken a word. Aside from Benny's constant wheezing and the gurgling of the opium juices in the smoker's pipe, the drug den was like being in a mausoleum.

At that point the door behind us was opened, letting a slash of light into the room, and a Chinese man, in his late fifties or early sixties, in a traditional Chinese black work robe, entered. When he saw Benny and me, he immediately became very agitated and started yelling at Benny in Cantonese. He gestured wildly, but his histrionics barely moved the four opium dreamers, only one of whom turned over on his bed to stare through a deep stupor. Benny grabbed me by the arm and led me out of the room, the Chinese man still yelling, while the Chinese guard boy at the door had a grin from ear to ear, evidently enjoying my discomfort at this outburst of anger.

Even though the drizzle was warm on my face, it was like a refreshing shower after the dirt I felt covered me from ten minutes in the opium den. "They don't like feeling like they're in a zoo, watched like circus animals," explained a chagrined Benny. "They don't even like it when we go up to look, but, man, when he saw your white face, it really made him lose it. It's a very private trip they take in that room, and you were a bad omen to him before he chased the dragon."

"What was he saying when he was screaming?"

"He said I was stupid to bring a foreigner. That I had no respect for what was happening there. The old guys, they are always talking about respect when they can't think of anything else to say. I don't think he has seen a white face there for a long time, maybe never. Maybe it wasn't such a good idea. I told you there was nothing there. Well, I don't have to argue with an old smoker. He's probably all fucked up anyway."

Less than one month later, 13,000 miles from Hong Kong, it was spring in New York City. There was no drizzle and no muggy weather like in Hong Kong, but on a very crisp April afternoon a black New York shoeshine man, J.J., a man with a twelve-year heroin habit, was escorting me to a drug "shooting gallery" on the Lower East Side of Manhattan. The shooting gallery is the modern-day American equivalent of an opium den, a place where addicts gather to buy heroin and share dirty needles and nod in a narcotic stupor.

J.J. was in his mid-thirties, although he looked ten years older. Tall and very thin, he sported a close-cropped Afro and had an enormous smile, which was notable for two missing teeth. He took me near Avenue A, a hectic part of the city, packed with tenements, filled with mostly Hispanics, a smattering of Italians, and recently an influx of New Wave punks who found some of the run-down housing cheap enough to afford. Across the street from a small bakery was a dilapidated five-story brownstone. The

first floor had its windows sealed shut with gray metal sheets. J.J.
took me to the third floor, past graffiti-pockmarked walls, to a
landing where a couple of enormous thugs were sitting by a cardboard box on which they played cards. The two toughs, one
dressed in black leather pants and a T-shirt, the other in jeans
with a leather vest, had long greasy hair and both sported various tattoos on their exposed arms—they could easily have been
members of a motorcycle gang. I thought of how different these
guards looked compared to the sixteen-year-old flyweight who
stood in front of the opium den in Hong Kong. If a guard was
supposed to intimidate, these two hoods certainly did a better
job than the Chinese bean pole on Ladder Street.

"Hey, man, you doing today?" (injecting or smoking heroin)
one of the bikers asked J.J.

"Nope, not now."

"How about him? Is he doing?"—pointing at me.

"Nope, he's just looking."

"Is he clean?" (not with the police).

"Yeah, he's okay."

"Well, no one just comes to look here. Unless you got a reason
for me to say okay."

J.J. had told me that I would probably have to pay something,
"tea money" as the Chinese call it, to get inside. J.J. had probably arranged my visit beforehand and would later split the $100
I handed over to the fattest of the pair of bikers. If he did split
it, I knew it would be quickly spent inside the third floor of that
building.

"Five minutes, jack. That's all. Come out on time so I don't
have to come and get you, and don't bother no one and don't
talk to no one," the biker told me as he unlocked a metal-rein-
forced door and let us inside.

My first impression was that it was very different from the
Hong Kong opium den. I was struck by the light. Shades were
pulled open, and some windows were even open a crack. It was
not merely one room, but an apartment, stretching into four
rooms. The place was run-down, chipped and peeling pale green
paint in every room. Chunks of plaster were missing from the
ceiling and some parts of the walls. There was less furnishing
than in the Hong Kong den, not even soiled beds.

There was no smell of narcotics. While the New York addicts

sometimes mixed other drugs with heroin, sometimes LSD, sometimes barbiturates or cocaine or amphetamines, they evidently did not smoke anything that left a drug cloud hanging about. The air was still foul and stagnant, but here the smell came from a mixture of human sweat and small, rotting piles of garbage around the apartment.

The shooting gallery was also much more crowded than the Hong Kong den. Almost twenty people were spread out in the four rooms, lying against the walls and sprawled out on the floor. Some were sitting up, nodding back and forth in a drug-induced hypnosis. One young black woman, her face soaked in perspiration, her hair matted in clumps across her forehead, her eyes dazed and staring at the ceiling, had a young baby near her feet, maybe one year old, a pacifier stuck in its mouth.

It did not take me long to realize that the initial feeling of the apartment being light and airy was an illusion. It was squalid. Near the front door somebody had urinated and now the smell of urine mixed with the remaining decay.

Most of the addicts were much younger than the four Chinese opium smokers I witnessed in Hong Kong. But they had the same emaciated faces, caused by the heroin monkey eating away their insides. The eyes were dead. They looked right through me as I passed in front of them. There were blacks, Hispanics, whites, men and women. A young woman, her face covered with acne, with a very short white punk haircut, leaned against the wall trying to tie a rubber tube around her arm so her veins would pop up enough so she could find them with a needle. Before she could even finish getting her arm ready, much less prepare her heroin hypodermic, the biker came in.

"Time's up, jack. Want to pay again?"

I had seen enough. I nodded no and walked outside with J.J., who explained to me that apartments like that existed throughout the city.

"That one's in between. Some are really the shits inside and some are really cool. The big ones even have junk [heroin] to buy. Here, this is small. A dude [a narcotics pusher] come in every couple of hours with some junk in case you out, but it ain't worth his time to hang out here."

"Do you bring your own equipment?"

"You can. But most shooters know if they come, they can get

a pin [a hypodermic needle] from someone. All the shit to get the junk ready, that's always here."

"Aren't you worried about AIDS? Don't you think by sharing needles you might catch AIDS?"

"Shit. Everybody scared of AIDS. You just got to know the people you taking the pin from. I ain't shootin' with no fags."

J.J.'s attitude is unfortunately not unusual among New York heroin addicts. There is a woeful lack of understanding of how acquired immune deficiency syndrome is spread, and New York police estimate that up to 60 percent of the 400,000 New York City addicts could be infected with the AIDS virus. According to the Center for Disease Control in Atlanta, intravenous drug users are the main infecting agent for the heterosexual population.

In that way J.J. was typical of heroin addicts I met during my investigations. Obtaining the drug was their overriding concern, nothing else mattered, not even life and death. The intense physical craving caused by the narcotic had developed a dominating addiction.

Separated by half the globe—a Hong Kong opium den with a few elderly Chinese and a New York City shooting gallery for heroin, filled with young people of all races, seeking the ultimate thrill from the most dangerous of narcotics. These addicts are related by their addiction, their inability to kick a powerful habit.

Despite heroin's devastating effects, the deep euphoric relief is inducement enough to keep the number of heroin addicts growing ever larger. In June 1971, when the American heroin population approached 500,000 users, President Richard Nixon declared a "war on drugs" and sent Congress an emergency appropriations bill of $340 million to "combat heroin." He called heroin a "deadly poison in the American lifestream," concluding that he "considered the heroin addiction of American citizens an international problem of grave concern to our nation." As I discuss in Chapter 5, while Nixon was declaring heroin public enemy number one, his own CIA was actively involved in the cultivation and encouragement of the opiate trade in order to win allies in the Vietnam conflict. Whether Nixon was aware of the complicity between the narcotics industry and the CIA is not clear.

What is clear is that the concerted effort of the United States to defeat the heroin problem has been a dismal failure. Even though Nixon targeted heroin, much as the Reagan administration has targeted cocaine abuse, the drug continued to spread across the United States. Today, sixteen years after the war on heroin was launched, the number of heroin users has increased to almost 750,000. The law-enforcement effort was unable even to keep the population static. And there are myriad problems caused for society by that large group of addicts. Nearly three-quarters of America's urban crime is caused by heroin addicts to maintain their habits. In New York City alone addicts steal almost a billion dollars a year to keep the heroin flowing. The average addict spends more than $20,000 a year on the drug.

The addict population consumes seven to eight tons of heroin a year, almost $20 billion of street-valued heroin. And most of that heroin comes from the mountains of Southeast Asia. America's heroin addicts are the final link in a chain of events that begins in early autumn every year when tens of thousands of farmers across a 4,500-mile stretch of rugged mountains from Turkey to Laos plant millions of tiny poppy seeds in their fields. About three months after planting, each poppy seed has blossomed into a narrow stem nearly four feet tall and topped with brilliant large flower petals, the colors ranging from neon oranges and shocking pinks and deep purples to blood reds. One of the most stunning natural sights is the annual late-November flowering of the poppy, when hundreds of thousands of acres throughout Asia are drenched in a solid floral carpet of glorious color. Gazing at that scene, it is hard to imagine that a plant so beautiful can produce a product that causes such misery and heartache. But this is precisely what happens. The only usable product of the poppy is opium. It is from these flowers that the destructive consequences of opium flows through Bangkok and Hong Kong on its way to the streets of America.

The process has been repeated for thousands of years. After the poppies have blossomed into their striking flower phase, the petals gradually drop to the ground and a green seed pod, about the size and shape of a small egg, is left standing. For reasons still unexplained by botanists, the green pod produces a thick white sap, which is opium. Once the pod produces the milky sap, the farmers have only a few days to harvest the drug. In the early evening hours entire families enter the fields and use primitive curved knives to cut the green pod with a series of shallow incisions. The white sap oozes onto the outside of the pod where it congeals. Overnight, exposed to the air, the sap turns a brownish-black color, and at sunrise the peasants enter the fields to scrape the dark sap off the pod's surface. Each poppy yields a morsel of opium a little larger than a pea, and after being wrapped into a poppy petal, the opium is placed in a wooden box carried on a string around the worker's neck. After a couple of hours the box is filled with the foul-smelling muddy sap, similar to bitter mold.

Each acre produces only two kilos (4.4 pounds) of opium. Yet the Golden Triangle, the mountainous, mist-shrouded area covering the four northern provinces of Thailand, the western fringe of Laos, and a broad stretch of northeast Burma, has increased annual production in recent years to nearly 1,500 tons of raw opium. Burma alone produces some 900 tons a year, enough when processed into heroin to supply the United States heroin population for more than ten years. To the hill tribes that produce the opium, it is simply their best cash crop. In order to sell it, the farmers do not even have to leave their homes. Drug traffickers and opium warlords send their agents to the tribal villages to buy opium. With other crops like coffee, rice, and potatoes, the hill tribe farmers must transport the crops to the lowland markets in order to make any money. If the market is flooded with an extra supply of food crops, the farmer must sell at low prices because the crops are perishable, and unless he sells he stands the real risk of losing his entire crop for the year. Sometimes the food crops spoil en route from the Golden Triangle to the lowland markets. In contrast, opium does not suffer rapid deterioration. It can be stored for a couple of years. Since there is no fear of losing the crop as time passes, if the market price is not good, the hill tribe farmer can hold onto his opium until the price improves.

Opium is also the best complement to the style of farming preferred by the hill tribes of the Golden Triangle. At the end of each rainy season the farmers use bush knives and axes to chop trees and local vegetation, let the wood and brush dry for nearly a month, and then burn them. Each year small fires cover large portions of the Golden Triangle, leaving a thick acrid smoke lingering over the countryside. When the fires have died out, the hill tribes strip away the topsoil and pulverize the ash into the fresh ground. The ash acts as an astringent fertilizer, ideally suited for opium, and produces excellent opium yields. The hill tribes do not replace any minerals in the soil, and the poppy plants rapidly exhaust the nutrients, so that this slash-and-burn agriculture ravages the arable land. Within a few years the soil is completely exhausted. During the ten to fifteen years it takes the soil to replenish itself, the hill tribes move on and settle elsewhere, leaving behind barren hilltops and deforested slopes. If the population increases too quickly and the hill tribes return too often to areas already despoiled, the land becomes so degraded as to be permanently useless. But the semi-nomadic hill tribes do not recognize the devastating effects of either their agricultural methods or their crop.

In addition to the good cash prices for opium and the ease with which hill tribes market the crop, combined with the way opium complements the slash-and-burn agriculture, there is a final reason for the hill tribes' involvement with opium—addiction. For over two hundred years these native tribes have not only cultivated the drug but have smoked it for both medicinal relief and as a soothing escape. Opium plays many roles in the hill tribes' existence: it is prepared with sugar and eaten as biscuits and cookies as well as many other traditional cooking recipes; it is mixed with liquids and used as a sleeping aid, and in its raw and refined states it is eaten, smoked, and offered as a sacrifice during tribal ceremonies ranging from funerals to prayer sessions. Even in the important ritual of marriage, opium, cattle, silver, and guns are the only treasured commodities that can buy a bride for a man. To the hill tribes opium has become an integral part of their culture—a socially accepted usage similar to a cocktail at the end of the day in Western culture. While missionary groups have had some success in convincing the hill tribes that opium has devastating side effects, a significant percentage of the ten million hill tribe population still use opium or, increasingly, one of its derivatives, morphine or heroin.

Although the hill tribes are an indispensable first link in a narcotics chain that culminates with diluted heroin powder on the streets of Europe and the United States, their raw opium cultivation is not a very profitable business. Hill tribes are often paid by Chinese merchants or the opium armies in household goods

such as salt, matches, pots and pans, and cloth, for which they
are charged exorbitant prices. The cash payment for the opium
averages $40 per kilo, or $80 for every acre harvested (an amount
of opium worth more than $400,000 when processed into her-
oin and sold at the street level in the United States). If the hill
tribes need additional household goods or cash, the traffickers
will lend them the necessary money, charging an interest rate of
20 percent or more, guaranteeing that the farmers are slaves to
the opium crops in order to pay their debts. In recent years some
of the opium armies in northern Thailand and Burma have cultivated tens of thousands of acres under their own control, and
they invariably pay the hill-tribe people who harvest the crop in
small doses of refined heroin. Not only is this cheap for the opium
armies, but it ensures an increasing addict population and a work
force that will continue to make itself available in order to maintain its new narcotics habit.

The transformation from raw opium to morphine takes place
in jungle or mountain laboratories, many of them close to the
poppy fields. Transported to the labs by hundreds of horses and
mules in long caravans guarded by armed troops, the morphine
process reduces the raw opium to one-tenth its original weight
and size, making the smuggling of morphine bricks much easier. Although the quality of the labs and the proficiency of the
chemists vary widely, the process used to convert raw opium into
a pure morphine base is the same worldwide.

First, the chemist heats water in a large oil drum. When the
temperature is high enough, the raw opium is dumped into the
drum and stirred until it dissolves. At the key moment the chemist adds lime fertilizer, scoops out the layer of frothing white water at the top of the drum, and passes it through a flannel cloth
into another heated drum. While the solution is heated a second
time, concentrated ammonia is added, causing the morphine to
solidify into chunks and drop to the bottom of the drum. Special
care must be taken with the second heating, for if the water is
allowed to boil, the entire morphine production will be destroyed.
When dried and packed for shipment, it takes only a fraction of
the space and manpower required for the original opium.

Some of the drug warlords then process the morphine directly
into a form of heroin. Others ship the morphine base to more
sophisticated labs in the Golden Triangle, or the morphine may

be processed at labs in Hong Kong or, increasingly, at new labs in Europe. The refinement to heroin is much more complicated than the process to morphine, and a mistake can cause the trafficker to lose his entire shipment. A top-notch chemist can extract the most heroin from the morphine, and the best chemists in the heroin business are invariably Chinese. Although Marseilles had some excellent Corsican chemists before the destruction of the French connection in the 1970s, since then the Chinese have dominated the clandestine laboratory phase of the heroin business.

The chief chemist and several apprentices use an array of crude and basic instruments to chemically bond the morphine molecules with acetic acid to form virtually pure heroin. First, the chemist combines an equal amount of morphine and acetic anhydride into a large glass flask and heats it at exactly 185 degrees Fahrenheit until the two have totally dissolved, a task which can take up to six hours. Then impurities are removed from the flask, and both water and chloroform are used to raise the strength of the mixture. The solution is then drained into another flask. When sodium carbonate is added, crude heroin crystals form and start dropping to the bottom. A small suction pump pulls the heroin particles out of the flask, and then they are heated together with alcohol and charcoal, leaving a granular substance.

The next steps determine whether the chemist will make heroin number 3 or heroin number 4. Heroin number 3 is a whitish-brown powder that is 65 to 70 percent pure heroin and is only smoked, either in a water pipe or dusted onto a plain cigarette. Heroin number 3 is widely used in Asia and in Europe by millions of addicts, and it was also the major addicting drug for young GI's stationed in Vietnam. Heroin number 4 is only for injection with a needle. It is the heroin of choice by America's addicts. Heroin number 3 cannot be used with a hypodermic or it will clog the needle. Heroin number 4 cannot be smoked or it will evaporate. As produced in the labs of Asia, heroin number 4 is virtually pure heroin. When sold on the streets in America, it is often cut by middlemen to less than 3 percent purity.

If the expert chemist has orders to make a batch of number 4 heroin for the American market, he finishes the steps described above, places the heroin into a large flask, and dissolves alcohol over it. As he then adds ether and hydrochloric acid, white flakes begin to appear. In the hands of an untrained chemist, the volatile ether gas can explode, leveling the lab and destroying the heroin. But if done correctly, the flakes are then filtered out under strong pressure, and the resulting fine white powder is 99 percent pure injectable heroin. It is the purest form of the narcotic ever known, and in the drug trade it is called "China White." It is now ready for shipment and distribution to addicts around the globe.

The logistics of heroin, from the growth of the poppy to the cultivation of the opium to the refinement of the heroin, has stayed the same since the respective discoveries for the use of the drugs. While the cultivation techniques may differ among the hill tribes, and while the motivations may be complex, there is no question that the end result, about 1,500 tons of opium during a bumper crop, makes the Golden Triangle the number one narcotics-producing region on the globe. More than half of that amount may eventually leave Southeast Asia for export, after being refined into morphine or heroin. In contrast, the world's second-largest opium producers, the Middle Eastern countries of Afghanistan, Pakistan, and Iran (dubbed the "Golden Crescent"), produce some 600 tons. Less than 15 percent is exported, the vast majority being consumed by local addicts. Only ten to fifteen tons of opium are required each year to satisfy the world's legal medicinal demand. The extra production of more than 2,000 tons is used only for illicit consumption. And almost 70 percent of that illegal production is from Southeast Asia's Golden Triangle.

In large part the Golden Triangle has achieved this dubious distinction because Southeast Asia has had a pervasive and deep-rooted opium problem for hundreds of years. It was a narcotics curse forced upon the Asian countries by the greed of the great European colonial powers and later by the intelligence agencies of modern-day Western nations. Having had opium pushed down their throats for two hundred years by the British, French, Dutch, Americans, and others, Southeast Asians are now exporting their main crop with a vengeance.

3

The Triads

Hong Kong is a city where money is god, a city that consumes cash in such a conspicuous manner that even Beverly Hills seems tame in comparison. Hong Kong is all about making money and gaudy signs of success are plentiful—pink Rolls-Royces and pink mink coats on warm spring evenings, jewel-encrusted gold watches for sale in seemingly every other store, private nightclubs that charge businessmen $1,500 just to sit with a hostess for several hours, personalized license plates with lucky numbers that cost drivers up to $175,000, the world's most expensive office building cast in marble and glass at a cost of $1 billion. The list is endless. Hong Kong is a testament to the lives of its successful and wealthy residents. From a desolate group of scattered islands and a thumbnail portion of mainland China, Hong Kong has evolved into the world's third-largest financial center, right on the heels of New York and London. It is a city where a handful of mega-rich Chinese move from one social excess to another.

Yet it is also a jittery city. The Joint Declaration signed between the People's Republic of China and Great Britain declaring that Hong Kong would be returned to mainland China in 1997 has made many Hong Kong residents feel they are living on borrowed time. The result is an explosion of people trying to live out assorted garish fantasies of *Lifestyles of the Rich and Famous* before the People's Republic takes final control, a takeover that portends possible austerity. Even if the party continues, it is likely not to be the same no-holds-barred bash that is now consuming the city. Although Hong Kong probably will be an indispensable source of revenue and prestige for the People's Republic, the spartan leadership in Peking may well curtail some of the social excesses caused by the conspicuous rich in a city that prides itself on being the frenzied center of international capitalism. The uncertainty of what the mainland may do once the Communist flag flies over the British colony is accelerating the compulsive behavior of the ultrarich. Benny Kwong, an executive in charge of Manufacturers Hanover Trust's Hong Kong commercial development, has lived in the colony since his birth: "It is an unnatural world in many ways. People have a lot of money, and I mean as much money as any place in the world, and they spend it like there is no tomorrow. And for many of them the tomorrow is 1997. They have ten years left to finish an era that they believe is unique and will never exist again. It would be like someone coming to the United States in the middle of the Roaring Twenties and telling the country that the stock-market crash and the Great Depression were only five years away. As crazy as the Roaring Twenties might have been, I am sure if people had a certain date when they knew it would all be over, they would have pushed themselves even harder and closer to the limit. There is little saving for tomorrow. Oh, there is definitely a lot of legal and illegal money flowing out of Hong Kong to safe countries around the world, but a lot of it is staying right on this island and is being spent at unheard-of rates. It is as if everyone who has done well is standing up and saying, 'Look at me, I can spend $3,000 on dinner, or I can buy a new Mercedes every six months,' or whatever. It's their way of saying 'I've arrived. I've made it and made it in a big way.' No one in Hong Kong cares how you've made your money. They just are impressed that you have it and that you spend it."

In the middle of this glitzy fervor sits the Canton Disco, a temple to those who worship at the altar of capitalism. Situated in Harbour City, a sprawling, modern residential and shopping complex near the Star Ferry terminal in Kowloon, the Canton Disco is a multistoried, multimillion-dollar lighting-and-special-effects mecca for late-night revelers and dancers. Subtlety was not part of the design, which consists of layers of exposed high-tech machinery set against a backdrop of dark colors splashed on the walls. By midnight the club is packed with a thousand young Hong Kong partyers, lined ten deep at the curving bar, the latest thumping-bass-saturated disco song blaring over dozens of gargantuan speakers.

It is to the Canton Disco where Benny, the Buddha-shaped former gang member who had escorted me to the opium den on Ladder Street, directed me on a spring night. In this citadel of late-night Hong Kong money I was sent to meet a Triad member, code number 426*, an enforcer for the Sun Yee On Triad.

This encounter would put me in contact with a representative of a secret society with more than three hundred years of Chinese history behind it. Triad societies, represented by an equilateral triangle, each side signifying one of the three basic Chinese concepts of Heaven, Earth, and Man, were not founded for criminal purposes but as patriotic secret organizations. Their members, bound by blood oaths, were pledged to overthrow the foreign conquerors of their country and to restore the previous ruling house of China, the Ming dynasty, to the imperial throne. Although versions of secret societies are reported in Chinese history nearly 1,500 years before Christ, the modern-day Triad societies were founded in the late seventeenth century, only thirty years after the Manchus, the "barbarian" tribesmen from Mongolia, had swept over the Great Wall and placed the country under foreign domination. The Manchus had an iron grip on the northern two-thirds of China, but they faced continued rebellion in the south. A rallying point for the anti-Manchu sentiment in the south was the Foochow monastery, where 128 militant Buddhist monks organized the local population into pockets of resistance.

By 1674 the Manchus had consolidated their hold on northern China and were powerful enough to send a large contingent of armed troops through the unsettled southern provinces to the

*Triad members are assigned numbers, together with traditional titles, depending on their rank. The numbers are always divisible by 3, a number the Chinese consider magical. So a Triad leader is called the "Hill Chief" and also assigned number 489. The 426 I met at the Canton Disco is called a "Red Pole" and is in charge of all physical enforcement. All Triad positions have corresponding numbers, even to the ordinary members. The numbers are the intricate result of combining various Chinese superstitions with the numerical representations for creation, longevity, and rebirth. The numbers also hinder the police task of pinpointing Triad officers, since the gangster is always referred to by his number and never by his real identity.

monastery. According to legend, during the course of a relent-less military assault, the monks, who had developed and special-ized in a form of self-defense they called kung fu, remarkably held out against the Manchu assault for nearly three weeks. But a traitor among the monks helped the Manchu troops, disguised as coolies, to enter the monastery's sacred grounds through se-cret underground tunnels. Once inside, the Manchus torched the monastery and attacked the surprised defenders—only eighteen monks escaped the ensuing slaughter. The Manchus relentlessly hunted the escaping Chinese patriots, finding and brutally killing thirteen of them. But five of the Foochow monks escaped the wrath of the Manchus, and these five are credited with founding the first Triad society, with the avowed purpose of overthrowing the Manchu dynasty and restoring a Chinese imperial govern-ment.

Just as the massacre of Davey Crockett and a handful of Texans at the Alamo served to ignite Texas's fight for independence from Mexico, the bloodletting at the Foochow monastery served as a rallying point for further revolution against the foreign rulers of China. The first Triad members were bound together by an intricate system of secret rituals, oaths, passwords, and ceremo-nial intermingling of blood. Over a period of years the societies developed complex initiation rituals combining methods of an-cestral and astral worship, segments of Buddhist, Taoist, and Confucian philosophies, all mixed with mythology. New recruits were often given rigorous physical tests, instructed in the history of the Triads, and then sworn to thirty-six oaths promising al-legiance to the society and to fellow members before even one's own family or life. Sometimes animal blood or the blood of new recruits was mixed into a glass, and a small portion would be drunk by each new member to signify not only a blood broth-erhood but also that blood would result if they violated their freshly sworn oaths.

The secret societies spread like a fever across southern China and soon flourished throughout the entire country. As the Man-chu dynasty was increasingly riddled with corruption, it disen-franchised millions of people, and the role and stature of the societies expanded. The Manchu rulers fragmented traditional Chinese life, and rural China became filled with alienated citizens, among them drifters, former soldiers, vagrants, petty criminals, political exiles, and students. Hundreds of new Triads formed to accommodate the vast and diverse numbers that sought membership. These new secret societies became the primary instrument for the expression of social and political grievances for millions of frustrated workers and peasants. Crimes increasingly went unreported to the local police. The Triads became the arbiter of guilt and innocence, meted out punishment, and resolved disputes and feuds across China.

Triads became unofficial local governments, usurping many of the Manchu's administrative responsibilities. A proverb was repeated throughout China: "Armies protect the emperor; secret societies protect the people." Many of the Triads broadened their philosophy of opposing the Manchu regime to also oppose the presence of the "white devils," Europeans, particularly the British, involved in forcing opium on China. As the societies increasingly identified with the impoverished masses, they inevitably attracted adventurers and mercenaries to their ranks. Many radical critics of the Manchus who thought that legitimate avenues to the return of a Chinese-controlled government were too slow, joined the Triads in the hope of fomenting rebellions that would quickly overthrow the Manchu emperors.

When their ranks were swollen with these quasi-military adventurers, some of the Triads made prominent but abortive attempts at a successful revolution. The secret societies were instrumental in launching the seventeen-year Taiping Rebellion. It resulted in more than twenty million deaths and the utter devastation of some 600 cities. Triad societies also organized the unsuccessful "Red Turban Uprisings," which ended in devastating defeat for the independence movements. Following these rebellions, the Manchus embarked on one of history's most vengeful suppression campaigns. More than one million people were killed in mass beheadings, live burials, slow strangulations, and beatings of a thousand lashes. During this campaign of death many Triads fled China to Hong Kong and the United States. The exodus was so great that by 1847 British officials in Hong Kong estimated that while Triads had hidden behind the cover of artisans' guilds, workers' associations, and sports clubs, nearly three-quarters of the colony's population were Triad members.

In China the Manchus focused on crushing the secret societies, eradicating their popular support, terminating their members,

and cutting off their local sources of revenue. By the mid-1800s
their existence was threatened. Faced with possible extinction,
some segments of the largest secret societies reverted to an assortment of illegal activities, including piracy, smuggling, and extortion. The mainland Triads sent members abroad to Chinese
communities in other countries in order to organize and protect
the various kinds of vice and crime that thrived among homeless
settlers. Although the societies had almost always had some criminal elements as members, until the mid-1800s they were primarily legitimate and nationalistic organizations. However, by the
late 1800s the bulk of money for many popular Triads was from
illegal sources. Without those funds the Triads would never have
withstood the Manchu onslaught.

As the Triads realized that immense profits were to be reaped
from the criminal underworld, some of the secret societies turned
away from their political origins and concentrated on their criminal enterprises. Although one of the secret societies, the Eight
Trigrams Sect, or Fists of Harmony and Justice—whom westerners called the Boxers—led the aborted Boxer Rebellion against
the "white devil" Europeans in 1900, most Triads had abandoned
their patriotic underpinnings by the turn of the century. The deterioration of purpose was completed shortly after the successful revolution of 1911 in which the Manchus were overthrown
and a republic was established.

Dr. Sun Yat-sen formed the first government. He was a senior
Triad member, as were important new figures in the Republic,
including Charlie Soong, the international financier and a member of the powerful Red Gang, and Chiang Kai-shek, the army
general who lost China to Mao Tse-tung in 1949. Their political
purposes fulfilled, and officially recognized by Dr. Sun Yat-sen
for their assistance in establishing the Republic, the Triads became a powerful lobby group in the political and civic affairs of
the new China. They were well placed for a key role in the new
government for by the time of the 1911 revolution, Dr. Sun Yat-
sen estimated there were 35 million members of secret societies
in China.

The societies were so prominent in the new government that
many ambitious people in the military, private businesses, and
political life sought their assistance in order to advance their own
careers. Rewards for this assistance often took the form of ex-

clusive territories where the Triads could ply vice and extortion without interference from the authorities. Merchants and traders found that membership in the societies greatly enhanced their commercial enterprises, and they paid the Triads in stunning cash profits and goods. As the secret societies became increasingly corrupt they degenerated into vast criminal syndicates that rivaled in size and organization anything the Mafia ever dreamed of.

As they spread their control over China's underworld as well as the Chinese communities in other countries, General Chiang Kai-shek gave the Triads an unprecedented opportunity to gain formal recognition and power in national politics. Chiang's ambition was to lead a unified China as the military chief of a new imperial dynasty. He decided that only the Triads had the physical power to serve as the strong arm of his political party, the Kuomintang, or KMT. Chiang decided to use the societies for jobs his official army could not publicly be involved in.*

Chiang promised the Triads unlimited criminal control as well as prominent positions in his government if they cooperated with his newly established suppression campaign. He ordered the abolition of most labor unions, the arrest of Communist and left-wing leaders and spokesmen, and the closure of newspapers that Chiang considered "leftist" or critical. Triad henchmen were assigned the dirty work of carrying out Chiang's brutal campaign. A litmus test for the new relationship was Chiang's attempt to eliminate the Communist-led labor unions in Shanghai, then China's largest city. At the time Chiang decided to move against Shanghai, the criminal underworld was controlled by the Green Gang Triad. It was ruthlessly run by a Chinese gangster sometimes compared to Al Capone for his meteoric rise to criminal power, Tu Yueh Sheng, dubbed "Big-eared Tu" because of his prominent ears. Tu personally negotiated with Chiang to set the "fee" the KMT had to pay for the use of his Green Gang. Chiang and Tu struck a good deal, for on April 12, 1927, thousands of

---

*The inheritors of Chiang's KMT party, the government of Taiwan, still use Triads to complete dirty work that no official government agency wants to take responsibility for. A case in point was the 1982 murder of the Taiwanese reporter Henry Liu in Daly City, California. Liu was murdered because he was critical of the Taiwanese government. At the direction of the chief of Taiwan's version of the CIA, the United Bamboo Triad dispatched assassins to California where they murdered Liu near his house. The Liu murder is discussed further in Chapter 13.

Green Gang hooligans besieged union halls and leftist sanctuaries and began a reign of terror resulting in a virtual one-day massacre of Shanghai's Communist-led labor unions.

The details of the Green Gang deal with Chiang were soon evident. Tu was awarded the rank of major general in the KMT army and unofficially was allowed to fortify his position as the "Opium King" of Chiang's China. Chiang and Tu shared profits from the staggering prostitution trade in Shanghai, where it was estimated that one of every twelve Chinese houses was a brothel and one out of every 130 female residents was a call girl. Shanghai's prostitution trade was also infamous for its many houses of young boys as well as the largest population ever recorded of girls with bound feet, the ideal being feet less than three inches long. In the evenings Shanghai's whorehouses were the scenes of unrivaled sexual excess. Many of the more notorious houses specialized in a myriad of sexual acts and fantasies centered around the deformed feet of young girls. Tu's Green Gang and Chiang's KMT administered the prostitution trade in a brutal and relentless manner, and Chiang's sensibilities, which might otherwise have been offended at the perversion that was the hallmark of the Shanghai trade, were sufficiently soothed by the enormous profits.

In addition to Big-eared Tu, the acne-scarred godfather of the Red Gang, Pockmarked Huang, was appointed a senior advisor to the Nationalist government. Other Triad members became generals, officers, soldiers, intelligence operatives, businessmen, and financiers in the new China.

With the assistance and encouragement of Chiang Kai-shek, China became the first modern country where secret criminal societies were able to play a fundamental role in the legitimate administration of government. The very elements of the government that were supposed to limit and control the criminal underworld, the police and military, were themselves largely infiltrated, compromised, and even controlled by Triad members. This flood of Triad members in high-ranking government and civic positions ensured that few criminal enterprises in China were conducted without Triad involvement, protection, oversight, or acquiescence.

While Triad power had peaked in China, in Hong Kong the secret societies had barely begun their accumulation of influence and control in the British colony. Although Hong Kong Triads were involved in most criminal activities by the 1930s, they had never achieved the same level of government and social dominance as had their counterparts in China. The British had effectively kept limits on the power of the Triads. But all that changed with the advent of World War II.

The Japanese occupation of Hong Kong in 1941 presented the Hong Kong Triads with an unprecedented opportunity to solidify control over the black market and the vice trades. Opium, which had been legally available from British government stores, was unavailable except on the black market. Combined with a large addict population, this played into the Triads' hands as they quickly filled the void left by the British withdrawal. With the elimination of the British administration and police, some of the larger Triads reached accommodations with the Japanese invaders and were allowed to run the colony's illegal businesses in return for providing the Japanese with intelligence information and helping them maintain order. The Japanese openly encouraged prostitution, and the Triads controlled every aspect of the booming flesh trade. Also, as part of their agreement, the Japanese destroyed the bulk of the Hong Kong police records on Triads. All police files regarding previous investigations, personnel records, arrest histories, and information banks were obliterated.

By wiping the slate clean, the secret societies gained a tremendous advantage when the British again took control of the colony in 1945. The Triad societies had been active in Hong Kong since 1842 and the war gave them another four years to tighten their grip on the underworld without any interference from the police. But the British had the formidable disadvantage of having to rebuild their information files and investigations from scratch. It was no match. For the remainder of the 1940s, Hong Kong criminal bosses solidified their power bases, gained control of the docks, and made substantial inroads into the labor market, exerting influence over the construction and transportation industries as well as government workers. Even the thousands of hawkers, Hong Kong's street vendors, had to pay the Triads protection money in order to survive.

The police force, crippled by wartime deaths and injuries, attempted to rebuild but was understaffed and in disarray. Meanwhile, Hong Kong was racked by shortages of goods and currency disruptions that created a flourishing black market. The police could barely keep up with the daily volume of serious crime, much less focus on the syndicates behind the crime wave. The Triads used the police problems to their benefit. During the large postwar police recruitment drive, in which almost any able-bodied young man was eligible to join, Triad members swarmed into the force. Moreover, Triad societies formed ongoing relationships with many formerly honest members of the force. Bribes commonly supplemented the very low Royal Hong Kong Police salaries, and other police were compromised because they depended on Triad cooperation to pretend they were cracking down on criminals. Triad officials sometimes turned in expendable society members as well as helped the police plan "raids" on competitors' gambling and opium dens. The Triad infiltration of the police force and other government departments, together with the widespread corruption and staged cooperation, rendered the British administration an ineffective tool for a serious battle with the criminal societies.

Any hope that the British administration may have entertained of challenging the Hong Kong Triads ended with the events on the mainland of China during the same period, the mid- to late 1940s. By 1945 Chiang Kai-shek realized that a showdown with the Communists was inevitable. Chiang tried to save the Nationalist government by mobilizing the Triads in a final effort to stem the Communist armies sweeping from the north. Tens of thousands of Chinese were drafted into secret societies in brief mass initiation ceremonies, constituting a blood brotherhood against Mao Tse-tung's troops. The new recruits were sworn to obedience to the Nationalist government and told disloyalty meant death. The Triad societies also tried to mobilize the massive peasant populations against Mao's revolutionary army, but their efforts failed to halt the Communists' gathering momentum.

During the months immediately preceding the fall of China, Britain made the fateful decision of adopting an open-door policy for Chinese seeking refuge in Hong Kong. More than three-quarters of a million people streamed into the British colony. Included among them were many Triad members, initially large numbers of the Red and Green gangs. Big-eared Tu, the Green Gang godfather, fled to Hong Kong in 1949 with his senior lieutenants and most of his master chemists, including a one-armed chemist who was regarded as the finest heroin technician in the world. Tu guaranteed the Green Gang had enough funds to expand in its new Hong Kong home. As a parting shot upon fleeing the mainland Tu masterminded a robbery that garnered millions of ounces of gold reserves from the Bank of China. Shortly after Tu's Green Gang and other northern secret societies arrived in the British colony, the criminal gangs from southern China began flooding into Hong Kong. The largest of these was the 14K Triad, a name derived from a combination of the street address for their Canton headquarters and the Karat symbol for hard gold.

Tens of thousands of Chiu Chau, Chinese from the Swatow region of southern China, also poured into Hong Kong. The Chiu Chau have played a key role in Asia's crime world since the mid-1800s, analogous to that of the Sicilians in the Italian Mafia. While the Mafia is divided into many rival families such as the Gambino, Genovese, Bonnano, or other families, many of the Italians who fill the competing Mafia ranks are Sicilians. Similarly the Chinese organized criminal underworld is broken into rival Triads like the 14K, the Green Gang, and the Wo syndicate, comprised of many different regional Chinese, including Cantonese, Hakka, and others, but the core membership is often Chiu Chau. The Chiu Chau come from a seagoing segment of the Chinese population. They were early explorers and settlers and migrated to many Southeast Asian cities, later providing the ethnic ties to the Hong Kong Triads that proved crucial in the international narcotics trade. To the Chinese criminal, family is everything, and the Chiu Chau gangsters, many of whom have friends or relatives throughout Asia, became indispensable in helping the Hong Kong Triads expand their horizons in later decades.

This influx of mainland Triads and gangsters also created the first major rifts in the Hong Kong underworld. In the aftermath of the exodus from the mainland, 600,000 homeless refugees crammed into squatter areas, where the British administration was unable to provide any effective government service. These hordes of refugees, often distrustful of authority, built their own small communities, filled with shops, restaurants, and factories, and they seemed to expect that they would have to pay someone to survive. To the established Hong Kong Triads, the new refugees seemed a lucrative and ideal target. When the gang members moved into the squatter areas, however, they were shocked to discover that the refugees had brought their own secret societies with them. For the first time in the modern age, established Hong Kong Triads were faced with a serious threat to their control of the underworld, and the threat did not come from law-enforcement or a government crackdown but rather from migrating Triads from the mainland.

The Hong Kong syndicates could not penetrate the customs and dialects of the new refugees and by default allowed the new Triads to control the prostitution, protection rackets, and gambling in the squatter villages. But the mainland Triads brought with them a new vice that had been largely undeveloped in Hong Kong—the heroin trade. Big-eared Tu established the first large-scale heroin refineries by 1950, and locally produced heroin was supplying the northern addict immigrants by the end of that year.

Emboldened by substantial narcotics profits, the Green Gang became the single greatest challenge to the Hong Kong Triads. They expanded heroin sales, gambling, and prostitution beyond the squatter villages. Green Gang hoodlums terrorized hundreds of Hong Kong shopkeepers and were soon collecting protection money from a sizable portion of Hong Kong's retail establishments. The Green Gang also staged a series of spectacular armed robberies that rocked Hong Kong.

But the inroads the Hong Kong Triads had made into the police began to pay off in the battle for the underworld. Rather than start a bloody street war, the Hong Kong Triads first reached an accord with the 80,000-member 14K to stay neutral, and then aggressively used the police to eliminate their rivals. At the urging of the powerful Wo syndicate, the police formed a special squad to concentrate on the Green Gang. The police were suddenly inundated with confidential tips about pending Green Gang crimes and ongoing criminal ventures. Not only did the police receive widespread public praise for the suddenly effective crackdown, but the Green Gang problems alleviated pressure on the illegal activities of the other Triads.

Big-eared Tu did not live to see the Green Gang's problems. He had died in 1951. His successor, a solid and respected businessman, Li Choi Fat, was an energetic dragon head who fought back by trying to outbid other Triads in buying police "enforcement" directed against his rivals. For a year the police had hundreds of significant Triad operations and senior officers almost fall into their laps in one of the strangest gang wars in the annals of modern criminal history, one fought without a single shot but instead by bribing the city's police force to crack down against rival Triads. Evidently Li Choi Fat did not pay enough money, for he was arrested and in a kangaroo trial was deported from the British colony. The Green Gang was shaken to its core, abandoning many of its more profitable criminal ventures, and the gang continued to be plagued by arrests and deportations. By the mid-1950s the Green Gang's main influence was in bars, hotels, and nightclubs that catered to tourists, as well as among Hong Kong's tailors. Although they still had a number of heroin refineries, they increasingly relied on other syndicates for the morphine base as well as distribution to addicts. By 1966 the Green Gang had disappeared in Hong Kong.

The decline of the Green Gang did not mean that business returned to normal for the traditional Hong Kong Triads. They were also weakened from the underworld war. This was an opportunity seized by the massive 14K Triad. Led by the charismatic Nationalist General Kot Siu Wong, the 14K had remained neutral in the Green Gang–Hong Kong Triad battle. As a result, while the other syndicates had severely wounded themselves and compromised many of their profitable enterprises, the 14K continued to buy influence in the government and police, run the vice trades in the squatter areas, and expand their membership. Without much fanfare the 14K had become Hong Kong's most powerful criminal organization by the mid-1950s, even surpassing the traditional Hong Kong power gang, the Wo syndicate.

General Wong died in 1953, and a battle for leadership eventually ended in a grand council comprised of several dragon heads directing the Triad. The new leadership brutally expanded the 14K's underworld influence, embarking on a campaign of extortion and intimidation so ruthless that even other Hong Kong gangs were repelled. It was a campaign of criminal violence unparalleled in Hong Kong history, and by 1954 the 14K had eliminated much of its opposition. During its expansion drive the 14K attracted the toughest and brightest of Hong Kong's criminal world for membership. It also moved into substantial segments of the opium and heroin trade, purchasing the drugs from Chiu Chau gangsters in the Golden Triangle and arranging their distribution to Chiu Chau 14K members in other Asian countries. By 1955 the police, although heavily riddled with 14K penetration, were forced by the British government to crack down on the number one Triad. The result was 148 arrests of 14K officers and members, less than one half of 1 percent of their membership.

The limited police crackdown spurred the 14K leadership to attempt one of the most ambitious feats in organized criminal history—the control of every single aspect of illegal life in Hong Kong, the takeover of all other Triads, and the melding of the colony's 300,000 Triad members under the single 14K banner. It would be as if one Mafia family in New York decided to control all criminal activity throughout the United States and organized all Italian mobsters under the direction of that single family. The 14K attempt was even more ambitious in light of the much greater diversity and number of Triads present in Hong Kong.

Chiang Kai-shek's Nationalist government gave the 14K money and intelligence assistance. Chiang hoped that if the 14K could unify the Chinese crime empire it could wreak havoc with the peace of Hong Kong and politically wrest control away from the British crown, creating an opening for Chiang's KMT to grasp power. If effective, the magnitude of the new criminal organization, under the direction of a single dragon head, would have overwhelmed any possible law-enforcement efforts.

In order to finalize their Hong Kong takeover, the top echelon of the 14K planned to hold a Taiwan summit in late October 1956, meeting with key figures in Chiang's government. But a series of events intervened, exposing the 14K to a crippling government crackdown. On October 10 in Hong Kong, thousands of Chinese living in overcrowded resettlement blocks celebrated the forty-fifth anniversary of the successful Nationalist revolution. The celebrants pasted Nationalist flags on the walls of the resettlement blocks, an action forbidden by the British. When the Royal Hong Kong Police removed the paper flags, the massive crowds regarded it as an insult to Chiang Kai-shek and the Taiwan government and small-scale riots erupted.

In a serious misjudgment, the 14K decided it could manipulate the angry crowds into a full-scale popular revolt against British authorities. When the new Chinese government swept to power, the 14K would be at the helm. Triad members, wearing distinguishing armbands, entered the fight, organized street barricades, and spread the riots throughout the colony. Groups of Triads attacked foreigners, torched buildings, looted retail shops, and demolished Communist-owned businesses as well as trashing left-wing trade unions. As the rioting spread on the second day, the police made a desperate appeal to London. It responded by imposing an emergency curfew and calling in the British Army. The new orders were unequivocal—stop the disturbances at all costs. By the end of the third day the major riots were quelled, and although pockets of violence continued for nearly another month, the 14K threat had been repelled. Fifty-nine were dead (including the wife of the Swiss consul), almost 400 were injured, and hundreds of shops and factories were burned, with more than $20 million in property damage.

The British were infuriated at the blatant Triad involvement in spreading the violence of the October riots. Under strong pressure from London to clean its house, the Hong Kong police commissioner finally organized the Triad Society Bureau, a special arm of the police with the power to investigate and prosecute Triads and their criminal enterprises. London also dispatched Scotland Yard officials to reorganize Hong Kong's law-enforcement efforts. Emergency legislation was introduced and informers were encouraged to come forward in order to gain personal immunity. The British administration launched its first earnest war against the Triads. The results were initially impressive. More than 10,000 Triad members were arrested by mid-1957, many were deported, and others entered into a system of police supervision similar to probation. But the police action still reached only 3 percent of the estimated criminal population, and the real effect of the government crackdown was that the Triads entered a several-year period of consolidation, restrained from their more flamboyant enterprises as they waited for fresh opportunities.

The deported secret society members were sent to Taiwan where they settled into a Nationalist-supported Triad dubbed the "United Bamboo." The British authorities made a mistake by sending some of Hong Kong's key criminal talent to Taiwan. With Chiang Kai-shek as their long-standing friend, the deported criminals almost immediately returned to a life of crime. With their detailed knowledge of Hong Kong, these criminals later helped Taiwanese Triads like the United Bamboo establish effective branch offices in the British colony as well as form strong and critical ties to large Hong Kong syndicates. In the later development of the heroin trade, the Hong Kong–Taiwan connections were crucial.

Eventually the Triads emerged even stronger from the disastrous 1956 riots. An important lesson was learned—no single Triad could control the Chinese criminal underworld. The syndicates realized that in order to expand their businesses, they had to work together and learn to accept a smaller but safer piece of the illegal profits. By working together against law enforcement, they could still direct operations worth billions of dollars. Although the police might make occasional cases against them, that was an ever-present risk of doing business. The 1956 riots taught the Chinese Triads a lesson still not learned by the Mafia—that cooperation is much more profitable than fighting internal wars.

A second major factor helping the Triads emerge with even more power was that in their effort to find fresh opportunities to expand their businesses, they increasingly settled on heroin. As Chiu Chau syndicates in the Golden Triangle and in Bangkok and Saigon reported the profits made by French and U.S. intelligence agencies, the Triads embarked by 1960 on a narcotics campaign that would spread their heroin business far beyond the Hong Kong addict population. With Chiu Chau middlemen playing the key roles in forming the narcotics network, the Triads were poised to become key players in the narcotics world.

The upheaval of the 1940s and 1950s that marked the history of the Hong Kong Triads was finished by 1960. During the coming decade, Hong Kong boomed as an international manufacturing and business center and the Triads increased their power. Soaring business profits meant there was more money to be spent on vice, gambling, prostitution, and drugs. There was also more protection money for the Triads to squeeze from growing companies.

During the past quarter century no single Triad has attempted to take over the Hong Kong underworld. Although rival gangs have fought battles for control of a block of nightclubs or a group of gambling houses, there has been no major Triad war. The Triad unity was temporarily disrupted in 1969 when Red Guards fleeing Mao's Cultural Revolution fled into Hong Kong and formed the Big Circle Gang. These former soldiers had been through horrible abuses and tortures in China, and they were "vicious and tough as nails," according to a Hong Kong police superintendent. For several years they carved out a piece of the Hong Kong crime world. But eventually concerted police action and the attacks of rival Triads eliminated their threat and most of them fled Hong Kong for other countries.

The same Triads that dominated the underworld in the mid-1950s, the 14K, the Wo syndicate, and the Sun Yee On, are still the major players today. They have been joined by the United Bamboo from Taiwan. Hong Kong police estimate there are 300,000 Triad members in the British colony, one out of every twenty people. The significance of this number is evident when compared to the Italian Mafia—law-enforcement officials estimate that La Cosa Nostra consists of only 2,000 "made" members in the United States. Hong Kong police intelligence monitors more than fifty separate Triad organizations. And within large syndicates like the 14K there are nearly fifty subgroups.

The Triads have modernized, tightened their grip on the Hong Kong underworld, and expanded their influence through branch offices around the world. Fueled by staggering narcotics profits, they have expanded beyond mere criminal activity. "The big change from the mid-sixties to today is that the syndicates have gone into many more legitimate businesses," a Hong Kong police intelligence analyst told me. "They've moved into everything from home-decoration firms to fancy hotels to construction companies to car dealerships to licensed casinos. The old Triads wouldn't have thought about legitimate business. But today the Triads make so much money that if they don't invest it in legitimate enterprises, there is no way they can spend it in twenty lifetimes. And most of them are such good businessmen that they make another fortune from their legitimate activities."

For a modern-day criminal organization, the history of the Triads is unparalleled. From vast patriotic popular movements with a marked religious aura, they have degenerated into vast underground syndicates. They now cooperate in an extensive world-wide network based in Hong Kong and present in major international cities. It was with this background in mind that I met Benny and set out at 1:00 a.m., across the streets of a rain-swept Hong Kong, to meet with a Triad official.

4

The Red Pole

Benny and I walked down Nathan Road, the so-called Golden Mile, crammed with hundreds of glittering retail shops and restaurants all sporting the required sign of success—a neon sign larger and brighter than the one owned by a competitor. As far as the eye can see, thousands of neons are stacked one atop another. Even though Nathan Road has four lanes of traffic separating the sidewalks, at times the neon, most set at the second floors of the buildings and jutting out over the roadway, almost seem to meet. At night the street is awash with colors from signs blazing with oranges, pinks, yellows, and reds, a veritable canopy of psychedelic lights covering the walkway. Many of the electric lights, some the size of a building, flash into different shapes and slogans, some spin in circles, and others are surrounded with thousands of flashing bulbs, the entire effect being surrealistic, especially when the reflections of the neon sky are mirrored in the wet sidewalks of a rainy evening. The only other city that rivals this intense, man-made lighting show is Las Vegas, but because of the cramped conditions and the sheer volume, Nathan Road is far more intense than the American gambling oasis. This light show provided the background as Benny told me what to expect at the Canton Disco.

"In the last couple of years the Canton has become the favorite hangout for a lot of gangs. Starting around midnight you can see them arrive, almost always in groups. They come to see each other and to check out the girls. Everyone is trying to show 'face.' I mean all want to show how much money they are making or how popular they are with the girls and show how tough they are. Even tonight, with the rain, you still see them dressed to show off. They can feel safe at the Canton because it's become a Triad hangout."

"Is it owned by the Triads?"

"No, no way. It's owned by some English guy, a white man, but he is forced to do business with them. I mean he pays them, but everyone who owns a nightclub in Kowloon has to pay money to the Triads or you won't be in business very long. Actually, having your club picked as the hangout by the gangs is not so bad, it means nobody is going to give you any shit, because the protection is built in. Not everybody who goes to the Canton is a Triad, I mean you'll see tourists and some local Chinese also, but I know you are going to see something very different about this club."

"Tell me again about the Triad we are going to meet."

"He's an old friend of mine from the gang days. He has really done very well for himself, you'll see for yourself. He's nothing to laugh at, I mean a 426, a 'Red Pole,' that is the executioner for the Triad, and the Sun Yee On is one of the island's most powerful societies. Everyone is scared of this fellow because he is in charge of their enforcement, and there aren't many guys tougher, so no one crosses him. He's not even thirty and he's got a couple of dozen goons that answer to him and he's making lots of money. He is really going someplace. He's a good friend to have. Also he is real good for you to talk to because he is one of the few guys I know that has a real interest in the history of the Triads. I mean he knows all about the five monks and all that stuff, which is pretty unusual nowadays because most young guys couldn't be bothered by that crap, but he spends a lot of time studying the Triad past. That's one reason he's moving up so fast, because the elders like that he knows and studies the history. They think that most young people don't show enough respect for the origins, so when they find a guy like this who is real good at what he does and also likes the tradition, then bingo, he is on the fast ladder to the top.

"By the way, remember, don't ask him about crimes, or what

it's like to kill, or anything like that because you aren't going to get an answer and you might create hot water for yourself. It's a stroke of luck you're even meeting him. Remember, I vouched for you. He won't mind talking to you about some of the history of the Triads. If you want to try to find out more, be careful with your questions—he won't answer them if he doesn't want to, but don't go out of your way to get him angry. Don't expect too much."

There was a line of young Chinese at the Canton Disco waiting to pay a $10 cover charge to get inside. Benny pushed his way through the crowd, his quivering mass parting the small partygoers like Moses through the Red Sea. He nodded to a doorman and a red velvet rope was pulled up so we could enter. Once inside, the music, which was a dull thumping when we were waiting outside, became a deafening beat. Surrounded by flashing strobe lights and with a video clip from the rock singer Madonna staring at us through television monitors, Benny led me past the black bar. There, as promised, were young men in tight white jeans and tight T-shirts that emphasized their muscles, lounging around the bar, surrounded by young girls.

"There are the kung-fu toughs," Benny screamed at me, making sure I could hear him over the dance music. He stopped me and put his mouth near my ear to be heard. "Look at them for a moment. You aren't going to see so many of them in one place again, unless you come back here. They may look pretty scrawny, but I want you to study them. Most of them, they grow up on the streets. In order to survive here you must be able to handle yourself—these guys know the martial arts from a young age. It's survival for many of them. These kids you see at the bar, their muscles may not look very big, but I tell you that if they are in a fight, they are some of the toughest killers you will ever see. They can be half destroyed but they continue to fight. They are taught from the earliest age that no matter how badly they are hurt in a fight, even if their arm and leg are broken, they must cause greater suffering and damage to their enemy. So if I think like one of these guys and somebody breaks one of my arms and one of my legs, I will think to myself that I will break both of his arms and both of his legs. Then I will win. When you have two people who fight with this philosophy, plus you must remember that it is part of our culture not to show pain or hurt, then you will understand how many street fights lead to death. Until somebody dies there can be no stopping."

"There are so many of them. I'm just surprised that they are all attracted to the criminal underworld."

"Shit, you've got to remember they don't think of any of it as 'the criminal underworld.' For them the Triads are just the best way to make a good living. They only care about how much money they can make. That's the main reason that most of them want to be Triads today. They are fourteen or fifteen and they live in some half-condemned building with thousands of other families, and all they can dream about is owning one of those nice BMWs or Mercedes they see all over Hong Kong. And they don't want to wait twenty years working like their fathers in the kitchen of a restaurant serving tourists. They want the money now, and the only way they can get that money fast is by joining a Triad. A kid can make ten times as much in one month by collecting protection money from a nightclub like this than he can make in an entire year of breaking his back in a straight job. What do you think many of these kids will choose, especially when they see some of their friends who have joined the Triads come back to the old neighborhood with a solid gold ring and a nice silk suit? They want the same things.

"They don't care about the history. No one is joining because the Triads helped to establish modern China. That's bullshit. If the Triads couldn't give these kids a lot of quick money, then none of them would join. And when they are young none of them ever think that brains become the key factor as you start to move up in the world. When they are young they all think that only toughness gets them to the top. Many of these kids you are looking at are experts in handling choppers [long Chinese knives, similar to machetes]. They are quick like a fox with them. I have seen them chop people before the other is even out of the chair. Some of them are good enough to just cut the muscles in your neck or arms or legs so you cannot ever use them again—you are alive but crippled. And they all know the better they are with the chopper, there will always be a need for them in a Triad. Come on, enough bullshit or we'll be late, let's go see the 426."

We left the body competition and climbed the metal staircase to the second-floor dance room. Benny looked around for a mo-

ment and then shuffled across the jammed dance floor to a group
of cocktail tables spread out at the rear of the club.

A small and wiry young Chinese man, his face slightly pockmarked, eyes deep-set, very thick jet-black hair plastered straight
back, rose to meet us. He wore dark gray pin-striped trousers, a
freshly-pressed white linen shirt buttoned to the neck, and an
impeccably tailored light gray silk blazer. His fashionable clothing was a subtle advertisement for his status. Benny had warned
me that my Hollywood-based image of gangsters in garish pin-
striped suits with white ties would have to be abandoned for the
Chinese underworld.

The Red Pole put on his most ingratiating smile as he weakly
shook my hand and we sat at his table. Benny and I sat on small
stools separated by a glass-topped cocktail table, while the young
Triad officer sat on a narrow banquette. After the introductions,
Benny and the 426 officer spoke in Cantonese for several minutes, although Benny did most of the talking. The Triad enforcer
was reserved and taciturn. He kept looking over at me, furtive,
quick glances that sized me up. Benny leaned over the table toward me: "Remember, no names, right?"

"I know, no names. Right?" I looked at both of them, waiting
for a confirmation. The Red Pole had a bottle of vodka, a bottle
of cognac, an ice bucket, and two highball glasses in front of him.
Both glasses were filled and he would take a sip from one glass
and then a sip from the other. He snapped his fingers to get our
waitress, and he ordered sets of glasses for Benny and me.

Benny chatted with him for another ten minutes, the Red Pole
having little to say. Benny swung toward me: "He would like to
toast your visit to Hong Kong." We all raised our vodka glasses
for a loud clink, the Triad's face lit by a very broad and very
insincere smile. Following a large gulp of vodka, it was clear that
our host had decided it was time to work. He leaned over the
table, took a mother-of-pearl cigarette case from his breast pocket,
pulled out a filterless French cigarette, and as he lit it with a gold
lighter, he pulled up his suit cuff to display a diamond-studded
gold Rolex. As he blew out a long stream of smoke, he nodded
to Benny, who pulled close to my face. "He wants to know what
you want to know about Triads."

"Ask him about the initiation rites. I want to know what someone must go through to join a Triad."

Benny put the question at some length. At first the Red Pole was expressionless, then he gave a short burst of Cantonese to Benny. "He wants to know if you mean initiation rites like the old days or what happens nowadays." I told Benny I was interested in both. Benny relayed my question and the Triad officer answered quickly, jabbing the air with his cigarette as he spoke.

"He says you must remember, most of the initiation ceremonies have been cut very short because the old ceremonies, which took several days, are too much of a risk. Cops may find out what's happening. Even if it was safe from the cops, it's just not practical. Hong Kong is just too crowded, you couldn't do an old-style ceremony even if you wanted to. He says that nowadays the ceremony is simple and can be done almost anywhere. A lot of rites are done in Macao [the Portuguese colony located forty minutes away from Hong Kong by a hydrofoil ride] where there is very small chance of police problems."

"Ask him to describe in detail one of the traditional initiation rites and see if he will compare it to what goes on today." Benny looked dubiously at me but turned to him and put the question. The Red Pole went into a long monologue, with Benny putting his hand up every so often to stop him so that he could translate to me.

"Okay," says Benny with a broad smile, "he says he will tell you, but that when he finishes you will know more about the traditional Triads than most of the new members." I am not sure if I was supposed to feel fortunate.

"He says no one will tell you what the old initiation rite was like, but he knows it from the elders of the society. He will tell you. The ceremonies, they were a little different depending on which city the Triad was in, but the one he will tell you about is one of the most common. In the old days each Triad had its own headquarters, always a large building. Each recruit had to be sponsored by an official of the society—regular members could not sponsor, an official had to do it. That is almost the same today.

"The recruits dressed in silk robes and entered the front of the headquarters under a lot of banners, one for the Triad leaders, one for the new recruits, and one representing traitors. So the new members walked through several rooms past rows of other Triad members and they walked to the back chamber, which had an altar."

"An altar?"

"Yes. He says you must remember that in the old days it was all very colorful and membership in a Triad was just like becoming a monk, or like a priest for you in the West. It was also very serious. He says you will understand if you let him tell you what the actual ceremony was like. Over the door to the final room were banners saying, 'Do not enter if you are not utterly loyal,' and there several Triads crossed swords over the new members' heads, and forced them to crawl on their hands and knees— 'Crossing the Mountain of Knives,' it was called.

"The altar was usually in the middle of the room. Behind it and all around were banners announcing the heroics of the first five monks who founded the society.

"Most of the time the new recruits would have their faces washed at this point to show they were being cleansed and were starting a new life, like a new birth.

"Now concentrate, get this picture, he says. On one side of the main hall were the leaders of the Triad, and the member called the 'incense master' sat near the altar. Each new member had to write his name on a small scrap of paper and hand it to the incense master, and then the 489 [the Triad leader] would tell them the history of Triads. Nowadays he says no one gives a shit. Even if you tell them, they are probably not paying much attention. But in the older days you had to know the history because people would talk to you about it. Now they think you are an asshole if you talk about it too much. They want to know about what is happening today, not one hundred years ago. Well, that's not important for now, just let him get back on what he was saying."

It was surprising that the lack of interest in the history of the Triads seemed to be such a sensitive issue with some Chinese criminals. Certainly few new Mafia members would likely know that the Mafia was expanded under Giuseppe Mazzini in Palermo, Sicily, in 1860 as a guerrilla force to drive out a foreign ruler and unite Italy in the name of patriotism and liberty. As with any current-day criminal enterprise, the motivating factor was the ability to gain power and money. The Chinese I spoke to, however, seemed bothered by this practical side of the secret societies. They preferred the long-standing Chinese obsession with tradition and history, somehow feeling that by studying the patriotic origins and being able to recite that background, it legitimized or at least mitigated the current criminal activity that was their hallmark.

"He says that when the leader was done with his talk about the history, the incense master would take over the ceremony. He would light large bunches of incense and call for loyalty and strength. Then he would go to the altar and offer a service to those Triads who had given their lives for the society. After this all the officials would put on their ceremonial robes and gather the recruits on their knees in a single line.

"Near them would be three stuffed dummies and they would also be kneeling, with signs hung around their necks identifying them as the three traditional Triad traitors. A senior official then would get a long sword and chop off the dummies' heads while he told the recruits that this was what happened to all traitors. The incense master would then worship before the altar and talk about loyalty and the fact that once the new member has been accepted there is no turning back. No one can change his mind. Once you are in, it's for life, and the incense master would make this quite clear."

"Hold on a minute," pleaded Benny, holding his hand up to the Triad official and looking over at me. "This guy can really talk if he gets going. I got to have a drink or my throat won't make it. And with this music, it may be great for him because no one can hear him, but for me trying to think of what he is saying and then putting it the right way for you and not being too slow, man, do I have a headache." All I needed now was for Benny to fail me. Nearly two weeks of waiting for this meeting and suddenly I saw it going down the drain because of Benny's headache and the boom of the music.

"We can go back to my hotel room if it would be easier," I offered.

"No, I'll be okay. I just have to tell him to slow up. Don't worry, I'm catching all of it." Benny was sweating through his black turtleneck and his eyes were bloodshot. He took a swig of the vodka and spoke to the Red Pole. "He says I'm too fat. That's my problem. Huh, easy for him to say. Okay, let's go on. He says, where was he?"

"He was talking about loyalty and the dummies getting their heads chopped off as an example to new members."

"Oh, yes. Then the incense master would have a Triad fighter approach each of the kneeling recruits and press the sharp edge of a sword into his chest. 'Which is stronger, the blade of the knife or your heart?' the fighter would ask each new member.

'My heart,' the new guys would answer, meaning that even death could not make them betray their brothers. Then the incense master would read the thirty-six oaths, and the recruits would repeat them. The oaths are the main part of the rites. They say that you shall be killed by a 'myriad of swords' if you betray the society in any way. Each recruit was then given a small, burning piece of paper and he had to put it out in his hands as he promised that he would also be extinguished for any disloyalty. Each of the recruits then had to walk under a banner of yellow paper which said that death comes to all traitors. After they marched under the yellow banner it was also burned to show what would happen to them.

"Then the new members had to kneel inside a choppy bamboo circle and a sword was held at their chests. They had to recite an oath of loyalty as they stood up, and the bamboo was set up in such a way so to make it difficult to stand without falling, and if the new member fell forward, he could die on the sword. That was a way of cleaning out bad recruits. Some old-timers felt that recruits who might turn disloyal were weeded out in this way. It's never done anymore."

"Did he ever see anyone die this way?"

The 426 answered with a couple of grunts. "No," Benny translated, "he just heard about some of them but never saw it himself." After another toast of vodka, the talk continued.

"Following the sword test, the recruits had to walk across a 'fiery pit.' Actually, he says it was never a pit, just a lot of burning paper and sticks on the floor, and the recruits had to walk over some fire. That's another part of the ceremony that is almost never done today.

"Each recruit then knelt in front of the altar again and this time a cock was passed in front of him and then the incense master would chop its head off with one blow from a sword. He would tell the recruits that they would die like that if they ever betrayed the society, and the cut head was mixed in a bowl of wine together with the blood from the cock's body. That bowl was taken to each recruit, who would cut the middle finger of his left hand with a long needle and put some drops of blood into the bowl while saying that if he revealed the Triad secrets, then blood would be let out of the five holes of his body."

"What do you mean by the five holes of the body?"

"Like if someone sees too much, hears too much, and talks too much. Then they would get a bullet in both eyes, both ears, and the mouth. It warned other people not to betray their brothers. Everyone in the ceremony knew what it meant. And after they were warned about their loyalty, it was made clear to them. When the blood was collected from each of them, then the incense master burned the paper of the thirty-six oaths. He added that to the bowl of wine and mixed it with the cock's blood and head and the blood of the recruits. Each new member had to drink from that bowl.

"After all of that they would be dismissed and have to return three days later for more oaths, incense prayer, and then finally they would be allowed to pay a fee to join the Triad."

I was impressed that an organization could hold such sway over people to make them subject themselves to degradations and possible death for three days and then pay for the pleasure of having endured that ordeal.

Benny and the Red Pole did not miss a beat—they just kept talking. "Once the money switched hands, then everyone relaxed and there was usually a great celebration. He says he thinks you can understand why this type of ceremony can't be done anymore. Who is going to have the room or all the time to sit through this? Sure it helped give new members a feeling they were joining something very special, and it also helped to give them some sense of history, but it's just not possible today. He says he's not approving the change, that's just the way it is.

"Today it is all done in one day, sometimes in an hour. The main parts are the swearing to the thirty-six oaths and the constant reminder that death comes to all traitors. There is almost always some blood taken from the recruits and mixed with wine or something and then drunk by the new members. There are no robes and the people doing the ceremony are there to impress that there are only two choices for the new Triad member—loyalty or death. No one teaches the history."

"Ask him about his initiation rites. What were they like?"

"I wouldn't. It's very personal and not to speak of."

"May I ask him how many Triad members there are in Hong Kong, and specifically in his society?"

"He wouldn't answer."

"Ask him what he wants to tell me about Triads. What should I know if I am going to write about them?"

They launch into Cantonese. "He says people have so many

misconceptions. A lot is always changing with the Hung Mun [the Chinese name for secret societies]. People make it sound like a club, that some guy wants to get into the Triads so he goes someplace and says let me in and that's the end of it. It's not like that— no way like that. No one can join unless he is chosen. Oh they may want to get in, but they must be chosen to come in. If they are tough enough and they show some promise in their local little gangs, then maybe they will come to the attention of the Triad and it will say, 'Okay, you think you are tough enough to do more than squeeze some old hawkers on the street for a couple of dollars a day, then come and work for us.' And if they work for the Triad, they still won't be a member of the society until they have proven themselves and then only if the Hung Mun wants to invite them to join."

The 426 is sophisticated enough to know how his words will look in print. He makes it sound like an exclusive country club. What he fails to mention is that the credentials for admission are not pedigree and social status, but any young punk who is ruthless and calculating enough is welcomed with open arms.

"Do most of the gang members become Triad members, or do many choose to have their own business like you [Benny] have?"

The Red Pole laughs for the first time. Benny barely cracks a smile. "He says your question seems to say there is a difference between Triad members and people who have opened their own business. Not always. Most members are not former gang members, but they are people who have their own businesses and they make a lot of money from whatever they do. He has friends in the travel business, in the restaurant business, in the entertainment business, and they make a lot of money. They may also be Triad. They are loyal to the Triad before anything else in their lives and they serve their brothers. But he does not want to have you think that they sit around all day in some dark office planning how to control the vices of the world. Please, he says this image is not a correct one—just because someone may be Triad does not mean that they do not have their own businesses. Many times the fact that they are members helps them in their regular business."

"Can he tell me how?"

"It's easy. Think how many Triad members there are just in Hong Kong."

"I thought you told me he wouldn't say how many members there are in Hong Kong."

"Just let him finish. He won't tell you the number."

"If there are a lot of Triad members, some are very successful and have power in the city. He says would you be shocked if he told you that the wealthiest man in Hong Kong is Triad? Believe me, you don't know the half of it. You must remember, it is against the law in Hong Kong to be a Triad member—they can jail you for just being one. So not many people are brave enough to talk about it. They hide it, but that doesn't mean they aren't proud of it. Their first efforts will always be to help anyone in business who is a fellow brother. The top money people in Hong Kong are members. They never forget it. The police know it, the British know it, and the People's Republic knows it."

"So be more direct, Benny, how many Triads are in the government or the police?"

The Red Pole was expressionless and grunted a couple of times. Benny interpreted it, "Ask the police or the DEA."

I asked Benny if he could elicit a slightly more candid response. After having an animated and fast conversation and polishing off the rest of his vodka, Benny looked at me: "He says he has already told you enough. He says you must see if those in the police who know the truth will share it with you."

I asked Benny to see if he could ask the Red Pole point-blank about Triad success in bribing police officials. Benny said no.

"May I ask him about the heroin business in Hong Kong and how Triads may be involved?"

"He wouldn't answer. I wouldn't ask him."

"So there is certainly no point in asking him about Triad control of the casinos, the loan-sharking and extortion business, the prostitution trade, or the like, right?"

"That's right. You can't fool around with a guy like this."

The Red Pole crushed the butt of his cigarette into an ashtray and filled one of his glasses with cognac. He looked at Benny and spoke at some length.

"He says he wants you to understand one thing. Everything bad that happens in Hong Kong, everyone jumps up and shouts, 'Oh, it must be Triads.' A lot of this is wrong, it is junk. A lot of people say they are members to impress others, but really they are not. The Triads are not responsible for everything that is done in Hong Kong. He says you must understand that some things are part of human nature, like for a man to want to have a beautiful and young woman. You are not going to stop a man paying for such a favor from a beautiful woman. And some people shall always love to place a wager on the results of a horse race or the play of cards. Certainly to stop this wagering would be possible only if human nature changes. You must take the desire out of the people and this is not possible. And sometimes people have bad luck in their business or their family gets sick and they run out of money, and since they don't own anything and have no big salary, no bank will give them any money, so it will be human nature that someone will loan them money. But since it is business, a profit must be made on the money loaned. But in the West you call this loan-sharking, I believe, yet here the person who gets the money is happy to get it and the person who gives it takes great risk but the reward is his profit. So what is vice here? Is it the man who wants to spend an hour with a lovely lady? Or maybe the grandmother who wants to wager $5.00 on the outcome of a race? Maybe we should let the old man's wife die because he cannot get the money to pay for his wife's operation, even though he wants to borrow the money and pay any interest.

"If Triads control all of this, and he does not mean to say they do or could, just think for a moment that they might be doing the people and the government a favor. By one group running all of this it would be possible to avoid deadly fights over greed like you have in the United States, and it is possible to make sure everything is run smoothly and fairly. You know who to go to if there is a problem. So he doesn't know if there is any big problem like the newspapers always like to talk about, but if there was such a problem, and if one group controlled it, he thinks it could be a blessing in disguise. Do you understand?

"Now he says that he must get up early in the morning and unfortunately he must end our meeting."

Of course he would want to finish after telling me the most interesting piece of news for the night. He had justified Triad criminal involvement by arguing there was a demand. Obviously as long as people wanted something, the obstacle that it was illegal did not come into the Triads' consideration. The most interesting part of his answer was the implied conclusion that one single group of Triads controlled all criminal activity in Hong Kong. The Red Pole rose and started stretching at our table.

"Wait just a moment, Benny. Let me just ask a few brief questions I had in mind. Maybe we can talk another time and at least he will know the questions and can think about them before we meet again."

The Red Pole, who had been staring at me, looked away and started to talk to Benny in Cantonese. It was a lively conversation of some length, after which he chuckled and waited for Benny's response. Benny looked at me: "We just are getting to know each other. We don't need everything discussed in one day. Why don't you ask him a few more questions and then we can get together another night?"

I looked directly at the Red Pole. Although ostensibly fascinated with the action on the dance floor, he did not miss anything that happened at our table. He turned toward me and waited to see what I would do.

"Benny, ask him if Triads in the United States take orders from Hong Kong Triads."

"He doesn't know whether Triads in the United States take orders from Hong Kong, although he doubts it because he hears that some of the people who run some of the societies in your country are pretty independent-minded, and he can't imagine them taking orders from anyone. Of course this is just what he hears—he doesn't know them personally."

Every time I tried to get Benny to ask him another question regarding issues like drug trafficking, or money laundering, or the recruitment of youngsters at most of Hong Kong's schools, or the nature and extent of corruption within the government administration, Benny would nervously shake his head and refuse.

"You're walking on thin ice here. Let's call it a night," Benny suggested. "It's almost two-thirty in the morning, and I don't know about you, but I am going to get moving."

The Red Pole put a crisp $100 Hong Kong dollar bill ($13 U.S.) on the table as a tip.

It was clear that, as politely as a Chinese man would show you, this meeting was over.

"He says you still have a lot to speak about and we all must get together before you leave Hong Kong," Benny assured me as we started to leave. The Red Pole heartily shook my hand with a warmth that was not reflected in his eyes. I did not see him again during my stay in the British colony. Each time Benny tried to arrange a meeting, he claimed a conflict in his schedule. As we left the Canton Disco that night, Benny told me that it was unlikely he would meet again with me.

"You pushed him into too much sensitive material. He didn't mind talking about the ceremonies and the background of the Triads. But when you started to ask questions about today's players, you were stepping on too many toes. If he said something to you and it got back to the wrong person that he said something sensitive to a writer from the United States, he would be finished. Oh, they wouldn't kill him, but it would certainly be the end of his career. And by the way, he said he could tell from your questions that you were researching a lot more than the history of the Triads. He could tell by some of your questions that you have been talking to a lot of people, including the cops, to come up with some of the information you had. He just doesn't know you well enough to be frank about the things you wanted to know. He has to be a diplomat in order to save his skin."

"How could he understand all my questions, especially the ones you wouldn't ask him?"

"Oh, he understands some English, he just doesn't feel comfortable enough to speak to you in it. He feels better in Chinese."

"Well, it's too bad he was so careful."

"You don't know how lucky you are, man. No one comes into Hong Kong for several weeks and gets a senior member of one of the island's biggest Triads to sit down with him and talk to him about anything, much less the stuff he talked to you about. The rituals, the initiation ceremonies, they are still very proud of all that. They still consider it a secret. If I hadn't made the introduction for you, he would never have seen you. It would be like me coming to New York and getting a senior Mafia guy to sit down and tell me how you become a member and tell me his views on crime in America. It's not so easy, huh? Without this meeting you would have had to rely on the police to tell you about the initiation rites from the little they know. You are a lot luckier than you know. You are lucky he didn't get mad at you. He's not a good guy to have angry with you. Actually, I was surprised he was so talkative with you."

When I mentioned my meeting the next day to a senior member of the Royal Hong Kong Police intelligence department, it was my turn to be surprised: "We knew about your meeting. Oh, don't look alarmed. Do you think that we would fail to have some people inside a place as active as the Canton? We are always watching to see what is new and what is going on. You were lucky to get plugged in. When I heard about the meeting I knew you were making progress. And you shouldn't be disappointed that he was clever in what he told you. Of course he's careful about the current situation because you are dealing with billions of dollars. He's not going to risk telling you anything for your book that can in any remote way jeopardize their ongoing enterprises. He's a significant player, and I am surprised he even met you. It's not often you get to have drinks with a quintessential Hong Kong gangster."

That short meeting at the Canton Disco was a revelation far beyond the description of the initiation rites. I was able to judge firsthand a Triad officer, and what I saw stood in sharp contrast to the Mafia chieftains paraded before television cameras in the United States after their arrests or indictments. He looked every bit the yuppie out for an evening on the town. There was nothing sinister about him, no bodyguards hovering nearby, and no sign that he was carrying a weapon. Benny told me that he was quite representative of most Triad officials.

"You've got to change your image of people with lots of gold chains and white suits and all of that Hollywood gangster stuff. It doesn't really exist here except for some of the young kids who have to show off how much they are making. But the older guys, the more established people, they are very quiet. If you ever met any of the elders of the Triads they would look more like bankers than godfathers. They dress in dark blue and gray suits and conservative shirts and ties, they look just like the best businessmen in Central [the Hong Kong financial district]. Because in their hearts that's what they think they are—they are financiers for large narcotics deals, and they are businessmen dealing in the commodities of the underworld. It could be potatoes or pineapples or anything, it just happens to be heroin and prostitution and things like that. So they are businessmen who take high risks, and as far as they are concerned they deserve the high profits that come with the risks. They almost never have bodyguards.

They almost never fight about the business. They always seem to realize that there is enough of the pie to go around for everyone and so they negotiate their differences and adjust their take of the profits. They seldom kill each other at the highest levels. And when they get near the top they don't carry any weapons because it is not honorable to look like you are scared of anyone. If they were ever arrested by the police, they would admit they were caught—it is their shame to be caught. But they would never shoot it out with the police because that would not be honorable. Oh, they would have a policeman who was a pain in the ass killed, but they would never do it themselves."

The quiet gangster. Subtle in every way except his watch and cigarette case, the only telltale signs that he was sporting serious money. Yet the fact that he did not fit the caricature of a mobster meant nothing. I would later uncover information that exposed the Red Pole as one of Hong Kong's more ruthless criminals. During my investigations in Hong Kong and the rest of Southeast Asia, I would discover the answers to all of the questions that the Red Pole refused to answer that night.

Confidential police files and frank conversations with U.S. Drug Enforcement agents as well as senior members of the Royal Hong Kong Police later revealed the exact dimensions of the Hong Kong Triads, the nature of their tentacles into other countries, including the United States, their control of the international heroin trade, and exposés on everything from their methods of recruiting schoolchildren to laundering their illegal profits. But before the current stature of Triads is measured, it is necessary to view the development of the opium and heroin trade in Southeast Asia. Colonial European countries made the narcotic an accepted way of life throughout Southeast Asia. Then there was an explosive post-World War II growth fueled by the collaboration of intelligence agencies, primarily the CIA. This collaboration resulted in enormous profits, which allowed the Triads to expand worldwide. Indirectly, the CIA assistance catapulted the Triads into their present criminal dominance.

5

The Politics of Heroin

Asia's narcotics traffic has been shaped by the rise and fall of Western empires. Before the first Portuguese warships arrived in the 1500s, opium abuse and narcotics trafficking were virtually unknown in Asia. Starting with the "Age of Discovery," Europe's colonial empires sanctioned opium programs to generate enormous government revenues. After the colonies received their independence, the European administrations were replaced by Western intelligence agencies that directed the narcotics trade. Their legacy was the curse of opium and heroin addiction for millions of Asians as well as the ingraining of narcotics and smuggling into the very web of Southeast Asian life.

The Western powers laid the foundation for today's heroin problems. They showed the Chinese secret societies the region's full potential for narcotics and its incredible profits.

Before the European powers arrived, the Asian states were isolationist empires. The Chinese considered their country the only place on earth that mattered. With a population that was ten times that of France and Britain, and an area twice the size of the United States, they felt that whatever lay beyond their border was dark, ignorant, and hostile.

Less than a decade after Christopher Columbus discovered

America, Portuguese explorers reached China. The Chinese confined the "white demons" to the unoccupied coastline. Stymied
in trade because of Chinese self-sufficiency, the Portuguese, and
then the Dutch, tried to import opium from India to China. Lack-
luster demand limited their success for more than one hundred
years.

It took the pervasive bureaucracy and persistence of the British
to transform China into a nation of addicts. Britain became the
largest organized drug trafficker in history.

During the 1800s the European powers financed their colonial ambitions through the opium trade. The British led the drive.
They established a government monopoly over the large poppy
tracts in northern India and targeted China's millions of inhabitants as the most profitable market.

Prior to the British campaign, China had a small number of
opium smokers, leftovers of the Dutch efforts. The British mass-
merchandised opium. Together with the soldier–merchant–executives of London's East India Company, Britain became the first
Western government to traffic in narcotics. Moral objections were
overwhelmed by the enormous profits, almost 20 percent of
British India's revenues.

As the Indian opium shipments increased, so did the number
of Chinese addicts, despite the Emperor's objections. Opium use
was considered a desecration of the body and a violation of Confucian philosophy. The Chinese banned opium. But British cap-
tains ignored the imperial bans and sailed into Chinese ports
bulging with opium shipments. Indian opium shipments to China
zoomed from 200 tons in the year 1800 to 2,000 tons by 1840.

The Chinese resented being exploited because of British colonial aspirations. Although the Ch'ing dynasty was politically
weak and riddled with corruption, it tried to stop the drug. The
Chinese seized and destroyed $6 million in opium and arrested
some British traders. Opium dealers were exiled in the frozen
tundra of Central Asia, and one was even crucified on the Canton docks. The frustrations culminated in a Far Eastern Boston
Tea Party when Cantonese officials dumped several thousand kilos of British opium into the sea. Britain responded by shelling
the coastline.

Full-scale wars between Britain and China erupted in 1839 and
1856. Chinese junks and rusted cannons were no match for the

powerful British fleet. Dubbed "the Opium Wars" by the Chinese, a name resented by the British, they resulted in total British victory. China was powerless to stop the opium trade, paid the British onerous reparations, and ceded Hong Kong to British control.

Following the Opium Wars, the British accelerated their Chinese traffic. By 1880 some 6,500 tons of opium annually were instrumental in creating 100 million opium smokers and fifteen million addicts. Britain single-handedly made opium the world's largest cash commodity. Demand outstripped supply. Pressed for funds, the Chinese government finally tolerated domestic opium cultivation in two provinces. By 1900 it was turning a blind eye to an annual yield of 20,000 tons.

During the late 1800s a new wave of empire building was ushered in. Europe's sanctimonious real estate brokers divided the world into colonies, protectorates, and spheres of influence. Vietnam, Laos, and Cambodia became French Indochina, Burma became British Burma, and Thailand became a British sphere of influence and a buffer separating the British and French empires.

As opium addiction spread from China to Southeast Asia and then on to Europe and the United States, a worldwide anti-opium crusade formed. By 1906 the organized opposition gained such momentum in London that the House of Commons pronounced Britain's involvement immoral.

Although the British did not ban opium in Hong Kong until 1946, the House of Commons' vote marked the beginning of the end for Britain's control of the trade. Yet despite declining opium shipments and a suppression campaign, China remained a nation of addicts. Opium was ingrained into Chinese life. Even the Empress Dowager, who began the campaign against the narcotic, smoked an opium pipe. The drug remained a social grace for the wealthy and a means of escape for the masses. The 1911 revolution, in which the imperial government was overthrown and a republic was formed, worsened the problem. China ceased to be a unified country, disintegrating into autonomous regions controlled by powerful military warlords. Without a strong central government to provide enforcement, Chinese poppy cultivation and opium exports increased.

By 1900 missionaries tried to cure Chinese addiction with "Jesus opium"—morphine. Its addictive qualities were overlooked, and soon opium addicts were switching to morphine. By the 1920s a new "cure" for opium addiction made the rounds in China—heroin. A typical recipe for an opium "cure" called for two ounces of heroin, one-half ounce of strychnine, one ounce of quinine, five ounces of caffeine, and forty-eight ounces of milk and sugar. Thousands of kilos of legal heroin were shipped from France to China. Shanghai became a major heroin manufacturing and distribution capital. During the 1930s it was America's primary source of heroin.

While Britain made China a nation of addicts, the French did the same in Indochina. In Vietnam the royal court opposed opium smoking on moral and economic grounds and outlawed the drug. Yet any hope of avoiding an opium epidemic was shattered when the French captured most of South Vietnam in an 1858 invasion. The effects of the French victory were devastating. The Vietnamese were unable to pay enormous reparations without additional revenue. Submitting to the inevitable, the Emperor established an opium franchise in the north and leased it to Chinese merchants at a fee that satisfied the war penalty. At the same time the French created a government opium monopoly in the south. Colonial economists forecast that opium would have French Vietnam profitable within six months. They underestimated French inefficiency. The administration of the five separate colonies that comprised French Indochina was a model of bureaucracy at its worst. French Indochina ran at a deficit for more than forty years.

Opium came to the rescue. A clever budget analyst organized the five opium agencies into a single monopoly and aggressively expanded sales. The French built a state-of-the-art Saigon opium refinery and developed a new opium mixture that burned faster, thereby encouraging more use. Business skyrocketed, creating a Vietnamese addiction rate of 20 percent. In several years 1,500 government opium dens and 3,000 retail shops accounted for a third of French colonial revenues.

While the 1920s crusade against the "evils of opium" forced other colonial powers to reduce their narcotics operations, the French ignored the pressure. They waded through the Great Depression by increasing opium production, and even by World War II the drug accounted for a quarter of French Indochina's revenues.

The colonial successes in China and Indochina were duplicated in Thailand and Burma. Thailand was technically independent, the only Southeast Asian nation not a European protectorate or colony. Yet Thailand was under the British "sphere of influence," and while Thai citizens ran the government, Britain influenced most policies, including opium.

As in Vietnam, Cambodia and Laos, the opium problem arrived in Thailand in the early 1800s with a half a million Chinese immigrants. The King banned opium and instituted the death penalty as a deterrent. However, the British threat of a full-scale invasion forced the Thais to bow to the inevitable and establish a royal opium franchise. It was leased to a prosperous Chinese merchant, handpicked by the British.

Further British pressure forced the Thais to allow three Chinese-managed vices—opium, gambling/lottery, and alcohol. They provided almost 50 percent of government revenues. At the start of the great 1920s anti-opium crusade 3,000 Thai opium retail shops and dens supplied a quarter million addicts. International pressure forced the Thais to close more than two-thirds of the dens and shops by World War II. Even in a reduced role, opium continued to supply 10 percent of government revenues, and it had become an ingrained part of Thai life.

Burma stood in contrast to the booming opium businesses in the rest of Southeast Asia. Although the British established an opium monopoly after they colonized the country in 1852, opium was limited to registered Indian and Chinese addicts and prohibited to the Burmese. In Burma the drug provided fewer government revenues than in any Southeast Asian colony.

Burma also confronted the British with a unique problem. When Britain annexed northern Burma in 1886, the Shan States, composed of a dozen indigenous hill tribes including the Shan people, was the only Southeast Asian region with significant opium production. The mountainous region, roughly the size of England, is ideal for opium cultivation, producing enough to satisfy the world's entire annual demand.

The British never obtained a solid foothold in the rugged northern terrain. Divided by sharp mountain ranges and deep valleys, the Shan States' natural boundaries have historically created separate principalities ruled by feudal warlords called "sawbwas." When the British marched into northern Burma they discovered thirty-four sawbwas controlling separate fiefdoms ranging in size from that of New York State to less than twenty square miles.

The British avoided confrontation and recognized the sawbwas' powers. It was a critical mistake. When Burma received independence after World War II, the new government was saddled with a terrible legacy. The autonomous sawbwas, controlling the world's lushest opium land, tolerated no interference in their territory. When the British left in 1947 the Shan States had realized only a fraction of their potential for poppy cultivation. But as that potential was developed, the British-sanctioned sawbwas prevented the Burmese government from taking effective suppressive action.

In Southeast Asia, not only did the British and French opium monopolies create massive addict populations, but they also inadvertently formed a smuggling network that was crucial to the post-World War II heroin epidemic. Although the colonial administrations reaped huge profits, they never became involved in the drug's distribution and sale. That work was left to each colony's licensed opium merchant. Invariably they were Chinese. The British so successfully ingrained opium into China that Chinese merchants were a natural choice to run the monopolies throughout Southeast Asia. The French insisted that Indochina's opium franchise be leased to Chinese merchants. The British forced the Thais to accept Chinese control of all underground vices. In Burma the British allowed only Chinese to direct the opium trade.

Those Chinese merchants developed an unrivaled narcotics expertise. The Chinese families in the opium trade, from Rangoon to Bangkok to Saigon to Shanghai, became acquainted. The early Chinese traffickers, interrelated and tied together by business, virtually monopolized the supply of opium in Southeast Asia. With criminal elements from Triads in China, they were perfectly poised to take a leading role in the post-World War II heroin boom.

At the war's end, Southeast Asia underwent radical changes. The British returned to Hong Kong and a decimated police force fell behind the expanding Triads. In China the winds of change were represented by Mao Tse-tung's revolutionary armies. The

British gave Burma independence and for the first time in almost one hundred years it prepared for freedom. The French pressed their colonial claim to Indochina but were fighting a growing North Vietnamese rebellion.

French intelligence and the CIA became involved in clandestine activities that would seem farfetched in a spy novel but that played a major role in making the Triads and the Golden Triangle the greatest factors in the narcotics business. French intelligence dealt in narcotics to bankroll their costly war against Ho Chi Minh. The CIA, obsessed with the perceived cold war threat of monolithic communism, assisted criminal empires on the assumption that they would provide a buffer to postwar Communist expansion. The policies of these intelligence agencies transformed the region into the leading heroin-producing and -smuggling center. The French led the way.

When the French government finally banned opium in Indochina, French intelligence (SDECE) took the trade underground. The French military had decided the best way to fight the North Vietnamese was to employ tens of thousands of mercenaries in counterinsurgency warfare. But the problem was a lack of funds. The Indochinese war was tremendously unpopular in France and the government provided little money. Senior French intelligence operatives decided expediency outweighed legality and "Operation X" was born. From 1951 to 1954 the French developed a sophisticated opium distribution network, a feat which won the loyalty of the hill tribes, the population from which the French hoped to recruit their counterinsurgency army.

Each spring SDECE operatives bought opium at competitive prices from the hill tribes. Mountain guerrillas then avoided customs and police controls by flying the illegal drugs to a French military school. From there they were taken by truck to Saigon, where they were turned over to a syndicate of river pirates who worked for the SDECE. The river pirates transformed the raw opium into a smokable version in two large Saigon refineries. Then they distributed some to the city's underground dens and sold the substantial excess to Chinese merchants with Triad connections. The river pirates split the enormous profits with French intelligence.

Operation X initially boosted the military efforts with large infusions of money. And the hill tribes rallied to the French cause as long as they received high prices for their opium. But when the SDECE utilized non-highland minorities as middlemen, the hill tribes complained they were being cheated. The French ignored the complaints. As the money to the hill tribes dwindled, so did their support for the French. The intelligence service's opium policy unwittingly helped to end France's role in Indochina. The Meo hill tribes, the backbone of the mercenary army, were so dissatisfied with their opium prices, they allowed the North Vietnamese to infiltrate the surrounding jungles and surprise the French garrison at Dien Bien Phu. Without Meo reinforcements, the French surrendered on May 8, 1954, and signed an armistice two months later.

The entire SDECE opium experience was not lost on the CIA, which monitored the French operation and realized that opium was the key to hill tribe loyalty. In half a dozen years, when the CIA sent agents into the Laotian and Vietnamese hills to organize counterinsurgency armies, they offered the French colonel who created Operation X a senior position. Convinced the CIA would never give him real power, he refused.

The SDECE, in financing its Indochina war, made the Southeast Asian narcotics trade international in scope. While some opium was smuggled out of the Golden Triangle before 1950, the sheer bulk restricted the amount exported. But when French intelligence used the air force to move unlimited quantities, they established the foundations for large-scale postwar trafficking. By selling to Chinese merchants with Triad connections, they accelerated a narcotics network that expanded and paralleled the booming Hong Kong Triads.

Although the French signed a 1954 armistice, they merely agreed to withdraw from the northern half of the country and hold a nationwide referendum in 1956. The SDECE maintained its partnership with the Saigon river pirates, ensuring immense profits from the opium dens, gambling casinos, and prostitution houses, including the Hall of Mirrors, the largest whorehouse on the globe. The CIA wanted to cancel the referendum since the Communists were likely to win a popular election. The CIA asked French intelligence to abandon its underworld ventures and turn them over to the Americans. The SDECE refused.

By early 1955 the French mobilized the river pirates and some Corsican mercenaries into a wartime battalion. In April the CIA, together with the South Vietnamese Army, fought a pitched battle with the SDECE forces. It was the first and last time that two Western intelligence agencies entered open combat. Colonel Lansdale, the CIA chief, directed operations from the presidential palace, while Captain Antoine Savani, the SDECE chief, moved into the river pirates' headquarters. For six days a savage house-to-house battle raged for Saigon.

The river pirates offered a reward to anyone who brought Colonel Lansdale to their headquarters, where they promised to cut open his stomach and stuff him with dirt. There were no takers. The river pirates had grown soft through a decade of vice and corruption, and the CIA forces pushed them back into the Run Sat swamp. The outnumbered Corsicans withdrew. At the battle's end more than 500 were dead, 2,000 wounded, and 20,000 homeless. Ngo Dinh Diem, the Americans' handpicked choice, was in firm control of Saigon's political machinery and its extensive underworld.

During the next fifteen years the United States allowed the South Vietnamese to become deeply involved in the narcotics trade. The chief of the air force, later Premier and Vice President, Nguyen Cao Ky, became a principal smuggler, disguising his trafficking as intelligence and surveillance forays. His brother-in-law ran the Saigon port and oversaw a massive import and export of drugs. South Vietnamese officials worked closely with a Triad based in Saigon's Chinese suburb, Cholon. The Vietnamese used government planes and trucks to transport opium from the Golden Triangle into Saigon. The Cholon Triad negotiated the price with the Chinese growers in the Triangle, refined the narcotic in jungle labs and then distributed it to Vietnam's addicts and sold the excess to large Hong Kong syndicates. During this time Bangkok became a key transshipment point, a role it retains to this day.

U.S. military files are replete with the names of South Vietnamese government leaders who spent more time dealing in narcotics than in fighting Communists. Money poured into a system held together by corruption. But the United States not only overlooked its allies' illegal activities, it also assisted them. The CIA followed the path of French intelligence. When operatives went into the Laotian hills to organize counterinsurgency units, CIA agents assisted the Meos in planning maximum harvests. It then transported the drugs. Air America, a CIA-owned subsidiary, flew opium loads from Laos to South Vietnam as late as 1973. This was two full years after President Nixon declared heroin "public enemy number one" and promised every possible effort to eradicate it.

But the opium-heroin tool used by U.S. intelligence was the same one that backfired on the French and caused their humiliating defeat at Dien Bien Phu. Now it came back on the United States like a boomerang. This time the damage was a sudden burst of heroin addiction among GIs. Starting in 1970 the Cholon Triad imported the first Hong Kong chemists capable of producing number 4, injectable heroin. Never available before in Vietnam, suddenly number 4 heroin was everywhere. Fourteen-year-old girls sold it at roadside stands on the main highway; South Vietnamese soldiers offered vials with 99 percent purity for $5.00; prostitutes always had a supply of China White for a special treat; street peddlers stuffed free bottles into GIs' pockets as they strolled through Saigon. The aggressive Triad marketing campaign succeeded. By mid-1971 the U.S. Army estimated 15 percent, or 40,000 GIs, were addicted, and the number was growing.

Vietnam was a giant test market for the Triads. Hong Kong sent 14K and Wo Shing Wo gangsters to Vietnam to see the effects. They were impressed. They saw that a demand for heroin could be created among Westerners similar to the way the British had created an opium demand among nineteenth-century Chinese. Eventually an estimated 100,000 GI addicts consumed as much heroin as two million users would in the United States, more than twenty tons a year. That is why when the GIs withdrew, the market initially collapsed in 1972–73. The Triads' solution was to ship more heroin to other Asian cities and the United States. Combined with a fortuitous ban on opium in Turkey in 1972, Chinese heroin increased from 8 percent of the U.S. market in 1971 to 30 percent by 1974. Although large crop failures later temporarily lowered that share, Vietnam taught the Triads that America was a receptive market. It whetted the Chinese appetite for selling heroin in the United States.

At the same time these events transpired in Vietnam, CIA activities in neighboring Burma, Thailand, and Laos transformed the Golden Triangle from a minor opium producer to the unrivaled world leader. At the end of World War II the Golden Triangle annually produced 100 tons of opium. Within fifteen years CIA policies were instrumental in increasing production to 700 annual tons, on its way to today's 1,500 tons.

Following the 1949 collapse of Chiang Kai-shek's Nationalist Chinese (KMT) government, the Truman administration decided to stop communism at all costs. The United States gave military aid to the French in the Indochina war and supplied arms to the new KMT government in Taiwan. Truman also allowed the CIA to regroup those KMT armies that had retreated from Mao over China's southern border and had settled into the Burmese Shan States.

By the spring of 1950 some 2,000 KMT troops were in Burma. U.S. intelligence was convinced the KMT lost armies were not only a barrier against further Red Chinese aggression but, if properly armed, could retake China. The CIA support for the KMT is crucial in understanding the current heroin empires, for one of the world's largest traffickers, General Li, is a KMT officer and still directs a KMT army in the Golden Triangle.

When the KMT settled into northern Burma, the Burmese demanded they surrender or leave. The KMT refused, and the CIA gave them the strength to resist. Under CIA direction the KMT underwent an intense expansion and within months Taiwanese intelligence agents arrived. Scattered KMT survivors joined the armies, doubling the number of soldiers to 5,000. The KMT pressed another 6,000 hill tribe residents into service. The new troops and an incredible assortment of supplies arrived through CIA front companies, Civil Air Transport, renamed Air America Corporation, and Sea Supply, Inc.

While the CIA covertly supported the KMT, the Triad tycoon Charlie Soong orchestrated the overt campaign. Together with his sister, Madame Chiang Kai-shek, he helped form a Washington lobby group called the "China Lobby." Its purpose was to generate popular American support for the KMT. It did this admirably, claiming a notable roster of members, including columnist Joe Alsop, FBI Director J. Edgar Hoover, former California Senator William Knowland, and former State Department Chief of Intelligence Ray Cline. The China Lobby counted influential allies, like Soong's close American friend *Time* magazine publisher Henry Luce and Richard Nixon, who received a quarter-million-dollar contribution in 1968 from the Lobby for his presidential bid. The CIA interpreted the widespread public support for Chiang Kai-shek as a mandate to help the KMT in the Golden Triangle.

With CIA supplies, the KMT launched invasions of China in 1951 and 1952. They engendered little popular support among the millions of peasants, and each ended in a crushing defeat by Mao's troops in less than a week. After the second failure, General Li, the KMT commander, abandoned the idea of retaking China and focused on increasing his power in the Golden Triangle. Equipped with state-of-the-art CIA weapons, the KMT captured all of the opium-rich Shan States.

At first General Li was content with taxing the hill tribes for growing the opium. Then he taxed the smugglers who brought the opium out of the hills. Realizing that bigger profits were to be made, General Li "rented" KMT troops for protection on the smuggling routes. The KMT used strong-arm methods ranging from public executions to torture and forced most small traders out of the Shan States. The KMT progressed to buying the opium directly from the hill tribes. It then smuggled tons by mule caravans, up to a mile long, through the Shan States into Thailand. There remnants of the KMT Fifth Army, under the leadership of General Tuan, arranged for further transport.

During the 1950s, while the KMT gained control of the opium trade, the United States and Taiwan generated propaganda that Communist China was the world's largest heroin exporter. The United States maintained that the "Reds" were flooding the world with heroin as part of their Communist philosophy. Taiwan echoed these accusations. In fact, opium production in China virtually halted after the 1949 revolution. During the 1950s it did not export opium or heroin. The stories were intended to deflect the spotlight from the guilty parties, the KMT, the CIA, and Taiwan.

The KMT boosted the Shan State opium crop from forty tons when they arrived in 1949 to 350 tons within a decade. They changed opium cultivation from scattered individual farmers to hundreds of thousands of organized plantings. The Chinese Nationalist generals, with their Taiwan connections, brought the Triads into every stage of the heroin business, from the source to the refinement to the distribution and sale. Hong Kong Triads sent chemists to KMT heroin labs, and the Chinese armies reserved their best narcotics and lowest prices for the Hong Kong syndicates.

Although the CIA knew of the KMT's opium involvement, it did not alter its support for the Chinese Nationalists. With CIA backing, the KMT stayed in Burma until 1961, when they were dislodged by a joint Burmese–mainland Chinese military strike. The KMT lost armies moved to Laos, where the CIA employed them in its secret anti-Communist operations. By 1965 the KMT moved its operations to Thailand. U.S. pressure, combined with the Thai fear of communism, made the KMT an accepted buffer force in the north. General Li's Third Army and General Tuan's Fifth Army, more than 10,000 troops, always had an unexplained supply of current U.S. weapons. They created autonomous communities, even including Chinese schools staffed with Taiwanese teachers. Taiwan government and intelligence officials made frequent visits. Until they were later challenged by other Chinese warlords in the Golden Triangle, they monopolized the trade. Their power expanded together with the heroin business. But they owed their existence to the CIA, which rescued them in 1949. The ramifications of the CIA action are still felt today. Although General Tuan is dead, the result of an overdose of a Chinese aphrodisiac in 1980, General Li is one of the world's largest heroin traffickers. Although he maintains a close relationship with the CIA, his still powerful army now fights only for narcotics.

And while the CIA oversaw the KMT's emergence as a narcotics army in neighboring Laos and Thailand the CIA's policies laid the groundwork for the explosive growth of heroin syndicates and Triad influence. In Laos the CIA organized large-scale opium cultivation. Laos is one of those few countries that is virtually without natural resources. Its only crops are rice and some poppy fields. Unable to finance itself through taxes, exports, or industry, Laos has been plagued with fiscal problems since its 1954 independence. As a result it became a transit center for international smuggling, from which it reaped considerable revenues.

After the 1954 French departure, some Corsicans established "Air Opium." Until 1958 they reliably flew opium, gold and currencies from Laos to Saigon. The Laotian military was content with bribes to allow the traffic to flourish.

The U.S. cold war hysteria fundamentally changed Laotian

opium involvement. In 1958 a leftist government won a surprising election victory. Paranoid that Laos would turn Communist, the United States suspended all economic aid, forcing the new government to resign. The CIA's handpicked man in the new right-wing government was a young colonel, Phoumi Nosavan. With CIA support, Phoumi became a general, built secret anti-Communist armies, rigged local elections, and infiltrated CIA agents into the fabric of Laotian life. But in 1961, President Kennedy, against CIA advice, halted $3 million in monthly aid. The CIA decided the only way to keep the right-wing Phoumi in power was to raise funds through opium.

Under CIA direction, Phoumi stopped collecting Chinese and Corsican payoffs and instead imported opium directly from another CIA client, the KMT. It was not long before U.S.-supplied planes were ferrying bulging opium shipments to Saigon.

Through the 1960s and early 1970s Air America and the U.S. military further organized the Laotian narcotics trade. Meo farmers were encouraged to grow opium and American intelligence agents oversaw the annual harvest just as French operatives had twenty years earlier. Laotian production zoomed from twenty-five tons to more than 200 tons. Although Laotian production stopped for several years following the fall to communism in 1975, since 1980 Laos has reverted to the single profitable cash crop that Western intelligence agencies showed it to rely on. The current annual Laotian opium production is estimated at 250 tons and growing. The CIA and French intelligence taught the Laotians well.

The last Southeast Asian country affected by CIA meddling was Thailand. While the CIA's Thai policies did not increase opium production as they had in Burma and Laos, they initiated a widespread system of disciplined corruption. Marked by remarkable bribery, patronage, and greed, it opened the door to the Triads.

Until 1946 Thailand maintained the last Southeast Asian opium monopoly, but international pressure forced its demise late that year. Burdened with a large addict population and no legal opium, Thailand authorized poppy cultivation by the northern hill tribes. But the domestic production was small, and Thai addicts were increasingly served by Chinese Triads based in Bangkok.

The KMT armies provided the opium. The Chinese traffickers bribed Thai officials to ignore the trade. The key official was the corpulent General Phao Sriyanonda.

The right-wing Phao was chief of the police. His vehement anticommunism complemented the CIA's cold war fever. With CIA military aid, Phao expanded his single police force to include an air force, an armored division, a maritime fleet, and a paratroop squad. The CIA introduced him to General Li's KMT.

Phao boosted the KMT political aims in Thailand, sold their opium, and raised considerable funds for them among wealthy Bangkok Chinese. While serving the CIA, he also served his own considerable greed. In addition to the opium traffic, he formed a partnership with the Triads over the vice rackets, rigged the Bangkok gold exchange, and extorted money from some of Bangkok's wealthiest citizens. *The New York Times* called him a "superlative crook."

By the mid-1950s Phao's police force was the largest trafficking organization in Thailand and the Bangkok Triads had grown with him. Police guards escorted the opium from the Burmese border. Once in Thailand, it was brought to Bangkok in police trucks or planes, and then maritime police boats escorted it to ocean freighters bound for Hong Kong. Triad officers regularly met with Phao, gaining an unprecedented familiarity with a generation of Thai government and military leaders.

In September 1957 a military coup forced Phao to flee to Switzerland. The new government threw out Phao's CIA advisors and arrested senior police officials. Inadvertently, the Thai decision to clean its own house gave the narcotics business to Phao's partners, the Chinese Triads. They aggressively filled the void. Triads arranged for direct deals with General Li's KMT. Triad middlemen moved the opium to refining centers and then to Bangkok for distribution and further transport.

By the time the CIA returned to Thailand in the early 1960s, the damage could not be reversed. The Bangkok Triads had monopolized all stages of the heroin trade. The CIA's man in Thailand had opened the door to the Triads. Today the network is exactly the same.

"Does any of that surprise you? It shouldn't. You're dealing with a bit of everything in that part of the world. Don't forget about the strategic importance of the area, right under Communist China, within striking distance of the Soviet Union, and blessed with incredible natural resources. The French understood how important it was and we understood as well. And to try to work in that region you must work within the local rules, and the local rules say that opium is part of the social fabric. The French and the British colonialists ensured that was the case. So don't be so surprised that every Western government that has gone there has had to play in the opium game."

The man talking was a retired CIA agent who had spent fifteen years in different Southeast Asian assignments. I was sitting in his Virginia farmhouse only a week before Christmas. A large Christmas tree, heavily decorated with garlands, ornaments, and lights, flashed incessantly while we talked.

"Nobody in Washington ever made a conscious decision to move opium around Asia. The French did make that conscious decision with Operation X, I mean they actually used it to pay for operations the government wouldn't fund. For us it was different. We had all the money we needed. For us, helping a little in the opium business just ensured loyalty from people we needed to rely upon.

"In retrospect, I don't know if it was worth it. Vietnam and Laos went to the Reds anyway. We just helped a lot of people get wealthy there. In Burma and Thailand, well I guess that helping the KMT was pretty stupid. They looked real good in 1949, but I think they screwed us pretty well. General Li wouldn't know a Communist if he tripped over one today."

The years from the end of World War II marked a period of tremendous change in the Southeast Asian narcotics trade. Governments made decisions that helped create major powers in the crime and drug world, and the intelligence agencies of France and the United States formed partnerships with organized criminals. The ramifications are still felt today.

In Indochina, French intelligence launched Operation X to help the hill tribes market opium. Later the CIA fought the French and their Corsican enforcers for control of the opium market and vice rackets in Vietnam. The CIA allowed the South Vietnamese to become heavily involved in the narcotics trade—the payoff was 100,000 addicted GIs. Western intelligence involvement in Vietnam gave the Triads the organizational expertise to move opium from mountain growing areas to urban consumer centers. It was a crucial step forward in the development of their heroin business. In Burma the CIA supported the exiled Chinese Nationalist armies, the KMT, and molded them into the largest private heroin armies in the world. The KMT increased opium production in the Golden Triangle by 500 percent in just fifteen years. In Laos the CIA used the opium trade to fund a right-wing government, and in so doing increased opium production by 800 percent. In Thailand the CIA's major government contact developed a partnership with the Triads to run the narcotics trade. When he was forced to flee a coup, the Triads quickly filled the gap.

The politics of heroin in Southeast Asia have been highlighted by a series of crucial mistakes from colonial powers to modern-day intelligence agencies. Inevitably the Western powers ingrained opium and heroin into the very web of Southeast Asian political and social life. They sowed the seeds that have developed into a heroin epidemic and a Triad bonanza.

"I know that when we left in 1975 the place was starting to boom with heroin," the retired CIA agent told me. "It was everywhere and the Chinese were all around. I hear things, but I don't know what it's like today. There are a lot of open questions. To find out what a mess we left, I guess the only way to do it right is to go up there and find out for yourself."

I knew he was right. The answers were to be found in the hills of the Golden Triangle.

6

Princes of
Darkness

Chiang Mai is Thailand's second-largest city. Since it sits at the Golden Triangle's southern flank, it is also the starting point for expeditions into the heart of Asia's heroin fields. "You've got to cruise around Chiang Mai before you do anything else in northern Thailand," a veteran DEA agent told me in Bangkok. "Just walk around and get a feel for the city and you will start to get a feel for the northern part of the country. It's very different. When you go into the Golden Triangle itself you'll be in one of the last great lawless regions left on the globe. Kids actually go fishing with rocket-propelled grenades and M-16s outnumber radios. You won't see anything like it anywhere else. And Chiang Mai is a good introduction into what you will run into up the road in the Triangle. Everything is just simmering under the surface, the craziness is almost in the air. Just around the bend you'll feel like you are going to run right into trouble."

I started my walk at dusk near the river, vainly hoping for a breeze to relieve the 100-degree heat. I was at a multistory wooden building resembling a traditional Thai pagoda. The facade was covered with hundreds of strings of Christmas lights, thousands of flashing bulbs illuminating the gaily decorated but empty souvenir shops. I was the only tourist mad enough to be there.

Although this was one of the newest and most ambitious tourist developments in northern Thailand, it seemed I was the only person who did not know that the single success of this tourist mecca cast in a swamp was in attracting hundreds of thousands of tropical insects. As I stood at the water's edge watching a man paddle a canoe down the river until he disappeared into the deepening darkness, I suddenly realized that even though the dozen large electronic bug lamps were intensely working overtime zapping an endless variety of insects, I was getting bombarded by a growing and exotic assortment of crawlers. Under my feet I could feel and hear the crunch of bugs, some seemingly as large and hard as jawbreakers. Other bugs started flying directly at me. Since the sun was setting, the lights of the tourist center had attracted the swamp's insects. I was unprepared for it. The insect repellent I had bought back in the United States was obviously not intended for jungle pests. I covered my eyes and clamped my jaw firmly shut so nothing could pry into my mouth and down my throat, and I walked as fast as I could away from the river. Less than a hundred yards from the river, in dim lighting, I was safe from the attack. I stopped and vigorously shook off the remaining stubborn crawlers. At the roadside I found a three-wheeled motorcycle manned by a pubescent boy. For twenty-five cents he took me zooming down the dirt road toward downtown Chiang Mai. The DEA agent was right. It was like no other place I had seen.

Near the town's center a former police sergeant runs a restaurant that has caged bears and a snake pit in the middle. For $12 the waiter uses a pair of steel clamps to snatch a five-foot cobra from the pit. Standing at your table, he grabs the viper's head with one hand and slits the body from the throat to the tail with a straight razor held in the other hand. The oozing blood is drained into a large wine goblet and the resulting drink is considered a source of strength and a powerful aphrodisiac. The bladder is sliced out, and aficionados cap off the drink of fresh blood by swallowing the bladder, just like a western drinker might combine a mouthful of peanuts with a beer. Of course the rest of the snake is not wasted—it is cut into bite-size morsels that are fried in front of you. Entertainment is provided on weekends by a mongoose and cobra fighting to the death.

Near the snake-pit restaurant are Western-style clothing shops and electronic outlets blasting the latest Western rock 'n' roll. Behind these stores the side streets are crammed with sex bars, androgynous young Thais bidding welcome to men or women. The main streets are filled with hill tribe people in elaborate native costumes, many nursing their young. They travel to Chiang Mai's night markets to sell souvenir handicrafts to tourists. Walking between the hill tribes' street stalls, I stepped over dozens of terribly deformed beggars with rickets, many with no arms, their stumps pecking at the legs of tourists and their eyes pleading for one baht (four cents). But the beggars do not have a lot of success with foreigners because in Chiang Mai most of the tourists seem to be in a 1960s time-warp. It is as though San Francisco's "Age of Aquarius" Haight-Ashbury had been preserved in a time-capsule and reopened in 1987 Chiang Mai. Scruffy and dirty hippies flood northern Thailand, eating for less than a dollar a day at the hundreds of food-stalls and getting easy access to the north's biggest crop, the ever-present "black gold," opium.

It takes only a couple of hours' wandering through Chiang Mai to realize that the king of the city is the opium poppy. T-shirts emblazoned with the poppy are sold at outdoor stores. Barefoot children in tattered clothes run through the streets with buckets of dried opium poppies to sell to tourists, the remnants from the end of the recent harvest that the government claims does not exist. Sidewalk blankets are spread with opium pipes, from simple wood to ornate hand-crafted silver. Opium scales made in local factories are sold everywhere, disguised in carved wooden boxes resembling violins or elephant sculptures. The small scales are de rigueur for users and dealers alike. A visitor to Chiang Mai never gets far away from the ubiquitous opium poppy. The seats on the Thai domestic planes that fly you into the city are decorated with poppies. Local restaurants have poppy wallpaper and poppy place mats. At the best hotel in Chiang Mai you can dine at the Golden Poppy Room or dance all night at the Poppy Club. Souvenir shops are filled with postcards depicting hill tribe farmers at different stages of the colorful opium harvest.

But this is not just another mainstay crop that is celebrated in Thailand's second-largest city. Homage is being paid to something that is illegal. It is prohibited and banned by law for cultivation, use, barter, or sale. It would be as though the coca leaf were imprinted throughout Miami, with airlines, restaurants, and clubs named after the coca crop, postcards showing the coca harvest, samples of the coca leaf openly sold around the town, and the utensils of the cocaine trade displayed and sold in every other retail shop. It is the brazen defiance of the government ban on the poppy that is most startling. Chiang Mai is a year-round festival in honor of the Golden Triangle's poppy fields, the indispensable pipeline to the world's heroin addicts.

Each spring Triad middlemen flood into Chiang Mai to cement the deals that will determine where the next heroin crop is distributed. Young Chinese gangsters, with their gold Rolexes and Porsche wraparound sunglasses, are squeezed elbow to elbow at the Chiang Inn's coffee shop haggling over the price of a processed kilo and the degree of risk the Golden Triangle warlords will share with the Hong Kong Triads. Packs of local toughs are hired to stand at the coffee shop's entrance to scare away uninvited guests. Banks cram Chiang Mai's "business" section offering easy international transfer capabilities allowing dope deals to be clinched on the spot. In the middle of a city where the average annual salary is $385, sparkling new discotheques or hotels or limousine services are the hallmark of drug dealers with more cash than business sense. Just a mile from the snake-pit restaurant and the beggars of the night market is the palatial guarded compound of the Chinese Nationalist General Li, the commander of the KMT Third army. "Chiang Mai provides a 'who's who' tour of the Triangle dope trade," the DEA agent had told me in Bangkok. He was right.

As I walked back to my hotel, which I later discovered was owned by a heroin dealer, I took a shortcut through a side alley. There I passed an old grizzled man, with rotted and missing teeth. He was swaying back and forth while chanting a prayer over a small Buddha statue. Next to him a tribal woman was sprawled on her side. One of her young children, with enormous eyes, laughing as I imagine a mad child would, was running naked in circles, the curdling sound coming in an endless stream from his mouth. Near the end of the alley a beautiful tribal girl was sitting on the floor with her back against the wall, the neon sign advertising "Chiang Mai Bowling Alley" casting a surreal pink glaze over her face, fixing her as if she were a statute. Before I could get up the stairs into my hotel, the ever-present and pesky taxi drivers descended on me. No, I did not want a night tour for a special price. No, I did not want to rent a car for the morning. As most of them left, disheartened at their failed conquest, a couple of hardy hustlers stayed behind. One pushed in at me, revealing a glint of shiny metal coming out of his pants pocket: "Want a gold watch, very cheap and very good?" I shook my head as I continued bounding up the steps to the sanctuary of my hotel lobby. "You like to meet nice girl, do anything for you, mister?" And again a simple no. "You like smoke something nice, mister, have real good time?" They interpreted my pause as real interest, and they shifted into their high-pressure sales mode. They thought they had zeroed in on my vice—not counterfeit jewelry, not women, just dope. One peeled a soiled handkerchief apart and revealed a small black clump of what looked like dirt. "One hundred baht for good smoke all night"—he smiled the winning sales look that had won over dozens of drug addicts over the years. Four dollars for a packet of fresh opium. If nothing else, the price informed the traveler the source was nearby. I knew I would be seeing a lot more of this and other narcotics during the next several days as I journeyed deeper into the Golden Triangle. I turned to leave. "Okay, fifty baht, it's good deal, you not get any cheaper, believe me, mister." I took the last couple of steps to the hotel door. "Oh, maybe opium not enough for you. You want something special. How about China White, it is best in Chiang Mai, one hundred percent. It knock your head off, I swear it, you not get any better and I give you best price. Any amount, you say it, I bring it, you test and then you buy. Deal?"

I turned my back on the group of stragglers, entered the hotel, and closed the door firmly behind me. Chiang Mai was the first city I knew of where the taxi drivers servicing the town's best hotel were heroin pushers also servicing the foreign addicts or petty traffickers who were not connected to the major syndicates. I told the desk clerk that I had just been offered opium and heroin by the taxi drivers in front of the hotel and asked him if that surprised him. He smiled at me and looked as though I was the most naive man he had encountered in some time. "Welcome to Chiang Mai"—and he gave me my room key.

Chiang Mai was a full frontal assault on the senses. But I was only beginning investigations that would lead me to the doorsteps of the most powerful heroin warlords in the world, leading massive private armies in northern Burma's wild Shan States. The guides for the beginning of my journey were two petty young players in the heroin trade: Hu, a moon-faced, pasty-colored Chinese of twenty-four, and Chan, a short wiry man just turned twenty-one. Hu and Chan picked me up in their four-wheel-drive jeep the next morning, fully outfitted with automatic rifles and handguns. "Everyone has a gun in the hills," a smiling Hu informed me. "You have to remember that a life is only worth twenty cents here. That's what it costs for a bullet. So that's how easy you can kill someone. Cheaper than a beer. You never know when you need this," he said while patting an assault rifle. "Just want to make sure no one gets funny ideas." With that reassurance we were off on the narrow road leading to Chiang Rai, "the town that dope built" according to the local Drug Enforcement agent posted in the area. The goal of the trip was to illegally cross the Thai–Burma border and enter the Shan States, where the world's largest private heroin armies control millions of people and thousands of square miles just as an autonomous government would. The Shan States of Burma produce almost 1,000 tons of opium a year, almost as much as the rest of the world combined. Each year's crop could supply American addicts with enough heroin to last nearly fifteen years. The political situation in the northern Shan States borders on anarchy. No legitimate government exerts influence there, and about 40,000 armed insurgents belonging to a bewildering array of rival insurgencies control the region. As long as political and military chaos reign, there is no realistic chance of curtailing the massive opium production.

The Shan States, about the size of Greece, have been a problem for successive governments for more than one hundred years. The Mekong River, flowing out of southern China, cuts the Shan Plateau in two, creating a natural boundary. The region's physical isolation forced the British to forgo colonizing it. Political integration is difficult. Even today only two major roads extend into the Shan States, and not only are they plagued by banditry but they are very poor quality and subject to washouts. There are no services along the way, no airports, few doctors, and no effective government. The farther north one goes into the Shan States, the very geography that ensures excellent opium yields and protective cover for the insurgent armies deters central gov-

ernments from extending their influence. There are elevations
of 1,500 to 3,500 meters, deep gorges, thick jungle growth, and
hills covered in forty-foot-high bamboo. With unbearable heat
and humidity and visibility often limited to the next tree, it is
possible to understand how a hundred rebel armies could hide
in the Shan States and never be found. The current Burmese
government lacks both the resources and the willpower to over-
come these obstacles.

The British colonial masters struck a deal with the northern
warlords, the sawbwas, who were allowed to control vast tracts
of land in return for loyalty to the British. The sawbwas managed to keep peace among the many different ethnic groups that
populate northern Burma. Although they are called the Shan
States, after the Shan people, the largest minority there, the rugged northern provinces are also filled with large populations of
many other hill tribes, including, among others, the Ahka, the
Wa (renowned for headhunting as late as the mid-1960s), the
Karin, and the Kachin. These ethnic groups have sought independence as long as the Shans. Although they all fight the central government in Rangoon, they do not coordinate their efforts
into a single freedom movement, for they all want separate independent states. They often fight each other as much as they
fight the Rangoon government. Just listing the names of the hill
tribes does not fully indicate how complex the situation is in
northern Burma. For instance, in just one group, the Kachin,
there are at least twenty-five different and mutually unintelligi-
ble dialects. To add to the confusion, the political boundaries
drawn during colonization were done without regard to ethnicity,
and as a result the various ethnic groups are not geographically
localized but rather scattered in different pockets across the north
of the country. A majority of the Burmese population is made
up of these different scattered "minorities."

At the end of World War II the British granted independence
to Burma. The ethnic minorities in the Shan States expected the
same treatment. They reasoned that since they were never de-
feated by the British, and since their agreement with London had
allowed them to keep their own governments, the British had
no right to give "independence" to a Burmese government based
out of the southern capital of Rangoon and to ignore the separate northern requests for independence.

The situation appeared resolved in early 1947 when the George Washington of Burma, Aung San, promised to create independent northern states within ten years. But the chance of peacefully resolving the Shan problem was killed together with Aung San when right-wing Burmese Nationalists burst into a government meeting in July 1947 and assassinated the entire leadership of Burma, including San. The next ruler of the country was U Nu, a second-rate politician who lacked the decisive character of his predecessor. Although he vacillated on the question of northern independence, he publicly remained committed to the concept of freedom for the Shan States and he kept the ethnic revolts under control by sporadically negotiating with the different minorities. But in 1962 any chance for peaceful coexistence in Burma came to a halt. U Nu was overthrown in a military coup and fled to Thailand, where he tried and failed to form a government in exile. The new ruler was Ne Win and he remains there today, making him one of the longest-reigning rulers on the planet. But from the very start of his regime he made a series of decisions that laid the groundwork not only for the continuing ethnic revolt throughout the Shan States but also the groundwork that created the warlords and their heroin armies.

The first thing Ne Win did in 1962 was to arrest the leaders of the Shan States who had been in Rangoon negotiating with the government at the time of the military coup. He tore up the constitution, brought a radical socialist agenda to the government, and announced that his regime was not bound by the promises of earlier administrations. According to Ne Win, the Shan State minorities were Burmese, and he intended to extend the central government's control throughout the Shan States. Twenty-six years later he is still trying to accomplish that goal, with less chance of success today than ever before.

Ne Win's decision to control the north fomented a widespread rebellion. Although the names of the revolutionary groups in Burma change as often as the battle scenes, within a year of Ne Win's military takeover some of the largest ethnic minorities had formed movements like the Shan Revolutionary Army, the Wa National Army, and the Karin United Revolutionary Army. And the ethnic revolutionaries in the Shan States found an unexpected ally in the CIA-backed Chinese Nationalist armies of General Li and General Tuan. The KMT armies had carved out a monopoly over much of the opium and tax trade in the Golden Triangle. But the KMT had also faced increasing resistance from the central government in Rangoon, who viewed the lost Chinese armies as invaders seeking to capture Burma and establish a second Taiwan on China's southern flank.

So the KMT jumped at the opportunity to finance and organize some of the ethnic independence movements, knowing that if the ethnic rebellions could distract Rangoon's attention, the KMT could profit immeasurably in the opium-rich Shan States. The KMT sent some of the most promising freedom fighters to Taiwan for training. Taiwan intelligence sent agents into Burma to help plan battles and strategy. And Taiwanese intelligence offered the rebellion groups modern weapons and equipment. Short of funds, many of the groups tried to finance their independence movements by resorting to the only viable crop in the regions they controlled—opium. The Karen, who had the least cultivatable opium land, resorted to jade, gold, and ivory smuggling and taxing the opium caravans that marched through their territory. Within several years the northern Shan States had slipped into anarchy, involving a baffling number of Nationalist rebels, tribal chiefs, bandits, and opium smugglers, who fell in and out with each other in kaleidoscopic patterns and temporary alliances of convenience. The glue that held this fragile world together was opium. The situation is not much different today.

The major change is that a number of new players have been added to the already boiling recipe. In the early 1960s Communist China helped form the Burmese Communist Party (BCP), and that revolutionary group added a new dimension to the rebellions in Burma. Now in addition to ethnic insurgencies where the fighters are bound by their race, there was a well-financed revolutionary movement where the fighters were bound by their political beliefs. In 1963 Ne Win made a fateful decision which has since come to haunt him and the drug-flooded Western nations—he added yet another fighting element to the already confused Burmese scene. With full government and military backing, he formed more than fifty private armed militia, dubbed Ka Kwei Yei (fighting groups) or KKY. These KKYs were armed by the Burmese and were intended to fight the growing ethnic and Communist rebellions and help Rangoon complete a job it could not finish on its own. Rangoon did not pay the KKY volunteers, instead allowing them in their spare time the use of government-controlled roads, territories, and villages to dabble in opium and make some profits. Just as the Chinese Nationalist armies, formed and encouraged by the CIA to stand as a buffer to Chinese communism, decided it was more profitable to traffic in opium and heroin, it did not take the KKYs very long to realize that it was better to grow and sell opium than to fight rebellions.

From these KKYs emerged the men who became heroin warlords of the Shan States, the only men capable of successfully challenging the Chinese Nationalist generals. Today a flamboyant chain-smoking KKY fighter, half Chinese and half Shan, named Chang Chi-Fu, has become the general of a 15,000-man army dubbed the Shan United Army (SUA) and the world's greatest heroin warlord. Chang Chi-Fu is now called "Kuhn Sa," "Prince" in Burmese. Kuhn Sa, whose uncle was executed by the British for opium smuggling, had served with General Li's KMT Third Army and had been trained in Taiwan. As a paramilitary adventurer he was just one of many mercenaries wandering Burma before Rangoon gave him his own KKY militia and 400 troops in 1964 at the age of thirty-one.

The other warlord whose fortunes have risen and fallen and are now back on the rebound as this is written is the short, fat, moon-faced Chinese Nationalist Lo Hsing-Han. Together with his brother, Lo Hsing-Min, they became the most powerful warlords during the height of the Vietnam GI addiction explosion during the late 1960s and early 1970s. Lo started as a slum hood in the remote northern province of Lashio. He was a drifter with an interest in running guns and in women. He would have remained another of northern Burma's gun-toting bandits except that in 1963 he was drafted as a KKY leader and given 150 men. The Rangoon government badly needed a KKY in Lo's province, and the Burmese army had just seized a large shipment of Lo's opium. The government told Lo that if he formed a KKY, they would return his opium. Lo agreed. It was a better deal for him than for the Burmese.

By the late 1960s the KKYs had grown fat with narcotics profits, and they attracted adventurers from around Southeast Asia. Instead of fighting the insurgency movements, they largely ignored the rebellions and focused exclusively on the growing opium and heroin trade. By the early 1970s the KKYs had become such an embarrassment that Ne Win's government demanded that they dissolve. The KKYs universally refused and some of them, such as Kuhn Sa's militia, adopted names that made them sound like liberation movements, using the cover of legitimate independence rebellions to hide their narcotics trading. That is why today Kuhn Sa's army is called the Shan United Army (SUA), when in fact he has nothing to do with Shan independence. He has everything to do with the business of a criminal overlord, from forcing young men in his territories to serve in his army, to illegally taxing the villagers, to growing and processing almost half of the opium and heroin that is exported out of the Golden Triangle.

Kuhn Sa's rise to the top was marked by setbacks and events that almost finished his career as a player in the heroin trade. In 1967 Kuhn Sa made a name for himself when he became the first warlord to challenge the heroin monopoly of the Chinese Nationalists, the KMT. Kuhn Sa had concluded an agreement with the CIA's man in Laos, General Ouane Rattikone, Commander in Chief of the Lao army. Kuhn Sa's deal was for direct shipments of enormous loads of opium to General Rattikone's heroin refineries on the Lao–Burma border. The problem was that Kuhn Sa's opium caravans had to pass through Chinese KMT-controlled territory, and when General Li demanded the normal opium transit tax, Kuhn Sa refused to pay. For a while it looked as though Kuhn Sa had pulled off a major coup and that the Chinese Nationalists had suffered a terrible public loss of face. Kuhn Sa took 600 mules and 500 troops with almost ten tons of opium and arrived safely at the Laotian border. But General Li knew that if Kuhn Sa was not punished for his rebellious attitude, then other warlords would challenge the authority of the KMT armies. So more than 1,000 of General Li's troops ambushed Kuhn Sa and a fierce battle, dubbed by the press "The Second Opium War," raged for three days. More than 200 were dead and the two sides were in a stalemate when the CIA's General Rattikone intervened with Laotian troops on the side of another CIA client, General Li and the KMT. With the Laotian air force supplying air support, the KMT gained the upper hand and Kuhn Sa was forced to abandon the massive opium shipment and retreat with his battered force back to the sanctuary of the Shan States. General Rattikone was the big winner, as he charged General Li $250,000 for the Lao military support that turned the battle's tide and General Rattikone kept the opium without paying for it.

At that point Kuhn Sa appeared finished as a viable power in the narcotics world of the Golden Triangle. Most law-enforcement agencies wrote Kuhn Sa out of the Golden Triangle picture and considered him a player of the past. After the battle with General Li, Kuhn Sa had less than 800 troops, waning popular support, and he had earned the hatred of the powerful KMT. Kuhn Sa's fate seemed sealed when he was captured in a surprise 1969 raid by Burmese troops, tried for treason and opium smuggling, and given a life sentence.

Although Kuhn Sa and Lo Hsing-Han are major rivals, they have both demonstrated tremendous resiliency over the years, their careers often moving in opposite directions. While Kuhn Sa's star had fallen with his 1969 arrest and imprisonment, Lo's was on the rise. Lo was building a fully integrated narcotics empire, from cultivation to processing in his own refineries to delivery to the Chinese middlemen representing the Hong Kong Triads. Lo was ideally poised to take advantage of the great market opportunity of the 1960s, the influx of over 500,000 GIs into Vietnam. His brand of heroin, neatly packed in plastic bags with its own Double U-O Globe trademark, became one of the most sought after in Southeast Asia. Lo helped his army grow from 150 men in 1964 to more than 5,000 in 1972. His brother, Lo Hsing-Min, ran the heroin laboratories and made the deals with the Hong Kong Triads.

The arrest of Kuhn Sa in 1969 removed the only other major warlord from the Burmese scene. Lo filled the void. He was satisfied with his growing share of the heroin trade, and he avoided any clash with General Li and the KMT with its extensive Taiwanese and U.S. support. Lo established his headquarters at the remote mountain town of Tachilek, which one observer called "the capital, the stock exchange, the processing and refining center of the Golden Triangle." Answerable to no one, contemptuous of beleaguered Burmese army units and graft-ridden local police forces, the then thirty-eight-year-old Lo ran an empire that collected taxes, directed punitive military actions, and presided over the collecting, initial transport, and sale of the bulk of the Triangle's opium production.

Although Lo and his army grew fat from the narcotics profits, he was caught unprepared when the United States decided to withdraw its military forces in Southeast Asia. Lo was hooked directly into the Vietnamese and Laotian end of the business but had never bothered to develop contacts with Triads expanding into new markets in Europe and North America. And as had happened before, as Lo's business was declining in 1973 and 1974, Kuhn Sa's fortunes started to rise again. The warlord who had been forgotten in a Burmese jail was about to be freed.

Kuhn Sa's chief of staff and likely replacement, Chang Tsechuan, a native of Manchuria and a Triad member, has a reputation throughout the Shan States as a bloodthirsty leader. He is famous for having cut up an Ahka chief alive for having betrayed Kuhn Sa's Shan United Army. He then threw pieces of the body to a pack of dogs and the dying man lived long enough to watch parts of his body cut away and eaten by the mongrels. Chang came to Kuhn Sa's rescue by organizing the kidnapping of two Russian doctors with the Soviet Embassy in Rangoon. Unknown to Chang, one of the two Russians was a KGB agent, and the Russians placed intense pressure on the Burmese to rescue the prisoners. Meanwhile, Chang promised to release them unharmed for a single ransom demand—release Kuhn Sa. The Burmese had no choice, and Kuhn Sa was a free man by 1974.

At the same time that Kuhn Sa's star had begun to rise again, Lo's fortunes plummeted. In July 1973 he fled a Burmese army sweep and sought sanctuary on the Thai side of the border. But unfortunately for Lo, he fled almost directly into the arms of a waiting Thai patrol and was promptly arrested. Although he offered the Thais more than $1 million for his release, the arrest had attracted such publicity, as well as the intense scrutiny of the United States, that the Thais had no choice but to favorably respond to a Burmese extradition request. By the time Kuhn Sa was free, ready to reenter the heroin trade, Lo was in the court docket in Rangoon, charged in an elaborate show trial with treason. By the time Kuhn Sa had chosen a new base of operations, Ban Hin Taek, a small frontier village in northern Thailand, Lo had been sentenced to death by the Burmese court. Although the highest court in Burma granted his appeal to dismiss the death sentence, it ordered life imprisonment, and by the mid-1970s Lo looked as though he was finished as a force in the heroin trade, just as Kuhn Sa was "finished" after his 1969 arrest.

While Lo languished in a Rangoon prison, Kuhn Sa increased his forces to almost 8,000 and expanded his role in the heroin trade. Taking a page from Lo's successes, Kuhn Sa integrated his enterprises and not only taxed the people and the opium shipments passing through his territories but also cultivated the crops, refined the products in his own laboratories, and sold directly to Triad representatives in Thailand. Kuhn Sa became the first of the warlords to use the press to his advantage, and he gave a series of interviews claiming that he was not involved in the narcotics trade and that his Shan United Army was a legitimate liberation force. Many believed him. The number of his troops swelled to more than 10,000 by 1980 and today approaches 15,000, even though he now freely admits he is the world's largest trafficker.

During his years in Thailand, Kuhn Sa established key contacts in the Thai government and counted on his payroll some of the most influential police and government figures in the country. He converted Ban Hin Taek into a luxurious headquarters complete with a movie house, modern television and video machines, manicured lawns, tennis courts, a soccer field, indoor and outdoor pools, rooms made of imported marble, a basketball court, and shops that sold electric guitars, imported food, liquors, and leather furniture, these among other items that Kuhn Sa considered necessities for a "liberation" army. Ban Hin Taek cost more than $2 million a month in upkeep, but it was the "loose change" the Shan United Army raked in from the drug trade. Kuhn Sa established more than thirty large heroin refineries straddling the Thai–Burma border. Always ambitious to carve out an ever-larger chunk of the heroin business, the Shan United Army fought pitched battles with the rival Wa National Army, the Burmese Communist Party, and General Li's Third KMT Army.

Kuhn Sa also used his sixth sense for flamboyant press coverage when he made an unprecedented offer in the summer of 1977 to sell the United States the entire Golden Triangle opium crop for $12 million. Although General Li and the KMT sold the United States twenty-six tons of opium in 1972 for $1 million,* Kuhn Sa claimed he could sell the entire crop, at that

---

*Classified CIA documents indicate that General Li had an excess of opiates in 1972 because of the GI withdrawal from Vietnam. The twenty-six tons were overproduction that the general could not sell. If the United States had not paid $1 million for it, General Li would have had to destroy it. Instead he pocketed a handsome profit and looked like a hero to his CIA benefactors, who made it appear as though General Li was merely rounding up hill-tribe opium as a favor to the United States' fight against narcotics.

time nearly 500 tons. The offer was taken so seriously that Congressman Lester Wolff of New York, the chairman of a congressional committee on narcotics, traveled with a delegation to Kuhn Sa's northern Thai camp and tried to hammer out the details. The offer was eventually rejected when the State Department concluded there was no way to ensure that Kuhn Sa could deliver such an enormous consignment of opium. Although the United States rejected his offer, the fact that the American government sent a congressional delegation to meet with a warlord on his own turf gave him instant prestige not only among the other Burmese insurgency groups but throughout Southeast Asia. A Thai police official in Bangkok told me, "The Lester Wolff trip was the stupidest thing the Americans have ever done in the war on drugs. It gave Kuhn Sa great 'face' among his rivals and friends. Overnight they made him a major force to deal with. No one in Washington even asked us if they should talk to him— they just arrived and said we are going to see Kuhn Sa to buy the Golden Triangle crop from him. Stupid."

By 1980 Kuhn Sa had gained such notoriety that the United States urged the Thais to move against him. Events came to a boiling point when Joyce Powers, the wife of an American Drug Enforcement agent, was kidnapped and killed in Chiang Mai. She was executed within inches of her husband, who was vainly negotiating with the abductor to let her go free. While the "official" Thai police investigation concluded it was a robbery attempt that went awry, the country's leading antidrug law-enforcement official, a man termed by the *Bangkok Post* and United Press International the "incorruptible cop," Colonel Viraj Juttimita, concluded that the killing was the work of Kuhn Sa—the mission was supposed to be a kidnapping but the abductor panicked when he could not make it safely out of town and killed his hostage instead of giving her up. The Powers killing brought the full pressure of the United States to bear on the Thai government. The result was a 500,000 baht ($40,000) reward for the head of Kuhn Sa, a reward that the Americans guaranteed to pay if Kuhn Sa was brought in dead or alive. Kuhn Sa responded by telling the press that his "death would not halt opium growing in the Shan State because this has been going on for more than 200 years," and he posted $25,000 rewards on the heads of DEA agents stationed in northern Thailand. The rewards seemed aimed more at public relations than for any real effect. None of Kuhn Sa's 15,000 troops made a single attempt to attack the large and prominent DEA compound in Chiang Mai, and the Americans and Thais never made an effort to stop Kuhn Sa from visiting Hong Kong, or his house in Bangkok, or his jade shop in Chiang Mai.

But the growing public focus on Kuhn Sa placed him in a spotlight that would eventually force law enforcement to strike at him. And as had happened in the past, as Kuhn Sa came under increasing attack in 1980, the fortunes of his longtime rival, Lo Hsing-Han, began to reverse. The former chief Golden Triangle warlord, who was supposed to serve the rest of his life in a Rangoon jail, unexpectedly had his sentence commuted by President Ne Win. According to one source, the release was clinched with a $3 million payment to Ne Win and his cronies. To add to the initial shock of the release, the Burmese gave Lo a new KKY armed militia. Lo was given 2,500 troops (called the Shan State Volunteer Force) and modern arms, and told to fight the rebel armies once again. Although the Burmese had lost control of him before, they counted on the fact that if Lo was ambitious enough to regain a prominent role in the heroin trade, he would have to fight the main players. And since virtually every ethnic insurgent group and revolutionary army had become deeply involved in opium since the late 1960s, Lo would have to fight all of them in order to regain some stature in the narcotics trade. As Rangoon considered Lo the most vicious warlord that it could release again in the Shan States, it hoped that Lo's KKY might have the military success against the insurgents that had eluded the Burmese army. Lo got his second lease on the dope trade just as Kuhn Sa's problems started to multiply.

By 1981 the United States State Department announced that "the Shan United Army, under the leadership of Chang Chi-Fu, controls approximately 70 percent of the heroin refining in the Golden Triangle." The press attacks on Kuhn Sa gained momentum and U.S. government officials pushed the Thais to eliminate Kuhn Sa's free hand in Thai territory. The Thais first tried their old trick of releasing press statements that they were conducting military operations against SUA units along the northern border and not only inflicting heavy casualties on Kuhn Sa's troops but also destroying his heroin refineries. Most of these "actions" received prominent page-one banner headlines in the nation's newspapers and in the weekly newsmagazines of Southeast Asian periodicals. These stories were invariably fables created for the purpose of making the Thais look intent on cracking down on Kuhn Sa when they were actually quite pleased to profit from his heroin trade. But this time the Americans refused to let the Thais engage in a cosmetic war. The opportunity for serious arm twisting was left for Thai Prime Minister Prem's visit to Washington in October 1981. Figuring that he needed to impress the Americans with Thai sincerity, Prem scheduled a military operation against one of Kuhn Sa's heroin refineries on Thai soil. The operation was to coincide with his visit to the White House. Instead, American drug agents believe that a Thai official on Kuhn Sa's payroll leaked word of the impending attack to the warlord. While Prem was in Washington he received the results of the operation—his elite troops had been ambushed by SUA forces and most of the Thai troops were dead while the refinery had been moved. Prem was humiliated, and the Reagan administration, in the throes of yet another "war on drugs," was adamant that Thailand expel Kuhn Sa. Not only was a cutoff of military aid threatened, but a significant bonus, said to be $15 million in additional aid, was promised if the Thais took quick and decisive action.

The Americans were persuasive. On January 21, 1982, 800 soldiers of the Thai Border Police were helicoptered in for a surprise dawn raid on Ban Hin Taek. The Border Patrol Police, sometimes suspected of corruption, had only two hours' advance notice that they were about to attack an undisclosed location. Thai officials tried to prevent another leak resulting in another disaster. But word had gotten to Ban Hin Taek in time for Kuhn Sa to flee to Burma before the Thai units arrived at dawn. The Thais demanded that the several hundred SUA defenders surrender, but upon their refusal a pitched battle began. Kuhn Sa's Triad chief of staff, Chang Tse-chuan, led the attack and escaped while the battle raged. Only when the Thais called in air strikes did the well-armed SUA forces surrender. Seventeen Thais were killed and forty wounded, while Kuhn Sa lost eighty dead and almost 200 wounded. The Thais picked up ten tons of SUA military equipment, including nearly 1,000 assault rifles, 300 hand grenades, 25 grenade launchers, shoulder rockets, crates of bazookas, and 52,000 rounds of ammunition. "It makes the arms seizures in a drug bust in Miami or New York seem like child's toys in comparison," Colonel Viraj told me in Bangkok. Although no heroin was found, the Thais did find 60,000 plastic bags bearing the Double U-O Globe brand, capable of holding almost forty-two tons of processed heroin, enough to supply the United States addict population for almost seven years.

The Ban Hin Taek strike was a major disruption of Kuhn Sa's operations. It interrupted lines of transportation and banking and routing that he had developed over ten years. It also let the other heroin armies think that he might be weak enough for a death blow. They underestimated his resiliency. When he tried to move his SUA troops into the strategic mountain-pass town of Doi Lang along the Burma–Thai border, the Wa and Burmese Communist Party forces fought him in what was dubbed "the Third Opium War" by the press. Hundreds of troops were killed on each side during the 1983 fighting. At battle's end the different groups were forced to share the strategic pass. Again observers said that Kuhn Sa's days were over and that his army could only decline as it had no strong base of operations. Again he confounded the so-called experts. He moved most of his operations back to Burma, where he had not operated in force since his 1969 arrest, and he established his headquarters at Mong Kun, some twenty-five kilometers from the Thai border. By 1984 Kuhn Sa had again broken new ground. He reached an accord with the Burmese Communist Party to buy their opium and refine it in SUA labs. It was the first time that the avowed anti-Communist Kuhn Sa had decided to work together with Communists in the heroin trade (Kuhn Sa still publicly denies this alliance although it is common knowledge in the Golden Triangle). The Communists were desperate for such an alliance. Their financial support had been cut off by the People's Republic of China in 1978 when China decided to improve its international image by refusing to support revolutionary groups in many other countries.

This move scared the Rangoon government, who viewed the cooperation between a political revolutionary group and a warlord syndicate as a dangerous development. The Burmese feared that with the assistance of Kuhn Sa, the Burmese Communist Party could pose its most dangerous threat to Rangoon. As a result the Burmese government invested more arms and money into its hope for a new buffer force—Lo Hsing-Han's KKY. For the first time Kuhn Sa's good fortunes were now Lo's good fortunes. As Kuhn Sa's power grew, the Burmese strengthened Lo's army in the hope that Lo could slow the expansion of Kuhn Sa and the other warlords.

Thus far the Rangoon plan has failed. Since 1984 the last group that Kuhn Sa was fighting, General Li's Third Army, has finally reached an uneasy truce with the SUA forces. Kuhn Sa had actually gone so far as to bomb General Li's house in Chiang Mai in 1984, and the general, while spared, lost face in that he could not even protect his family's home from attack. Throughout 1985 and most of 1986 Li's KMT Chinese fought Kuhn Sa's SUA—hundreds were killed in skirmishes in Laos, Burma, and Thailand. But the Kuhn Sa forces were a much stronger unit than the one General Li routed in 1967 in the First Opium War. This time they held their ground and inflicted heavy casualties on Li's troops. The result of all this fighting was that at the end of 1986 the KMT and the SUA troops reached a fragile truce that has held to the present day, each respecting the other's territories. "They appear to realize there is more money to be made if they work together than fight each other," says Colonel Viraj.

By reaching truces with almost all of the insurgent groups, Kuhn Sa has been able to devote the full energies of his Shan United Army to the heroin business. The results are impressive. He has rebuilt the elaborate and successful operation he had in Ban Hin Taek and is even less accessible to legitimate government authority. He has single-handedly expanded opium cultivation in Burma and boasted in a 1987 "press conference" at one of his training camps that opium production in Burma was expected to double in 1987 to 1,000 tons. He admitted that his SUA as well as the Communists and Li's KMT had numerous large mobile heroin refineries. Even though the reward on his head has increased to 5 million baht ($200,000), he said, "I'm not worried. I'm not going anyplace soon." And he continued to grab headlines with his use of the press and some controversial coverage. He announced in early 1987 that the Russians were willing to supply him with modern weapons, and while the Rangoon bureaucrats shuddered at the thought, it helped ensure that he had a constant supply line to Western powers, who were afraid of Kuhn Sa's army developing ties with the Soviets. By the spring of 1987 Thai newspapers reported a new and expanded threat from the warlords—Kuhn Sa had deployed his first American-made air-to-air missiles along the Thai–Burmese border.

And just when it appeared that Kuhn Sa could not be challenged, there were intelligence reports of fierce skirmishes between SUA troops and a new group of able fighters. DEA internal reports identified the new fighters as Kuhn Sa's old nemesis, Lo Hsing-Han, now fifty-three, attempting a comeback in the Shan States. "If anyone is wily enough and brave enough to take on Kuhn Sa, it's Lo," a DEA intelligence analyst told me in Chiang Mai. "I think he is one of the most interesting characters in the Triangle today. Many people write him off and say his glory days are over and that he can never challenge Kuhn Sa, but I am not so sure. Lo has come back from worse spots before. And this time Rangoon is giving him a lot of help. He won't be dumb enough to engage Kuhn Sa in an open battle, but he'll wait for Kuhn Sa to have other problems and then he will exploit them. He might even be able to make an alliance down the road with General Li's Third Army and together they could give Kuhn Sa a very hard time. Plus, Kuhn Sa has become the clear-cut 'Prince of Darkness'—that is a high-visibility spot and it is difficult to maintain. Everyone is trying to take a shot at you and to knock you off the top spot. Lo will be waiting in the wings should Kuhn Sa fall."

These are real criminal titans, the survivors of a deadly game competing for the biggest stakes of all, control of the Golden Triangle. Three warlords who ran the opium trade in the 1960s, General Li, Kuhn Sa, and Lo Hsing-Han are still the major players twenty years later. Kuhn Sa, now fifty-four, has become the most powerful of the group. General Li, now in his mid-seventies, remains the second-largest supplier of heroin in the world, and Lo Hsing-Han, given yet another chance by the Burmese, is setting the groundwork for a comeback. Other powerful warlords in the business have come and gone, and many facets of the heroin trade have drastically changed since the mid-1960s, but in the Golden Triangle there is one constant—the "Princes of Darkness" have remained the same.

7

"The Town That Dope Built"

At midnight it was still a humid 90 degrees, a sweltering tropical summer night in Southeast Asia. I was crammed into a brown Toyota jeep with four other men, without air-conditioning, a fully loaded M-16 machine gun strapped onto the side of the left front door, and two chrome-plated .38 revolvers resting on the center divider. In addition to Hu and Chan, my two escorts from the heroin trade, I was joined by two provincial police officers. Hu was sweating through his jeans and T-shirt. His breath reeking of local whiskey, he kept slapping me on the back and assuring me I was lucky to be on this excursion. Chan, our driver, the youngest of the group, was barely tall enough to see over the dashboard. His hair was plastered back in an Elvis Presley-style pompadour, and he sported a peach-fuzz mustache and was missing an index finger. I watched him at the wheel, knuckles white, eyes wide, as he hurtled the jeep down the twisting potholed roads. Suddenly we swerved down a narrow back alley, now enveloped in almost pitch darkness, the jeep screeching to a stop in front of a large, battered, metal gate. Chan impatiently honked the horn three times, and the gate slowly rolled open.

We pulled onto a gravel driveway, revealing a group of young, armed thugs sitting around a small barbecue in the adjoining courtyard. Behind them was a pack of mongrel dogs, skeleton-like, kicking up a small cloud of dust as they ripped apart a chicken carcass. At the back of the makeshift driveway was a rickety two-story wooden building with its windows boarded shut with planks. Hu told us to get out of the jeep and wait while he made further arrangements. As we waited, swatting at dive-bombing mosquitoes, a rat the size of a jackrabbit scurried past me and nestled near the metal gate. I started to get back into the jeep, but Hu nudged me and indicated that I should stay. He said something to one of the thugs in Thai and received a grinning acknowledgment.

A young tough, a Colt .45 automatic pistol stuffed into his jeans, strutted over, sized me up, and then signaled to follow him. He took us under a strip of corrugated tin supported by a couple of bamboo sticks, which served as a covered walkway to the wooden shack. Before entering, each of my escorts stopped and bowed, hands clasped as if in prayer, in front of a small black metal shrine of a meditating Buddha, illuminated in the darkness by a large mound of smoldering incense and burning candles encircling the bottom.

Entering the shack, I was immediately struck by a strong odor, an unusual mixture of fresh sawdust and cheap perfume. My eyes blinked rapidly to adjust to the very bright lights. As they focused I noticed I was in a single large room, about sixty feet long and nearly twenty feet wide. Sawdust covered the floor, while the walls were draped in floor-to-ceiling shocking-pink satin sheets. A large, faded, black-and-white poster of Marilyn Monroe, her dress flapping over an open grate, hung lopsidedly over the door. The wooden foundation pillars were tattooed like a sailor's arm with initials and dates and graffiti. At the far end of the room a giant-screen television flickered, while on the other three sides were low, narrow wooden benches on which women and girls were crammed together like fish for sale at the local market. Most were in their early to mid-teens, but a few veterans ranged in age to the mid-sixties, most of them dressed in silk dresses, chartreuse and black the predominant colors. Their faces were heavily made up with white powder, a touch of pink rouge, and crimson-red lips. All seemed to have had their hair cut by the same person, long over the ears and blunt straight bangs covering the forehead—the "China Doll" look perfected on an assembly line.

In the middle of the room a dozen girls sat around a low, round brass table, desperately trying to look older and sophisticated. Later I would learn that the oldest was twelve and the youngest was six.

When our group entered the room the girls turned, almost in unison, away from the television and started primping for us, smiling and squirming on the benches in order to give us a better view. Some were quite nervous and uncomfortable, but most seemed blasé and stared passively through us. A small black boy brought glasses of warm water on a teak tray. Hu, my moon-faced escort, now soaked in perspiration, gulped down the water. The rest of us sat on old packing cases covered with a native cloth, assembled near the table of young children. In a couple of minutes, when the girls realized we were just there to look, they lost interest and either pulled out small makeup cases and freshened their painted faces or simply turned back to the television screen. It was filled with a close-up news clip of former President Jimmy Carter.

My escorts had driven me to the town of Chiang Rai in Thailand, only twenty miles from the Golden Triangle. The building I was in was dubbed the "chicken coop," having been the town's largest up to five years ago, before it was taken over by local drug traffickers and transformed into one of Chiang Rai's biggest whorehouses. The girls are bought or kidnapped from their families in remote provinces. Then they are forced to be whores for the pleasure of locals as well as to earn some pocket money for the heroin dealers and provincial police who form the partnership that runs the chicken coop. The evening I was there Hu bragged that some of the girls had been taken off a rice paddy less than a week before.

Chan struck up a conversation with a girl at the table of young children. She was dressed in a neatly pressed red-and-white schoolgirl's uniform, her hair different from the others in that it was pulled into pigtails. She looked no more than ten years old. "She says she's been here about six months," Chan explained, looking at me over his shoulder. "She lives with her auntie, probably how she got into this in the first place. Auntie is probably an old whore." Chan laughed heartily at his own comment, looking at Hu and the police for a smile but not getting any response.

"Ask her where her parents are."

Chan put the question to her, and she hesitated and looked at the other girls before answering. "She says they are dead. I think she lies. She is real nervous, talking to us in front of everybody, they all pretend they don't listen but they all have big ears."

"You seen enough?" Hu looked at me. "We don't want to make things bad for other customers. Ready?"

"Just ask her how much money she makes here."

Hu shook his fat head. "No good. No one talks money here with the girls. Just not done."

"One last thing. Ask her how old she is."

Hu looked at her and shot off a query in Thai. When she answered my escorts and the young thug who had let us in all started laughing. The girl only weakly smiled. Hu looked over at me, his stomach still quivering from the laugh. "She says she sixteen. Every girl here says she is sixteen. That's because all men, especially American soldiers, like to have a sixteen-year-old never used before by other men. If not sixteen, then they are too young. Older, and they are soiled goods. Sixteen is perfect. So even the old ones here will tell you sixteen. This girl is maybe twelve. She's got a long way to go. Come on, let's get moving."

If the girls can avoid degenerative syphilis or AIDS, and if they are not battered senseless or killed by a drunken or drugged john, and if they show real promise as whores, they will eventually be shipped to Bangkok, where they will join an army of more than 500,000 prostitutes. To buy a girl for the night costs a local resident 100 baht, less than $4. For a foreigner the price is 300 baht, almost $12. If a customer wants more than one girl, the guards will negotiate a better price.

A customer can take the girl of his choice outside the chicken coop—the only rule is that the girl must be brought back conscious. Customers can also use the six-by-four-foot cells on the second floor, with curtains instead of doors and soiled mattresses as the only furnishings. I walked to the second-floor landing, and while the curtains may give some visual privacy, they do not suppress any noise. The moans and the grunts sounded much more like pain than pleasure—I hoped it was just my imagination. After hearing that, I certainly understood why the television was played at high volume on the first floor. Without the T.V., the waiting girls would have been constantly and graphically bombarded with the abuse from the second-floor cells.

The chicken coop left me rattled, a result I believe my escorts planned. On this first stopover with Hu and Chan I had an eye-witness view of the flourishing partnership between local crimi-nals and the provincial police. You could tell the difference only because one group wore uniforms. Hu had no doubt about the role of the chicken coop. "It's only pocket money for us. But it also lets us keep track of police and politicians—most of them are regulars here. I guess they feel safer here than most [whore] houses because they have a piece of this one." The message was clear. Hu wanted me to know from the start that I was entering his world, and that my Western preconceptions of how police and government officials operated for the public good would have to be drastically altered. A local U.S. Drug Enforcement of-ficial would later confirm that what I saw at the chicken coop was not unusual: "The provincial police meet every requirement set forth by the FBI to define organized crime, with the single exception that they aren't that organized." The chicken coop also confirmed what a DEA agent had told me in Bangkok—that the Golden Triangle was one of the last "great lawless regions in the world."

The next morning we were on the road by sunrise, after a breakfast of fried rice topped with an egg at an open-air food stall in the town's center. "It's good you eat Thai style while you are here. Makes you stronger," Chan assured me. The grumbling in my stomach told me he was not right.

The police from last night were left behind. They are posted to the force in Chiang Rai and could not leave the city. About five kilometers from the town Chan turned off the paved two-lane road and started down dirt roads leading to the hills. "If you want to see the Triangle, you have to get off of the main road. You've got to see the mountains to understand how the opium can be brought here so easy."

For the rest of the day we drove along dirt roads that became ever narrower. The vegetation was dense and closed in on all sides of the jeep. As we climbed the back hills we had to keep the windows closed because otherwise the hanging plants and tree branches would have slammed into the interior of the jeep. "You should see in rainy season," said Chan, "then all this stuff is ten feet taller and you cannot even see another car until it almost hits you." Occasionally we saw a few towns—a gathering of small

wood huts qualified for the title—but there was not a sign of life
in a single one.

"No one's crazy enough to go out in this heat," Hu explained.
"They are all inside now—all the work is done in the morning or
late in the day. And now there is nothing to do anyway. If you
had been here a month ago, you would have seen all this covered in opium."

"I thought the government had done away with a lot of the
opium crop."

"Bullshit. It's a lie. Sure, they are planting some coffee and
other crap in some of the villages, but they are also growing
opium on the next square of land. Come on, don't believe that
stuff. These people have been growing opium for hundreds of
years and they don't think anything is wrong with it. You come
and tell them about heroin and they don't know what you talking about. It's just good stuff for them. So why should they stop
growing because someone comes from Bangkok and says 'Please
stop, it's bad because it is made into heroin and sold in New York
and the King and Queen of Thailand would like you to stop.'"
Hu turned around in his seat to look at me, his voice rising as he
was getting agitated. "Shit, they don't know where New York is.
You might as well say the moon. It means no more to them. And
the King and Queen want you to stop is crazy because these people don't even consider themselves Thais. They are Meo first or
Ahka or whatever. None of them say they are Thai if you ask
them. So why should they listen to people that come as Thai big
shots and say stop growing opium because it's bad in some place
you never hear about and we are Thai and you are Thai and
this is Thai land, so you have to listen to us. Shit, they don't even
know this land is part of Thailand. To them it belonged to their
father and to his father and it goes back that way. So they say
this land is ours to do what we want with, so fuck you. That's
why this whole area is covered in opium every year—it don't matter what they tell you in Bangkok."

As we continued along the dirt roads Hu and Chan kept pointing at barren slits in the hills that were horse trails. "Those are
the paths where the caravans come with mules and horses and a
lot of packs of opium," Hu told me as he offered me a canteen
of water.

"I can hardly see them," I mentioned almost to myself as I

squinted at the faint lines that snaked through the dense rain forest.

"That's just the point," said Hu, jabbing his pudgy finger into the air. "They can hardly be seen in this time of year, so imagine when the brush is all grown much higher—then you can't even see the trails with a helicopter, because the ground stays wide enough for the men and horses to pass but the trees and bamboo grow so tall that they touch each other at the top and make like a roof so you can't see the ground. And you have to remember, hundreds of trails like that come out of Burma into Thailand. So where are the cops and your drug agents going to look? Which ones are they going to sit and wait at? And new trails are always being made. It just takes five men and some tools and it can be done in a week. Kuhn Sa even uses bulldozers to open up new roads and then he uses them once and never again. And everyone who brings opium down these hills knows each of these paths like he made it. So they can escape and use them to get away. The cops don't know where the trails go so they get lost and everyone with the opium gets away."

"Aren't helicopters used to discover the opium caravans and then watch where everyone tries to escape to?"

"No way. Look how quiet it is around here. We are the noisiest thing they hear in a while. They don't see many cars around here. If the cops try to bring a fucking helicopter in to watch from the air, you can hear the motor coming from a couple of kilometers away and the whole caravan is off the path and under the trees by the time it flies over. And the opium is only brought in at night. No one moves it in the day. So if that's the case, what can the helicopter see at night? I tell you—nothing!"

In only a day of driving through part of the Triangle it was possible to understand how caravans with hundreds of horses packed with tons of opium could move with total impunity. Insurgent armies could hide in the nearby villages or under the cover of the rain forest and be invisible. And never once during the entire day did I see another car or jeep. With the exception of two Meo hill tribe girls who jumped out of the way of our speeding jeep, I did not even see another person. Except for the hill tribes who lived here, this part of Thailand was no-man's-land. I have trekked in the Andes, the Sahara Desert, and through northern Canada's ice fields, but I have never seen a region as rugged as that section of northern Thailand that led to Burma. Even if the insurgent armies did not populate the Triangle, the authorities would have difficulty in establishing a full government administration in this wilderness. But coupled with 40,000 armed insurgents, the task seems insurmountable unless a major military operation is undertaken and then followed by large infusions of foreign aid to develop the area and to wean it off opium.

"That was the border," announced Hu. I turned around and looked through the jeep's back window. "What? I didn't see anything."

"Exactly," said a proud Hu. "The border only exists on the map. Up here it is just marked with little stone posts. That tells you you're going from one country to another. Otherwise, the trees don't know it—they grow on both sides of the border. Opium, it grows on both sides. Don't stop at the border. So that is why if you have a lab on one side of the border, close to the markers, if one side of cops comes in after you, you just run to the other side of the border and they can't come after you. It's great. They fucked. They just stand there and afraid to come because they afraid of international incident. It's really good, huh?"

Now I understood why Burma banned land entry into its borders. It was the hope that by announcing you could get into the country only by air into Rangoon, everyone would follow that rule. Because if Burma allowed land entry, there would be no way of checking the flow in and out of the country. Anyone willing to take the bumpy mountain trip to the border could cross without fear of detection. No customs buildings, no clearance points, no guard posts, no fences, no walls, no signs or declarations trying to stop you from crossing.

"You're in SUA land now." Chan broke his almost trance-like concentration on driving to say something. "This is Kuhn Sa land all around. The villages, everyone, works with SUA. It's true he has a lot to say in Thailand, like he has some of his people in every major Thai city. But there he has influence only—here he is the only law."

"Aren't you worried that SUA forces will stop you up here in the hills?"

Hu answered. "No worry, my friend. Before we left Chiang

Mai we had to talk to the SUA man to say we are crossing this way. Everyone knows our truck so it's okay. And you are okay because we say you are. And for us, they know we are here as we cross the border. Word travel very fast from town to town. There is an old way of getting news out which never fails to let the SUA know that someone is walking on their land. They'll watch us here, make sure we don't get anywhere too interesting, and then watch us leave. I have something I want to show you not far from here. We can finish up and be back to Thailand by night. As long as we can hit the main road we can travel—I just don't want to be stuck in the hills overnight. No fun at all."

Near kilometer marker 15 Chan pulled the jeep off the dirt road and started a climb that took us over a small stream and settled in the middle of small hill. For the first time in nearly seven hours the jeep had its motor turned off. The silence was the most striking part of stopping. After stretching for a few minutes, Chan pulled the M-16 from the jeep and signaled for me to follow him. I couldn't see a road, but Chan and Hu seemed to know where they were going in the brush. It took us almost ten minutes to go one hundred yards, my ineptitude in the rain forest holding them back. If the land seemed rugged from the perspective of the back seat of a four-wheel jeep, on foot it seemed much worse.

Because I was concentrating intently on getting through the brush I did not realize that I was about to walk right into the side of a building until Hu put his hand out and stopped me by the shoulder. "Be careful," he chided, "never know what you can run into in Burma."

My face must have shown the surprise I felt, because both Hu and Chan found it all very amusing. I thought we had been climbing through the brush to get to a point where I would have a panoramic view of the Shan States. Instead I was at a large wooden structure, charred as though in a great fire, mostly covered in jungle growth. I stepped inside, following Chan. There was no ceiling, but within the long walls of the building were remnants of broken glass and beakers and contorted metal basins and oversized pans. Against one wall was a group of fifty-five-gallon black metal drums. Along another wall were makeshift lockers, rusted orange, their doors bent and hanging open.

"You are the first white man to be inside this spot," Hu suddenly told me. "It was one of the big labs for all the Shan States. This place could make 200 kilos a day." If Hu was accurate, that was two tons of processed opium a day. That is almost four times what the DEA thinks the average jungle lab can produce. "This place was built almost a year ago. Was in operation only two months and then was blown up with explosives. Planted very smart in the night with no one knowing and when it blew it killed twelve people and destroyed most things. Also blew some dope. SUA doesn't mind if you see it, because they think it was DEA or CIA here to do the blowup. No one else is good enough. And if that's the case, then in America you have to ask why they are here, because they are not allowed in Burma. This is off limits for them."

Hu obviously did not see the irony in a heroin trafficker, who lives by no rules at all, complaining because he believes that a law-enforcement agency did not play by the rules. Hu was getting agitated: "The people killed here, they were all peasants who get paid very little to work here. The chemist was not even here so they [American law enforcement] got nothing. In one week it's all up and going again."

"How did people get in and out of here? It's so thick with vegetation."

"Oh, that. When the lab was working there was a foot trail in. But that has been overgrown. Even though the place was always under the plants if you look from an airplane, now the green is all much thicker."

"How many chemists for a lab like this?"

"Only one chief one. This used to make number 3 [smokable heroin]. When it opened it was run by Nat Sa'Kui. He is the greatest number 3 chemist in the whole world. He lives on the road just outside of Mae Sai at the tip of northern Thailand. But he come here for Kuhn Sa to make sure everything working right. I saw it when it was new and it had everything here—good equipment, good shit everywhere. And had lookouts and guns here and that's why we know it had to be CIA or DEA—no one else could get in without being caught. But won't happen again, because there are new changes made by Kuhn Sa since this happened."

I had seen pictures of labs seized in the jungle. I always marveled at how rudimentary the refineries were. A collection of

tubes, flasks, and measuring devices that could be found in any
rural high school chemistry class. But somehow the picture always excluded the surrounding countryside and the quality of
the materials used in the building itself. Now that I was standing
in the middle of a heroin lab, I realized that the pictures made
them look better than they are. They are dark in the middle of
the day from the thick jungle canopy hanging overhead, and a
roof is seldom placed on them because the noxious fumes from
the refining process make maximum ventilation necessary. Stifling humidity and heat surrounded the building. When the fires
that cook the morphine and boil the chemicals are at full force,
the place must seem like hell. I stopped as my shoe twisted into
some glass on the ground. I had stepped onto a pair of eyeglasses,
the visible remains of one of the twelve victims whose body and
clothes decomposed long ago in this tropical weather. It was hard
to imagine that makeshift huts like this were a key part both of
the heroin trail and the Triads' business. But without these refineries the opium would have to be shipped in bulk to Hong
Kong or other refining centers. By placing labs at the source of
the opium, the shipments leaving the Golden Triangle are a tenth
of their size and weight for easier smuggling and are already processed for maximum profits. Even if the shipment is intended
for Hong Kong or Dutch labs,these jungle refineries at least convert the opium into heroin base or morphine.

At this stage of the heroin trade there was no glamour. This
was the blue-collar part of the business. Backbreaking work was
done by low-paid workers in makeshift labs across the Golden
Triangle. Only the chief chemist was usually a partner in the lab
and reaped profits second to the warlord whose opium was processed.

We stayed there for almost a half hour before Hu said that if
we did not start the return journey, we would never get back to
Thailand by nightfall. The return trip was quiet. Hu slept most
of the way, Chan was fighting to see over the dashboard and concentrating intently on driving, and I contemplated where I had
just been. That heroin lab in Burma was a long way from the
Triad headquarters in Hong Kong, or from the youth gang members that peddled the drug on the streets of New York, or from
the offshore banks that helped to launder the billions of dollars
in illegal profits, but the laboratory was as integral a part of the

chain as any of the other elements. This was the source. Without the insurgent armies, without the crop and the refineries, the heroin pipeline was never turned on.

It was indeed Kuhn Sa's territory. I had seen that lab courtesy of his Shan United Army. Nobody was coming onto his doorstep, the Shan States, without his permission. I thought back to the Triad enforcer I had met at the Canton Disco in Hong Kong. His gold watch and fancy ways, much of what he owned, depended on the ability of these Golden Triangle warlords to continue to turn out bumper heroin crops. And the best business partner they ever had in these parts was Kuhn Sa.

He is the most aggressive and flamboyant of the warlords. To drug-enforcement agencies worldwide he is evil incarnate. To the veteran Chinese KMT generals he is an obnoxious upstart. To armed insurgents in the Shan States he is an opportunist who has misappropriated the independence movement to cloak his narcotics trafficking. To local hill tribes in the Golden Triangle he is a feudal warlord, a sort of modern-day Robin Hood fueled by opium. To some government officials in Burma and Thailand he is their most profitable and important source of money. But to the Triads in Hong Kong he is the most important and first link in the multibillion-dollar-a-year heroin business. Somehow, visiting one of his burned-out heroin labs in Burma had helped me realize that.

8

Too Few Good Men

"That's a lot of crap," said the DEA agent as he leaned toward me over a massive wooden desk. "We don't plant bombs at heroin labs. We can't even cross the border into Burma. Our work stops at the border. The State Department would have a shitfit if a drug agent from Thailand was found on Burmese soil. And I can tell you that the DEA in Burma is an advisory and intelligence-gathering office, not an operational one. No black-bag jobs are done out of Rangoon. And if you think the CIA around here is interested in spending its money and effort on blowing up jungle labs, you're mistaken. They have their own priorities, and controlling dope isn't necessarily the highest on the list. Any burned-out SUA lab in Burma was done by one of the other insurgent groups, I guarantee it. Either the KMT or maybe the Wa—somebody hit that lab who is in competition with Kuhn Sa. It wasn't from us. We have our hands filled hitting the labs we find on this side of the border."

I was at the Drug Enforcement compound in Chiang Mai, less than a week after I had crossed the Burmese border with Hu and Chan and seen the shell of the burned heroin lab they claimed had been destroyed in a DEA operation. The man talking to me was Ben Yarbrough, Drug Enforcement Administration station chief for northern Thailand, "the DEA's combat assignment," according to Yarbrough. "Only the cowboys in the agency volunteer for this spot. You don't come here unless you want to get your feet dirty in some action. You know that in Chiang Mai you are going to get to shoot some dope traffickers, and you are going to get your ass shot at as well."

Yarbrough is clearly ready for combat. At six feet three inches and almost 250 pounds of muscle, he looks as if he could crush your head in a fight and not be out of breath when it was over. Sitting in an oversized leather chair with his arms folded behind him, he is the image of a clean-cut American serviceman, tan, with a pair of oversized aviator glasses and a Yankee baseball cap pulled low over his short-cropped brown hair. Married and the father of two children, Yarbrough would be perfectly cast as the sidekick in an Arnold Schwarzenegger or Sylvester Stallone action movie. He not only looks as if he is ready for action, but he loves the excitement of being on the front lines in the heroin battles. His office is a testament to his action-oriented philosophy. Plaques announcing his citations for bravery fill the walls.

"Look, this is really a war up here and we are trying to fight the damn thing with a police action. How do you expect us to stop the heroin flow with a single office? And some of the Thais we work with are great. They put their lives on the line, they don't earn crap in pay, and they get no respect from the Thai people. These guys and their men have stood side by side with me in machine-gun fights with traffickers, and they don't budge. They are honest and they'll give their lives for you. But that doesn't mean that there aren't a lot of corrupt Thai cops. So many of them are on the take it makes you sick. And not only cops.

"Sometimes I can't wait to get to a country where the damn traffickers can't buy their way out of jail. If they don't buy their way out from the prison warden, they bribe the prosecutor or the judge—somewhere along the line, no matter how many honest people you get, there always seems to be someone with his hand out who is willing to take some money and let someone go free. It makes you sick to make a case against a big trafficker and then see him go free because the system is riddled with corruption. But that's Thailand, and if you don't get used to it, you'll go crazy thinking about it. But you also get to do something here that you can do in few places. The Thais give us more leeway to operate than any other country the DEA is based in."

He looked over at an assault rifle resting against the wall in his office. "See that? Well, that is the real court of appeals in this country. Traffickers love to fight it out with the cops so you get a chance to put a lot of them away—permanently. So far this year I have killed four dope traffickers. In the States that just doesn't happen. Last year [1986] we raided a heroin lab together with the BPP [Border Patrol Police] and we had a firefight with twelve men armed with machine guns and hand grenades. This year we busted a lab with thirty guards—they had machine guns, M-16s, Russian AK-47s, M-79 rocket launchers, and grenade launchers and booby traps and land mines. It's no picnic up here but it's never dull, that's for sure. Of all the DEA offices in the world, we are the most operational and have the least emphasis on just intelligence gathering. This is the front line in the war on drugs."

Yarbrough took me around the DEA compound. It was like a small fortress. Surrounded by a tall concrete wall, complete with elaborate electronic security, it is where DEA agents and their families live their own lives, cut off from Chiang Mai. The compound is situated in one of the poorest parts of the town, surrounded on the outside by tin shacks and makeshift homes. When you drive through the massive steel-reinforced gates, it almost looks like Hollywood has recreated a little American town. Tan young men and women in tennis whites play doubles matches on newly built courts. The houses are beautiful two-story American country homes resettled in the middle of Thailand. Manicured lawns, swimming pools, cases of Coca-Cola, and large stocks of T-bone steaks and corn on the cob easily help you to forget that you are 13,000 miles from the shores of the United States.

"In 1974 one of the first DEA agents posted here, George Shoaf, and his wife, Sheryl, were attacked on the back roads near town by a couple of kids with sawed-off shotguns. It was like a welcoming committee from the Chinese in the area, and Sheryl ended up in the hospital. And then in 1980, Mike Powers, one of the best agents we had up here, lost his wife, Joyce, when she was kidnapped and killed. We don't talk about the Powers case much, it still hurts too much. It all just comes down to the fact that the compound is important for us. We need this type of security."

"What about the threats from Kuhn Sa that he will put a price tag on DEA heads?"

"The families here actually evacuated after he made that threat the first time about five years ago. But now when the KMT or SUA or some of the other Chinese traffickers get angry because we have just had a successful operation, and they put out rumors that they might move against the DEA, we always let them know that if anyone gets hurt, then their business will really suffer. They understand that. To the Chinese, making money is more important than just about anything except his family. Sometimes I think it's more important than family to them.

"They are a lot smarter than the Mexicans. In Mexico, drug traffickers tortured and killed a couple of DEA agents figuring that it would scare the U.S. and the DEA out of Mexico. It shows how stupid they are. It only made everyone angrier, more agents were sent in, and the U.S. kicked the crap out of the Mexican government to make them move against the traffickers. The end result is that it is worse for Mexican traffickers now than before they did anything against the DEA.

"The Chinese aren't stupid. They are very clever, and guys like General Li or Kuhn Sa perfectly understand that if they get rid of every one of us, then more replacements arrive the next day and the U.S. government starts kicking some real ass up here. So for them it's better that they allow us to run around picking up as much dope as we can and shooting as many traffickers and they still make a fortune. They're still getting tons through even with us here. They just factor us in as part of the cost of doing business."

"But if they are still getting so much heroin through, is your presence here really effective?"

"You bet your ass. Without us it would be a real flood up here. The Thais would not catch half a ton of dope without us. And we are always pressuring the Chinese: they don't feel comfortable with us up here. They know we pay good money for information and we buy a lot of CIs [confidential informants] that way, and after a while they don't know who to trust so it gets them jumpy. And we hit their labs wherever we find them and that costs them money, and we take out their chemists. We may look like only a finger in the dike, trying to hold the dam from busting with a lot more dope coming in, but we are also a pretty good pain in the ass to the traffickers up here. They know we are around, and we give them an occasional kick in the ass to remind them that we are serious.

"I think the problem basically is that there are too few of us. We're fighting fucking armies up here. If we are ever going to get serious about taking out the heroin business up in the Triangle, it's not going to happen until we send in F-16s and bomb the refineries and armies in northern Burma. When we realize it's a war and we fight it like one, then we'll stop this shit. But without that commitment, we are just going to nickel-and-dime. Come on, we'll talk later, but we've got to get our asses moving and on the road."

I was going to the tip of northern Thailand on an overnight reconnaissance mission with a DEA team acting on information provided by a confidential informant. I followed Yarbrough out of his second-floor office and through the main headquarters building. Most of the second floor was taken up with an enormous, ornate, dark wood Spanish-style conference table surrounded with a group of high-back velvet-covered chairs. Off the side of the conference room was the briefing room, a ten-by-twenty-foot room covered from floor to ceiling with maps of the Golden Triangle and colorful markers indicating the latest intelligence on heroin labs, movement of the insurgent armies, and new smuggling routes through the hills. The windowless briefing room also served as the office for the unit's intelligence analyst, Steve Worobec. In sharp contrast to Yarbrough, Worobec, who has a Ph.D. in philosophy and wrote his dissertation on Southeast Asian drug trafficking, was every bit the young university professor. Studious, he looked up from his desk, cluttered with papers and books, peered at me through a thick set of wire-rimmed glasses, and barely got off a hello before Yarbrough slapped him on the back, "Great guy, Steve. Knows more about dope trafficking in Southeast Asia than anyone else in the U.S. government. We'd be in a real hole without him. You'll have to talk to him when you get back." And with that Yarbrough grabbed me and we were on our way downstairs to the equipment and gun locker.

Although the insurgent armies of Burma are armed with some of the best weapons available from arms merchants worldwide, the DEA office in Chiang Mai was not stocked with mere cap pistols. Ben opened the iron grille that separated the room that was dubbed the "locker." Inside were rows of assault rifles, powerful handguns, riot shotguns, explosive devices, and seemingly enough ammunition to blow up Chiang Mai.

"Come on, Ben, we've got to get our asses moving," a voice at the door boomed out, "or we'll never make it to Chiang Rai." Ben introduced me to the second DEA member on the mission, Mike Bansmere. As with Yarbrough, Bansmere reminded you that this was an action DEA assignment. At six feet one inch, his black hair shaved into a crew cut, the forty-four-year-old agent was even more muscular than Yarbrough, but because of his smaller frame seemed to be more agile. Mike was a decorated Special Forces Vietnam veteran. He liked wars. This was the closest he was going to get to one in "peacetime."

As we left the headquarters we passed a makeshift weight room in the first-floor lobby, Nautilus weight-training machines crammed one on top of another. We walked outside to a four-wheel-drive truck. As I had learned from the trip with Hu and Chan, no one was going to make it through northern Thailand without an all-purpose vehicle. The guns were locked into the truck, and as we loaded in, a middle-aged oriental man came and jumped into the back seat. Mike turned around in the front seat to look at me. "That's Pep. He's Laotian and he's one of our best guys. Aren't you, Pep?" A small grin cracked across the man's face. "Pep doesn't say much. But you won't find anyone tougher or braver. He worked for the CIA during the war in Laos. Then he escaped when the Communists took over. He went back in to bring his family out, and he swam down the Mekong River pulling a raft his family was on while the Commies were shooting at him and cut his whole back up. He should have been dead a long time ago. But since he doesn't want to die, we're giving him another chance to get killed with us. Right, Pep?" Again a smile. "Pep doesn't say much," repeated Bansmere as he turned back around and kicked the truck's motor on.

Ben jumped out of the front seat for a moment and yelled to his secretary, standing on the staircase, "Get Posner and his wife a new hotel reservation at the Suriwongse and get them moved out of the Chiang Inn while we are away." Settling back inside, he turned to look at me. "Forgot to tell you that the Chiang Inn is owned by a heroin trafficker. Not a good place for you to be. I know the manager at the Suriwongse. He's queer, but he's okay."

"I didn't know the Chiang Inn was a heroin hotel."

"A lot of places around here are funded by dope money but you would never know it." It seemed I was one of the few peo-

ple in Chiang Mai who did not know the Chiang Inn had a narcotics connection. When it first opened in the late 1970s the police
got a tip and raided it, finding 200 kilos of opium in the cellar.
The owners were arrested, but the next day one of the janitors
came forward and claimed it was all his. No one asked any questions, like how he could afford it since he did not have any money.
But he went to jail, his wife got a new house, the owners went
free and are back in business.

Yarbrough turned around in his seat. "When we travel up
north if you notice the stone houses in town, those are always
the dope dealers. Once they make some money, they replace their
wooden huts with a nice stone house. Keep your eyes open."

The first half of the trip to Chiang Rai was on the same road
I had been on a week before. Ben and Mike were on walkie-
talkies the entire time coordinating an attempted undercover purchase of heroin from a couple of young Chinese traffickers near
the airport. I wondered for a moment if it could be Hu and Chan.
Too much of a coincidence, I thought. But I never had a chance
to find out since by mid-trip the undercover agent was unable to
get the unidentified traffickers to show him the dope and Ben
canceled the operation.

"They are really clever, these Chinese," Ben mused half to himself while looking out the side window. "They know that DEA
policy is never to part with flash money [the cash used to make
an undercover purchase of narcotics] until we have the dope. The
DEA just won't give us any flash money unless we have dope in
our hands. So the Chinese just started to demand money up
front, and since the Chinese are interlocked by this great trust
created by family and by knowing everyone through somebody
else, the real Chinese dope buyers were willing to part with their
money before they ever saw the dope. You could never do that
with the Colombians or Cubans—they'd take the money and run,
but with the Chinese, if they say they will return at five o'clock
with the dope, that's exactly what they'll do. So for a while that
policy of money up front screwed us up the ass. But recently we
got headquarters to let us make a buy by giving the dealer flash
money without getting the dope. The trafficker was so cocky that
he was actually telling our UC [undercover agent] how he never
gives dope at the same time he gets the money because that way
he can never get arrested. And when he brought the dope the

next day and we pounced on him, you should have seen his face. He shit in his pants. He couldn't fucking believe that we were cops. It was great. So now even though they are damn smart, they have to be scared that we can give them flash money up front and still bust them later. That'll scare the crap out of them for a while."

"Do you find the Chinese have different traits as a group of criminals and traffickers than other groups you've worked on?"

"Yeah, sure," replied Ben. "I've been around Chinese dealers a long time. In 1970 I was on the New York City Chinatown squad and I was posted to Asia for the first time in '73 and was in Chiang Mai for the first time around '75. A Chinese partner of mine, Steve Tse, and I made the first bust of Chinese heroin the Dutch ever had in the mid-seventies. And when I was in Seattle from '76 to '83 I dealt again with a lot of Chinese. So I've seen Chinese traffickers for almost twenty years. If you get three Chinese together, you'll have gambling, prostitution, dope, numbers, extortion, you name it—"

"Seriously," Mike interrupted him, "Ben will tell you, and so will other agents in the DEA, the Chinese are just a lot smarter than most other criminals. They are more patient, disciplined, loyal, and low-key. They will outwait law enforcement. I mean some of them are flashy and have the gold watches, the Mercedes, and the bottles of Hennessey XO reserve brandy, but most of them are pretty low-key. And even the ones who aren't flashy still get involved in gambling games worth millions of U.S. dollars."

Ben turned around to look at me to make a point. "And they are the toughest bunch of bastards I have ever come across. If you bust them, they will never break in interrogations. I have seen the Thais conduct some damn tough interrogations. I have seen a guy pass out from pain, be brought back, and then pass out again, and that continues until he is almost dead. There's nothing I can do about it, it's the Thais' country and they do things the way they want. But I have never seen one of these guys break down and talk."

"Never." Surprisingly, Pep spoke. "They die first."

"And they do die sometimes instead of talking," added Bansmere. "If you've busted them, they'll always admit that they are guilty, but they'll swear they were a one-man syndicate and that no one else was involved."

Ben turned back in his seat and looked out the side window again and picked up the conversation. "See, they are afraid that if they talk, they will certainly get killed by someone in the dope business. But if they keep quiet, then the big bosses will take care of their legal affairs, might buy them a shorter sentence, and will certainly take care of their family. If they talk, they are fucked. I've never seen another race as tough as this. The Mexicans can't wait to sing if you pick them up. Just looking at them crossways and they say, 'Oh, please, señor, no more, don't hurt me anymore.' The blacks, they talk easy. Italians want to talk to you straightaway about making a deal. Only the Chinese are like a wall of silence."

The Triad oath of silence I had heard about in Hong Kong was obviously effective. We drove the rest of the way to Chiang Rai talking about some of the cases they had worked on since arriving in Thailand. It seemed as if no matter how big a success they thought they had in a single case, another Chinese trafficker would fill the void and restart the operation within weeks of their action. The frustration level on the job was very high. So was the stress of working in a country where heroin armies were shooting at you and the police were often not to be trusted. They each knew of DEA agents who had become heavy drinkers from the job, or whose wives could no longer stand the untold days and nights without knowing where their husbands were, much less if they were alive or dead, and had just packed up and left.

"I don't think anyone really understands what we are trying to do up here or how damn difficult it is," Ben said. "We've got our asses on the line twenty-four hours a day. I am in the office by seven in the morning and I am never home before ten at night, and I make less money than if I was selling real estate or was a stockbroker somewhere. I see my kids for an hour in the morning and I can't remember the last time I had a vacation with my wife. But I also think what we are doing is real important. I think the average person in the United States thinks of a drug agent as someone in a suit and tie going around like a bureaucrat trying to find someone smoking a joint or selling a gram of cocaine. They have no idea that we are fighting syndicates that are connected around the world. If you ask most people in the U.S. where Burma is, they probably couldn't tell you. And if you told them there were armies up here running heroin that landed on the streets of their cities, they probably would be shocked. Sometimes I wonder if anyone gives a shit. I wonder if it's really worth getting my ass shot at if no one cares. But I guess in the end I feel it's important enough to do even if no one acknowledges it. So that's why I'm here. And Mike, and all the guys. We can get pretty down at times, but in the end we know without us it would be a lot worse."

That night in Chiang Rai was a sharp contrast to the one I had spent there with Hu and Chan. We stayed at a new, modern, six-story hotel, a multimillion-dollar extravaganza erected in this otherwise sleepy town with few tourists. "Dope money," said Mike as we checked in. "Too much money, and they don't know what to do with it so it ends up in a place like this. It can never make a profit, but it sure makes a nice place to stop over on the way up north."

That night Ben, Mike, and Pep had to meet confidential informants who were waiting to give information and receive their payoff money. But before they left for the evening, Ben took me to the back of the hotel to show me "a private club." A broad Thai with a Fu Manchu mustache blocked a nondescript door to a white stucco annex. When we showed him our hotel keys, he opened the door and we entered an interior designer's fantasy of what a Roman bathhouse must have been like at the height of the ancient empire. "Marble" columns, which turned out to be painted concrete, rose from the floor to the top of the fifteen-foot ceilings. The floor was covered with white marble tiles, and girls dressed in skimpy togas ran up and guided us to a cocktail lounge. We sat facing a bad reproduction of the Venus de Milo spewing pink- and green-colored water. The girls spun our chairs around and suddenly we were looking at a wall of solid glass, behind which some fifty girls sat lounging on large, brightly colored satin pillows decked out across marble steps.

I was in another whorehouse, the opposite end of the scale from the chicken coop. These girls were all young, none of the weather-beaten veterans or the young children that were the special "treats" of the chicken coop. Here all the girls ranged from their mid-teens to their mid-twenties. Their clothes were glamorous and expensive, and they seemed much more "professional" than the girls I had seen the week before. Each girl wore a large red-and-white number tag on her shoulder. Hotel guests came in, had a drink while they studied the girls, and then told the manager which number or numbers they wanted. The charges were $4.00 an hour or $25 for a night. Again, a television was at the front of the room, with its back to us, and the girls were uniformly mesmerized by whatever was on the screen. While I sat there a middle-aged French couple came in; and after ten minutes they left with a young Thai girl in a purple satin evening dress.

"Thought you should see this." Ben turned toward me. "It's a side business for the dope dealers who run this hotel. They have the girls here to pocket a couple of bucks, but mainly it's for servicing all the dealers and reps who come in from Hong Kong during the buying season. Not everyone gets up to Chiang Rai. A lot just finish their deals down in Chiang Mai, but for those who come up here this is the only place they stay at and they all want a girl and they want one who is 'clean.' There are forms of venereal disease in Thailand not yet invented in other parts of the world. So one of the big selling points for a place like this is that the girls are supposed to be free of disease. I wouldn't bet on it."

I asked him about the chicken coop. "I've heard about it. It's notorious throughout the area. It doesn't surprise me when you say that cops were all around. I would never deal with the provincial police. They are a very dirty group. Come on, let's get out of here before they realize we are just looking and kick us out. I thought if you're going to write about this hotel, you should know it doesn't have a health club like one in America. Dope traffickers maximize their investments in a different way."

From two trips to northern Thailand I was becoming convinced that the flesh trade went hand in hand with the narcotics trade in the Golden Triangle.

The next morning we were due to leave Chiang Rai by eight o'clock. At seven I went for a walk in the neighborhood around the hotel. It was already almost 90 degrees, the weather being the same as Chiang Mai. But this was a poorer town than Chiang Mai; as I looked at the motley assortment of stores and houses, it was difficult to imagine this was a key stopover on the heroin pipeline. The poverty made places like our luxury hotel stand out for its garish use of narcotics profits. Other places of dubious investment cropped up along the way. A cafe with neon lights and Art-Deco-styled counters, a place that would have been at home in the trendiest sections of Manhattan. It was sandwiched between a shack that served as a shoe repair shop and a gas station. Another white-tile-and-glass building held forth a dazzling array of the latest foreign motorcycles. It had an enclosed reception area complete with the latest European magazines spread across its expensive coffee table.

I settled in for breakfast at an open-air garage. It was filled with metal tureens and was the only place I found that was open. One look at the tureens, filled with indistinguishable soups and curries, and a vat of overcooked rice made me ask for a simple coffee. I think mine was the first request for coffee in some time as the cook looked about frantically until he finally and triumphantly held up a soiled jar of Nescafé. Two heaping tablespoons later I had coffee, Chiang Rai style. As I was transcribing notes from some of my taped interviews, the blast of a car horn broke my concentration. I looked up to see Ben, Mike, and Pep. "You're checked out and we've got your bag. Pay the bill and let's go," yelled Ben.

Ben and Mike were in jeans and T-shirts. Both wore aviator sunglasses and Ben wore his trusty Yankee cap. Pep was in an old army shirt and a pair of black work pants. The DEA was on its way to wave the American flag in the Golden Triangle. As with Hu and Chan, Mike left the main road only fifteen minutes out of Chiang Rai, then looked back at me in the rearview mirror: "We are going a way that we've never gone before. We're going to try to drive right along the border, and then if we can cut through the hills, we will drop in on Mae Sai from the north. I don't think there's any road up there. We'll make a new one. I'm sure they've never seen a car drop down on them from that direction, because I don't think anyone has ever made the ride we are going to."

On the way Ben and Mike would point out the homes of known traffickers or representatives of Kuhn Sa or General Li. Ben pointed out a large green house off to the right of the road. "And there's a home of the son of a former agricultural minister in this country. We have him under investigation. We think he is responsible for sending about 200 kilos a months to the United States."

"So if you know where so many of the traffickers are, why don't you have better success moving against them?"

"It's the laws of the damn country. There is no way to seize somebody's assets here. So if he has spent a fortune on himself and you can prove his phony import-export business can't explain all that money, you might get him some tax problems but that's all. And the conspiracy law is really screwed up. You might as well have no conspiracy law at all. You have to catch the guy with the dope in his hand. Well, you know, you never catch the top guys even near the stuff. You won't find them in the same room with a kilo of heroin. When they get to the top they are too smart for that. So I have heard of cases in which the Thai police have been so frustrated that they just take the dope trafficker and take him over to where they seized his dope shipment and then they take pictures of him together with the dope. At the trial they testify that is how they found him and arrested him. That's how the Thais deal with the shortcomings in their laws. But since we have to play strictly by the rules or we get our ass handed to us, the laws can be a real hindrance. We don't have a problem in knowing who the major dopers are—we just have trouble making cases against them under Thai law."

For the next six hours I had a journey that rivaled the one Hu and Chan had given me for its difficulty. Mike was right. We spent most of the time with the truck crunching down bamboo and tropical plants trying to forge a new path. Three times the truck got stuck in seemingly intractable spots. One time we had to hook a rope around a boulder and around the front bumper to try to help it out of a hole—we lost the bumper but did get back on the road. One time Ben was ready to radio for help, camp out for the night, and wait for a pickup in the morning, but again, with all of us pushing at the back, we were able to get the truck off the side of a ridge where it was precipitously perched.

Our trip took us through the back hills past SUA-controlled towns. Our destination was the northern tip of the border where a town called Wan A Ti sat just over on the Burmese side. "It's a Kuhn Sa town," explained Ben. "The last time we came near Wan A Ti the tribal chief came running at us with his M-16 and screaming at us to get away. This time we will surprise him by driving out of the bush instead of coming near him on the dirt road. That should excite him."

Before getting to Wan A Ti, as we passed the town of Ko Phak Hi, Mike saw a couple of figures on a hill spot the truck and start to run back toward the town. "Want to take a look?" Mike looked at Ben and got an affirmative nod. Mike ripped the jeep up the incline toward the village, and suddenly I saw three figures running down a small hill behind the village at breakneck speed. Ben grabbed the M-16 and cocked it ready. Pep picked up a pistol and rested it in his lap. The atmosphere inside the jeep had changed instantaneously. No longer were the men lounging and talking about the dope trade in the Golden Triangle. Suddenly they were on the hunt, and their demeanor changed to all business and they were upright in their seats, all eyes on the three runners. They didn't appear to have any guns. "Stay low"—Ben looked back at me.

Before the jeep could make the incline, the three men had made it to the bottom of the hill and were into the village. By the time we drove into the front of the village, there wasn't a sign of life. Mike stopped the truck and we sat silently inside. "What do you think?" Mike asked.

"Well, I think if we stay here, we're sitting ducks if they want to try something," said Ben. "If we get out, where do we go? We don't know where they went and we don't know what they look like and everyone will deny it was them. We don't even know if they were doing something dirty. I just would have liked to have gotten to talk to them. Drive through real slow and let's see if anything pops out."

Nothing did. But for a few minutes it was almost possible to feel the adrenaline that makes men like Mike and Ben tick. They thought they were ready to have a fight and they were armed and looking forward to it. If one of those three men had pulled a weapon, he would have been blown away where he stood. There was no nervousness about the work. Just a determined attitude that made it seem like carrying guns and chasing criminals in the Golden Triangle was almost mundane.

By the time we reached Wan A Ti it was four o'clock, the hottest time of the day. We were all exhausted from the truck excavations, but arriving at the trip's destination gave everyone a second wind. Mike positioned the truck behind tall bamboo, out of sight of the village. Then we started to climb the side of a hill. It took almost half an hour in the sun to make a ridge where we could look directly into the town but not be seen from it. After several minutes Ben handed me his set of high-powered binoculars.

"Just follow my finger and look right down there. Tell me what you see."

"I see a bunch of chickens in a wire coop."

"Look to the left a little."

"I see a group of rocks, like the entrance to something. It looks boarded up."

"And what do you see right in front of the rocks?"

"Nothing. Oh wait, I see a hatch door, looks like an entrance to a cellar or something."

"Something, my ass," laughed Ben. "You're looking at a cache site for number 4 heroin. It's all neatly wrapped and packed in waterproof packages and it is sitting right under that ground. There are three cache sites in Wan A Ti, more than 300 kilos of pure heroin. And we know it's there but we have to wait for them to move it and that's the tricky part. Because it's a kilometer on the wrong side of the border, there's nothing to do about it until it gets on our side. But if we can pull this off, it will give Kuhn Sa a damn good headache."

Ben had a confidential informant who had provided the exact time that a group of twenty armed SUA guards were supposed to take the almost 600 pounds of heroin into Thailand for a rendezvous with Hong Kong drug buyers. We hiked to the other side of the ridge and looked down into a narrow gulch.

"They'll come down that trail there," Mike pointed out. "We have to wait until they get inside a couple of kilometers before we open up on them."

Ben was glued to his binoculars, scanning the terrain for miles around. "And we'll have to place some of the Border Patrol back here where we are right now. This is the perfect spot. If the SUA start to make a break back to Burma with the dope, then the Thais can be sitting here and pick them off like dead ducks."

The three DEA agents spent the next hour taking notes and marking locations and comparing them to a detailed intelligence map of the area. When satisfied they had enough information for a successful ambush, we packed into the truck and were off again down a torturous road leading into the Thai border town of Mae Sai.

"Too bad you won't be here when the operation goes off." Ben looked back at me. "It's not supposed to happen for at least another month. And that is of course if the CI doesn't change his story at the last moment. This is the first time we are dealing with this guy, and you can never tell if they are just trying to shake down the rich Americans for some money or if they are serious about giving you good info. This guy could easily turn around and say the dope was moved to a new set of buyers and he didn't find out about it until it happened. But then I'll make him pay the money back to Uncle Sam, I guarantee it.

"There was even one major in the Border Police who set up an entire lab in the jungle for us to bust. He knew that we paid a lot for labs, so he and a couple of crooked cops got together and made an entire lab and then pretended they got a tip on it, collected our money, and then busted it with us. We found out it was a phony because it was clear that none of the equipment had been used and it didn't fit into any of the intelligence we had for that area. We got our money back and the little bastard was transferred to southern Thailand. I'll break his neck if I see the little prick."

As we headed into Mae Sai, Ben gave me a quick lesson on the town's role in the heroin trade. "It exists only because of heroin. It has only one main street, a dirt road, and when we get inside, tell me what you see the most of along that part of town. In Mae Sai it costs 1 million baht [$40,000] to buy the police chief's job and you have to pay 300,000 baht [$12,000] a month to keep the job. And the stinking job officially earns only 2,500 baht a month [$100]. But that's how much heroin is flooding through here. To make sure the police keep their noses out of the traffickers' business, the Chinese pay very well. But the police have to pay the local town council in order to be appointed and hired for those jobs. It makes me sick. I tell you ninety-eight percent of Thai police are crooked. See, the Thais are smart. They give us the freest hand of any host country in the world, so then we can't complain about being restricted. But they know there's so much goddamn dope coming through Thailand that we are only making a dent. So instead of trying to stop us, they let us do our stuff, and they still pocket a bundle of money for turning a blind eye to the big Chinese syndicates.

"I mean I could give you file folders filled with cases of corrupt Thai police, military, diplomats, government officials, and the rest. It would amaze you. The dope trade can't exist without that type of institutionalized corruption. And Thailand is a heaven for corruption. And if you have money in Thailand, everyone respects you and no one asks where it comes from. Some of the biggest dope traffickers have become fucking heroes in this country. One of the biggest dope movers to the U.S., a Chinese fellow in Chiang Mai, Lu Hsu-shui, was actually awarded the highest award, the Order of the White Elephant, from the King. Can you imagine it? He gets a medal from the King of Thailand because he is giving so much money to charities. Meanwhile, his heroin is responsible for a quarter of the addicts in Bangkok. But no one cares about that. Oh, forget it, if I get going on this…"

A drive down the several hundred yards of Mae Sai's main street took less than a minute. It was clear what Ben wanted me to spot. In this little dusty border town in the middle of nowhere was an almost unbroken string of banks. The telltale sign of the drug trade. Banks with international connections to clinch dope deals at a moment's notice.

After lunch in a Mae Sai open-air diner, we were off again on the main paved road back to Chiang Mai.

Again it was Ben who wanted to talk. "You see this road we're on? We know that seventy to eighty percent of the dope that comes out of the Golden Triangle comes right down this and one other main road in the north. We know it comes on ten-wheel trucks and little vans and in all types of shipments, all disguised as regular commerce."

"If you know that, why aren't you more successful in seizing a lot more heroin?"

"Let me tell you why. Rice merchants will send a ten-wheeler down the main road from Mae Sai filled with 300 to 400 100-kilo sacks of rice. The dope is only in a couple of bags and that is a big shipment of dope. How do you find the heroin? You can't stop every commercial truck coming down the highway and search every bag. Even if you had the manpower it would take at least five men an entire day to carefully go through one ten-wheeler. We use a metal rod to poke through the sack to see if dope or rice falls out. But often the heroin is mixed with the rice, and if you hit the wrong spot on the bag, you'll draw only rice when the heroin is only an inch or two away. And by the fifth bag you've got so much crap on the rod, you don't know what you're seeing when you pull the rod out.

"Now, if you want to do it right, you slit open the bags at the top, have another set of bags with you, and pour the contents of one bag into the new empty one. Now you have to reseal each new bag if you don't find any dope. That's 400 bags you have to repack and reload. And the whole time you're tying up traffic. Remember this is only a two-lane road, and when you pull a ten-wheeler onto the soft shoulder it ties up traffic for miles. And the whole while the Thai police, who, by the way, you cannot do one of these stop and searches without, are busting your back to hurry up and finish. They tell you they can see the truck is clean.

"If you come up empty-handed, they will bitch for a week and promise not to allow you to do it again. And if you don't stand there with them and help them do the search, I guarantee they will never find a thing on their own because they just can't be bothered in the blazing sun to do that type of backbreaking work. They'll complain to the U.S. Consulate and then you'll have your ass in the ringer with the State Department for upsetting our Thai friends.

"And there are hundreds of trucks like that each month. Which ones do you stop? What it comes down to is that unless a CI pinpoints one for you, you just don't stop the trucks. And even if he does pinpoint one for you, it doesn't always mean you find any dope. I've been talking about the most obvious form of smuggling, which is hiding the dope in the sacks with the commerce. But what if it's been built into the transmission, or inside the tire rims, or dumped in airtight bags inside the gas tank? How do you find it then? What it means is that we know the dope travels down these roads and most of it slips right under our noses.

"And it's not just rice. It's ten-wheelers filled with 5,000 pounds of packed fish in ice blocks and the heroin is hidden inside the fish—try to search that. Or loads of two tons of cow shit with the 200 pounds of heroin placed at the bottom of that. Try to get a Thai policeman to rifle through cow shit and see how far you'll get. And one last thought. What if the dope is being transported in an official Thai government vehicle? You can't even stop that type to look inside so it's a guaranteed safe ticket for the trafficker, who can grease enough palms to put his load on board of one those headed for Bangkok.

"Assume for a moment that seventy tons of heroin comes down these roads each year. That would be a top number. That's 140,000 pounds, which could all fit into less than 700 100-kilo sacks. Hundreds of thousands of 100-kilo sacks come down these roads each spring. You give me a better way of finding those 700 and I will be happy to use it."

"You make it sound like it is an insurmountable problem."

"Now you're getting the idea. As long as we continue to fight this as a simple police action, we are bound to get the shit kicked out of us by criminals who have armies and are planning logistics and fighting this like it was a war."

We made Chiang Mai in several hours. Less than a third of the time it took us bouncing over nonexistent roads along the Thai–Burma border. The last couple of hours were spent mostly in silence, all of us exhausted from the long day. I thought about what Yarbrough had told me. There was no doubt that, given the terrain in the Golden Triangle and the politics of Thai law enforcement, the handful of DEA agents and honest Thai cops in the north were up against substantial odds.

During the next week in Chiang Mai I visited two Thai units for which Yarbrough had great respect. One was the Thai Border Patrol Police, and I saw the elite contingent that worked hand in hand with the DEA in attacking heroin labs and fighting traffickers. With four helicopters and one fixed-wing plane, they were responsible for covering the entire north of the country.

I also met Captain Wipon, a baby-faced Thai policeman who may be one of the few honest cops waging a serious battle against drug dealers in the north. I sat with him at his headquarters two days later.

I walked past simple wooden houses that served as barracks for his antidrug squad. Chicken and geese were running about in the large dirt yard, the entire place looking more like a run-down farm than an antinarcotics center. The main building, more like a hut, had no air conditioning. You entered past old rusty green lockers stocked with the men's uniforms. Captain Wipon's office was in a corner of the building. One side of the office was filled with battered, gray metal filing cabinets. Computers have not been introduced to Thai law enforcement. A sun-bleached poster of the King hung on the back wall. A large metal desk, rusted and pitted in the center, took up most of the middle of the room, two straight-back wooden chairs in front of it. The blades of a large overhead ceiling fan swung lazily in circles, recirculating the stifling office air. Since the two corner windows were boarded up with wooden slats for security reasons, the room seemed like an oven. "I'm used to it," said a smiling Captain Wipon, very slender in his uniform.

He earns a little over $300 a month for heading the antidrug efforts in Chiang Mai. He spent the afternoon telling me about his admiration for the DEA and men like Ben and Mike. He wanted to be like them, even to the point of having started to lift weights. He took me down a corridor from his office and we stopped in a large back room where a couple of his troops were sprawled out on sofas watching television. The contrast between Captain Wipon's primitive headquarters and the luxury of the DEA compound could not have been more pronounced.

We stopped in front of a small group of flowers and a picture of a young Thai boy. It was a photo of a twenty-six-year-old policeman killed six months before I arrived. He was the first man Captain Wipon had lost in his eight years on the force. And he had been killed by a fellow cop who was trying to complete a heroin sale. Now Wipon had made a small shrine in the back of the headquarters.

"Do you want to see pictures of the body when we found it?" he asked me. I nodded, feeling he needed to share his outrage with someone. I sat with him on a battered sofa and he showed me grisly pictures of a charred body that had been shot and left to roast in the tropical sun. His eyes glistened as he looked at the pictures for what I was sure was the hundredth time.

He looked up at me. "They say if I keep pushing like I am now, that I will end up dead. But Ben pushes as much, the same could happen to him. I won't be scared off. There has to be some way of stopping them. I don't know if I will live to see it, but one day I would like my children to be able to say that the dope dealers no longer own the north of Thailand. That the Chinese criminals have left. That honest people have come back and the place is theirs."

On that hot day in Chiang Mai I knew that people like Captain Wipon and Ben and Mike make a difference. Without them the Triads and their representatives in the Golden Triangle would do whatever they please. I imagined a Triad boss in his sleek Hong Kong office building laughing at an emotional figure like Captain Wipon and figuring if that was his foe, then his business was safe. But eventually little people like Wipon, if numerous enough, could make a difference. The problem is that at the source of most of the world's heroin, the Golden Triangle, there are too few good men willing to challenge the heroin warlords.

Within months of my departure from northern Thailand, the DEA and local Thai antidrug units made a series of large heroin seizures. They were substantial law enforcement victories. The warlords, led by Kuhn Sa, responded with threats against all DEA personnel in Chiang Mai. The United States government decided the threats were real. Agents and families were evacuated in November and December of 1987. Without the DEA, Captain Wipon pressed the drug fight alone. By early 1988, American drug agents slowly returned to their Triangle outpost. Ben Yarbrough was not among them. The DEA was convinced that a move by the warlords against Ben or his family was imminent. He was transferred to Miami. While his enthusiasm and expertise will assist in the battle against the cocaine cowboys of southern Florida, his removal from Chiang Mai has temporarily given the warlords the victory they sought. Their intimidation tactics succeeded in eliminating their major antagonist. The number of good men left to fight them had dwindled by one.

A Lisu hill-tribe woman harvesting opium from wild poppies in the Golden Triangle. (John Everingham)

A Lahu hill-tribe child collecting opium poppies in his father's field in northern Thailand. (Chusak Voraphitak)

Hill-tribe farmers use a sharp hook to place vertical incisions around the poppy pod, releasing raw opium sap. Ten kilos of this pure opiate paste can be refined into one kilo of pure heroin. (John Everingham)

Shan United Army units marching to protect a new opium supply route. (*Bangkok Post*)

A Thai soldier guarding Bangkok's annual bonfire of seized narcotics. This fire destroys nearly $1 billion of illegal drugs, mostly heroin, each year. (*Bangkok Post*)

A father cooks and smokes raw opium as his daughter leans against him. Hundreds of thousands of addicts in Southeast Asia call this ritual smoking "Chasing the Dragon." (Royal Hong Kong Police)

Kuhn Sa gang presses local hill-tribes people into service in his opium army. Not even children are exempt from his military training. (*Asia Week*)

A Thai police colonel inspecting a crude heroin laboratory raided inside the Golden Triangle. (*Bangkok Post*)

Thai army units confiscating opium poppies, part of the government's eradication program. (*Bangkok Post*)

Lo Hsing-Han was spared from a death sentence in 1980 by Burmese President Ne Win. Released from prison, he has reestablished his prominence in the opium region by commanding several thousand soldiers under the banner "Shan States Volunteer Force." (*Bangkok Post*)

Kuhn Sa, the leading opium warlord in the Burmese Shan States, in a rare 1987 photo. Together with his 15,000-man Shan United Army, he controls 50% of all opium grown in the Golden Triangle. (*Asia Week*)

In the foreground, General Li Wen-Huan, commander of the Chinese Kuomintang (KMT) Third Army. Having fled Mao Tse-Tung's Communist victory in 1949, General Li's 10,000 troops have been a major force in the Golden Triangle for nearly four decades. (*Bangkok Post*)

The Ma Boys: Ma Sik-yu, "White Powder" Ma, on the left, and Ma Sik-chun, "the Golden Ma" on the right. According to law enforcement sources, they are among the largest international heroin traffickers. Wanted by the Hong Kong police, they currently reside in Taiwan. (*South China Morning Post*)

Ng Sik-ho, nicknamed "Limpy" for a battered leg that resulted from a Triad fight in his youth. One of Hong Kong's dragon heads during the 1970s, he is serving a thirty-year sentence for drug trafficking. (*South China Morning Post*)

Lui Lok, a former Hong Kong police sergeant, fled corruption investigations, first to Canada and then to Taiwan. He is called "the 600-million-dollar man," the estimated size of his illegal fortune. He is one of forty ex-Hong Kong police millionaires living in Taiwan (*South China Morning Post*)

Chung Mon, dubbed "the Unicorn," a symbol of strength and magic in the Chinese underworld. The first Chinese dragon head in Europe, he was murdered by Triad rivals in Amsterdam, March 3, 1975. (Royal Hong Kong Police)

Raw opium, heroin processing chemicals, and refining equipment seized by Burmese army units from insurgent traffickers. (*Bangkok Post*)

Tse-Chiu "Eddie" Chan, an ex-Hong Kong police sergeant who became the undisputed dragon head of New York's Chinese crime world during the late 1970s. He fled a federal investigation in 1984, and his whereabouts are unknown. (*The New York Times*)

9

The Incorruptible Cop

This was the fight in which "Marvelous" Marvin Hagler was supposed to pummel Sugar Ray Leonard and stop his comeback in its infancy. The championship fight for the world's middleweight title was taking place in Las Vegas, with the undefeated champion Hagler fighting the popular Leonard, who was returning to the ring after a two-year hiatus. But with every punch Leonard landed on a surprised Hagler, half of the dozen men standing around the twelve-inch color television gave a resounding cheer. When Hagler counterpunched and staggered Leonard, the other half of the group would whoop and shout as though their team had just won the Super Bowl. But none of these men was American. I was watching the fight on live Thai television, with the thirteen-hour time difference. It was Tuesday morning in Bangkok, but the fight was taking place on Monday night in the States.

I was at the office of Colonel Viraj Juttimita, often referred to as Thailand's incorruptible cop. He was the man who could not be bought. Chief of the Bangkok Narcotics Suppression Office, he waged a one-man war on drug trafficking before men like Captain Wipon even joined the force. No more than five feet six, slender, now in his late forties, he wears his thinning black hair plastered straight back and sports a very neatly trimmed mustache. He has Prussian blood mixed with his native Thai and received his law-enforcement training in the United States. He received a degree in criminology from the University of California at Berkeley, spent a year with the investigations squad of the San Jose police, another year with the San Francisco narcotics squad, and then turned down multiple offers from the CIA, FBI, and local U.S. police forces. "I told them Thailand needed more good men than the United States needed."

His American training, his arrogant refusal to be corrupted, his outspoken nature, his Prussian blood, all of these caused resentment in the Thai police force and the government. A DEA agent who had served six years in Bangkok told me, "He has the best record in the country in fighting heroin traffickers. The last person who held his job in Bangkok is a general now. Viraj should have been one by now. But too many people dislike his white-knight image, and they have done everything possible to hold him back."

I arrived at ten o'clock for my appointment with Colonel Viraj, but he and his men were crowded into the waiting room, glued to the start of the Hagler–Leonard championship fight. Money switched back and forth after each round as the men bet on the length of the fight and whether either fighter would get knocked down. Viraj was the only calm person. Leaning against a table in the rear of the room, dressed in a pair of neatly pressed dark gray trousers with an open-necked khaki shirt, he rested his trademark short-brimmed straw hat on the table next to him. As his men shouted and screamed as one of the fighters appeared to gain the upper hand, Viraj just smiled at them and looked over at me as if to reassure me that our meeting was still scheduled, just delayed. Between rounds his men gathered near him and asked his opinion on how he thought the fight was going and who was winning. Viraj was the leader of this group not just by rank but because it was clear the men respected him and what he had to say. His experience and reputation had made him a living legend.

At the end of the fight we waited to hear the result as the judges awarded the title to a new champion. The winning bettors among the men had a small celebration, almost dancing around the room. If they approached their work against drug traffickers with the same enthusiasm they showed that morning, I had little doubt they were an effective force.

"Come on inside my office," a smiling Viraj told me. He excused himself for several minutes and left me with coffee that tasted as if it was from the bottom of a two-day-old pot.

I looked around Colonel Viraj's long and narrow office. Most of his walls were covered with enormous maps of Thailand, making part of it look like a military planning room. One entire wall was lined with tall, gray metal filing cabinets, a large metal safe at the end closest to his desk. Along the top of the filing cabinets were pictures of Viraj with his American graduating class and various law-enforcement officials, as well as Thai and U.S. government commendations. Mixed among his plaques were framed plastic bags proclaiming Double U-O Globe, 999, Lions, all printed with illustrations of dragons and tigers. These were mementos of some of the Golden Triangle's well-marketed heroin brands.

His desk was a standard wood government issue. It was packed high with papers and file folders. A black rotary telephone that would be considered a museum piece in other countries occupied one corner. I was sitting at the side of a long table, which was bolted to the front of Viraj's desk. Except for the wall maps, the office was reminiscent of a 1940s detective's office, even down to the simple wood blinds that covered the windows.

I looked outside into central Bangkok, for Viraj's headquarters was in the middle of the sprawling Thai capital. There was a great contrast between Bangkok and the north of the country, where I had just spent a couple of weeks.

Bangkok is a teeming metropolis of five million, built on the edge of vast tropical swamplands that permeate southern Asia. It is an architect's nightmare. Rushing into the twentieth century with an excessive use of concrete, chrome, and neon, it is an unusual mixture of traditional Thai pagodas contrasting with mid-1950s Kansas City. The first-time visitor will never forget the Thai capital. Bangkok's smell will stay with you long after you have left.

Hundreds of roadside Buddhist temples dot the city, and they are filled with piles of smoldering incense and thousands of pungent fresh orchids. The perfumed incense clouds mix with hundreds of open-air food stalls frying traditional spiced Thai dishes. The incense and the cooking join a third predominant odor— the noxious fumes from the all-day traffic jams that assure Bangkok of having the world's worst traffic.

When the "Venice of the East" was built two hundred years ago, it was intended only for travel on connecting waterways. Today thousands of dilapidated autos, three-wheeled minicabs dubbed "tuk-tuks" (named after the sound of their piddling mufflers), swarms of motorcycles, food vendors' carts, pedaled rickshaws, wheelbarrow-pushing flower sellers, and the occasional elephant combine with ten-minute red lights and one-way streets to give "gridlock" a new meaning. Bangkok's rush-hour traffic crawls at three miles an hour—two-thirds slower than Manhattan. There is no mass transit except for a handful of rickety buses. This all-day rush hour, marked by a motor-vehicle population that is almost exclusively prepollution control, helps hang a perpetual cloud of gasoline and other noxious fumes over the city.

The only thing that can make it worse is visiting Bangkok during the scorching summer months of March to May, when the daily temperature zooms past a humid 100 degrees. I was there in the middle of April and discovered a fourth powerful Bangkok odor—piles of rotting garbage floating on the canals. This odor is reminiscent of a New York summer garbage strike, and it follows you around the city.

But Bangkok is much more than a colorful, disorienting world capital. It has a dark side—almost one in ten residents is a prostitute, an estimated 500,000 plying their trade in the red-light district and massage parlors, and more than one in ten residents is a heroin addict, an army of 600,000. Bangkok has become a victim of the free-wheeling and carefree attitude that is the hallmark of the Thai people. The government often refuses to acknowledge the seriousness of its own problems, only recently admitting that there is an AIDS problem in a city with the world's worst drug and prostitution epidemic.

Riddled with a staggering crime rate, massive consumer fraud, and a soaring unemployment rate, Bangkok struggles to cope with a population increasing faster than it is capable of servicing. Poverty is visible throughout the Thai capital.

Contrasting sharply with the festering side of Bangkok is a business and media center second only to Hong Kong in Southeast Asia. Gleaming glass skyscrapers house some of Asia's largest banks, many bulging with narcotics dollars. Wealthy Thais live in beautiful sprawling mansions in luxuriously maintained residential enclaves of the city. The Buddhist temples in the city are some of the best in Asia, and the Golden Temple, with its Em-

erald Buddha, is stunning. The turn-of-the-century Oriental Hotel, considered by many seasoned travelers to be the world's finest,
was the home away from home for such people as Somerset
Maugham and Noel Coward. Sitting in the Authors' Bar at the
Oriental, looking out at the Chao Phraya River, it is hard to think
of a more pleasant and genteel setting.

Thai hospitality for Westerners is fabled. It is called "the Land
of Smiles," Thai people being some of the friendliest and kindest
in Asia. For the occasional traveler to Bangkok, the warm and
open nature of the city's residents can create the image of a people who are eternally happy, never showing anger or disappoint-
ment. Yet just under the surface lies a potential for violence that
is unmatched in many Southeast Asia countries. "Oh, sure, lots
of smiles," a senior Drug Enforcement agent told me in Bangkok,
"they will smile while they shoot you. They have real tempers
here, it's just that most tourists never get to see it. I think that
the only people not carrying guns in Thailand are the *fahrang*
[the foreigners]. Don't let this happy-go-lucky attitude fool you.
This is a tough nation."

It is this city of sharp contrasts and extremes that serves as the
first major stopover for most for the heroin flooding out of the
Golden Triangle. It stops here on its way to Hong Kong and distribution around the globe. I had come to see Colonel Viraj hoping he could tell me more about how the heroin moved out of
Bangkok.

Viraj reentered the office and sat behind his desk, the lines of
sunlight filtering through the window blinds casting a striped
shadow across his face. His eyes were intense, a look that sized
you up instantly and determined whether you were to be trusted
or whether you were an enemy. It is the only way that Viraj has
survived. His reputation as Thailand's foremost honest cop has
not only earned him reduced pay and a stymied career, but it
has made him a marked man. He drives with a Smith & Wesson
9-mm automatic pistol in his lap, one bullet in the chamber and
fifteen more in the magazine. He has a Remington 12-gauge
pump-action shotgun loaded with five double-buck shells under
his seat and another at home, where his five sons are trained to
use it. His house is like a prison camp, surrounded by barbed
wire, with half a dozen guard dogs running the grounds. He is
a simple man who sees the world in black and white, knowing

without hesitation who is good and who is bad. And he knows that one day he might have to pay the price for his principles.

"I don't know why I'm still alive. Except they know that if anything happens to me, my men know who to go to and what to do. No one doubts that they will follow up on my death and make the score even. I don't think anyone wants that trouble."

But he realizes that he has created a reputation that is feared in Thailand. "They don't understand me here. In Thailand people believe no one should rock the boat. You just go down the middle until someone tells you to go one way or another, and then you do as you are expected to. But if you go straight all the time and you don't listen to anyone else, if you never become crooked, then you are feared."

A lot of people do not understand why Viraj prefers honesty to making a lot of money, especially because he is a policeman. "The Thai people think of a policeman like the lowest animal, like a dog to be kicked around. They think all police are corrupt and that they sell the people out to the criminals. They hear about policemen who are millionaires and they think that everyone in a uniform is a thief. But it is important that people can trust me. They can come to me and know I will not lie or sell them out. I want the police to be honest, and it may seem like an impossible task, but it is the only way I know to work."

Viraj earns slightly more than $500 a month. He barely supports his family with an average standard of living. But he has repeatedly rejected opportunities to fill his pockets with enormous bribes.

"I don't know how many times I have been offered money to look the other way or not to push so hard on a case. But it's been a lot. I have had suitcases opened in front of me filled with American dollars. I have been told I could have half a million to let someone go, another time $30,000 a month to take my men off of a case."

When he arrested Sukree Sukreepirom, one of the "untouchable" heroin kings of Thailand in the 1970s, Sukree sat in Viraj's office as arrogant as ever. "He told me that I could have anything I wanted. He was convinced that everyone had a price and that he would find mine. I told him I just wanted him in jail. He knew the system very well and told me that I shouldn't be so sure I could keep him in jail."

Sukree was right. Within three months a corrupt prosecutor freed the notorious drug king. But Viraj shook the boat by taking his case to the newspapers, and an embarrassed government fired the prosecutor and Sukree fled the country. Again, Viraj had followed the honest and right course, and again along the way he made enemies in both the government and in the narcotics world.

"I've been in this job twenty-one years. I have never had a sick day, never taken a vacation. My wife and children have been under terrible strain. They hear that I'm in a shoot-out with some criminals and they don't know until they see me that I'm alive. And if it's an important matter, a matter of life and death, people always call on me. I think as much as I enjoy being a policeman, if I had to do it over again, I wouldn't do it. Not again. It's just too tough on everyone."

"Do you feel that your twenty-one years of service have made a difference? Is there less heroin coming through Bangkok today that when you started?"

"No way. It's gotten much worse. There is a lot more opium being grown in the Triangle, especially in Burma, and even though we are catching a lot more than twenty years ago, there is a lot more coming down from the hills. So more gets through no matter how hard we work. Laos is producing again, maybe 200 tons this year. It had stopped producing for a while around 1980. Vietnam is putting maybe another twenty tons into the market. We don't know how much could be grown in southern China. Thailand is down to twenty-five tons. But Burma is up to almost 1,000 tons. The best thing that could help us now would be some bad weather and a couple of years of very poor crops. If the crops could be cut by two-thirds, that would do more to disrupt the syndicates than many of our efforts.

"We have more than 2,000 drug-related arrests a month. I know of a kid as young as ten being arrested for selling heroin, and a grandmother as old as eighty-six. But these are the lowest-level violators. The key is making cases against the top traffickers, and this is far more difficult."

"And who's at the top of the heroin business in Thailand?"

"Chinese. And the most important of them could not survive without the high-ranking international Chinese bosses in Hong Kong. Without the foreign Chinese, it is a much smaller business in Thailand. The Hong Kong syndicates have deep contacts here. Some of our Chinese criminals came from Vietnam in 1972 or 1973. Then when Vietnam fell the North Vietnamese claimed that the Saigon police records were destroyed, so it was impossible to check on which of these Chinese were involved in criminal activities while they lived in Vietnam. I actually believe the Saigon police records survived intact and that the Vietnamese Communists extort money from Chinese criminals here by threatening to expose their past.

"In addition to the Chinese, there are also some Corsicans involved here. Some of them also came here when Laos and Vietnam fell, and they have contacts in the heroin business. Now recently we have seen new and young Corsicans arriving in Bangkok, and they have been buying bars and discos in the Patpong area [the red-light district] with $500,000 or a million dollars in cash. You think they have to come 12,000 miles to own a bar? It's a bit more than that. They are still keeping up their contacts with the Chinese syndicates in order to get heroin to Europe."

Viraj's focus on the Chinese connection is key. Thai intelligence figures show that eight of every ten suspected drug traders in Thailand are Chinese, and the remaining two out of ten have Chinese connections and operate through Chinese middlemen. More than three million Chinese live in Thailand, all of them steadfastly retaining their Chinese identity. They consider themselves Chinese, not Thais, although they are required by law to adopt Thai names once they become naturalized citizens. They comprise the leading merchant class in Thailand, controlling much of the retail trade and important segments of industry and the professions. They control the bulk of the country's wealth.

Hong Kong Triads have established flourishing branches among Bangkok's Chinese. Since 1980 evidence of a large influx of the 14K Triads has been monitored with dismay by the Bangkok police. Six months before I arrived, the city was shocked when three 14K members armed with automatic weapons and hand-grenades were killed while staging a daring prison break of a convicted Triad, a former Royal Hong Kong Police officer.

Much of the information compiled by the Thais fits perfectly with intelligence gathered by the Hong Kong authorities. Top-level Hong Kong crime bosses make frequent trips to Bangkok to oversee what has become a critical branch office. "For young Triads on the fast ladder to the top, there is no better assignment to get in Hong Kong than to be in Bangkok for several years. It puts you at the front of a lot of the most profitable businesses the Triads are engaged in, especially drugs and the recruitment of prostitutes," a Hong Kong police superintendent had told me in the British colony.

And not only have the Hong Kong Triads sent their own representatives into Bangkok to coordinate the illegal businesses, but the Chinese who have lived in Thailand for generations have their own Triads. Although the Triads will sell heroin or prostitutes to the American Mafia or the Corsican syndicates, the best deals and terms are reserved for each other.

"Everybody at the top of the Triads knows each other," Viraj told me. "The top Chinese here are on very good terms with the top people in Hong Kong. So if the Hong Kong group makes a massive purchase of heroin, they only have to put twenty-five percent of the money down, and then the Bangkok group shares the risk with them. So until it arrives safely in Hong Kong there is no more money to pay. If the shipment is seized on the way, then they split the loss. No one else has a system with that type of trust but the Chinese."

While the top echelons of the trade are Chinese, the lowest rung of the ladder, the cannon fodder of the drug trade, couriers, is made up predominantly of young Thais and some Europeans and Americans. These people are employed for just over a thousand dollars to run a kilo or two in a false-bottomed suitcase or strapped onto their bodies out of Thailand and to a final destination country.

Traffickers have developed ingenious and sometimes gruesome methods of smuggling heroin. As soon as one method is discovered by the police, it is abandoned by the smugglers. Heroin has been found hidden inside furniture, behind the canvas of oil paintings, inside the metal walls of refrigerators, inside toys, aerosol cans, computers, batteries, television cathode tubes, underwear with secret compartments, shoulder pads, eyeglass frames, the heels of shoes, and even artificial limbs, among dozens of other hiding places. It has been discovered stuffed into the bodies of dead babies cradled in their "mothers'" arms and carried across the border. Some couriers who have swallowed a pound of heroin in a string of condoms have died when the heroin-filled condoms burst inside their stomachs.

Customs police are often confronted with television sets or aerosol cans that actually work as they are supposed to. The heroin is hidden in a part of the device where it does not hinder the operation. Sometimes only the extra weight to a spray can or a battery will alert the customs officer that something is amiss. Although they seem small, most of the smuggling devices can carry a very profitable amount of heroin. For instance, the aerosol cans have a vacuum spot that holds 750 grams of heroin, which costs $5,000 in the Golden Triangle and is worth $2 million when cut at the U.S. street level.

New developments by traffickers include a method whereby large amounts of heroin can be dissolved in a liquor bottle that appears absolutely normal upon close inspection. At its final destination the heroin is retrieved through a chemical process. Also linens and towels are now soaked in a special heroin solution and the heroin is retrieved unharmed by a later chemical treatment. Dissolving the heroin in bottles and on cloth even throws specially trained dogs off the track. One of the most perplexing smuggling developments is when heroin is packed into long custom-made straws and slipped between the perforated edges of a cardboard box. The straws are topped with some coffee grounds to mask any scent for the dogs. This is foolproof in that it cannot be seen when one looks at the box. Most of the time the customs officials are concerned with whether contraband is inside the box, not whether the box has contraband within its cardboard lining. This smuggling method was discovered only when a box was dropped at the Rotterdam port and white powder spilled from a gash in the side. Large cardboard boxes can hold up to two kilos of pure heroin, and in a shipment weighing 150 pounds the extra weight is not noticed.

The multitude of smuggling options makes the considerable number of drug seizures by the police seem even more impressive. Given thousands of ways for couriers to carry heroin across international borders, law enforcement is faced both with a sophisticated foe and ever-changing tactics.

"But the biggest amount of heroin is not moved by courier," Colonel Viraj told me. "No longer. Today it's done by trawler out of Thailand, in big loads of at least 200 kilos, and transferred to other trawlers off of Hong Kong and then taken to other locations. This method had been popular in the 1960s, then it lost favor for some time. Now with the large amounts of heroin that are involved, it has gained in popularity and is now the biggest way to smuggle. If a syndicate wants a thousand pounds, it would take them several hundred courier trips, a logistical nightmare.

"Instead if they split the order into five loads of 200 pounds each, and each is moved by a different trawler, it's much easier for the syndicate. And if they should be unlucky enough to lose one of the loads, then they still make enough money with the other four to last a lifetime, and they consider it the cost of doing business. Actually, the price for the drug increases so dramatically once it leaves Thailand that the syndicate could lose four of the shipments and still make a good profit with the one remaining load. So they lose money only if all five loads are intercepted. And of course this never happens, because they have different ships and times and destinations and some of it, if not all, gets through."

Thailand has an estimated 15,000 fishing trawlers spread along a rugged and large coastline. Most of the trawlers are unregistered, and even if narcotics are found on them, locating the real owner or who hired the boat is virtually impossible. No fishing trawler has to file destination plans with any Thai maritime authority when it sets sail. Whether it is going to drop a load of heroin in the South China Sea or whether it is going fishing in the Gulf of Siam is anyone's guess.

I asked Viraj to what extent the top drug traffickers in Bangkok had been able to buy respectable lives for themselves. It brought a broad smile to his face.

"Too many of them. I know who they are. They have become some of the most respected citizens in the land. And unless I arrest them with the heroin on their laps, no one will believe me if I say they are heroin traffickers. And even if I arrest them with the heroin in their hands, people will still not believe they are guilty. Instead they will think, that crazy Viraj, he must have some personal grudge against this great man in the community, so he has set him up to make it look like he was involved in heroin. And almost any court will free the trafficker and lock me up instead for fraud. Maybe that is the real reason that I am still alive. They know I am there and am coming after them, but they are sure that I cannot make a case against them stick.

"And they are almost all Chinese. Sometimes I see articles in the paper and they have given big money to this charity or that charity. They are even some of the biggest contributors to anti-drug campaigns. They are really very smart. How could anyone believe that a businessman who has led the crusade against addiction among young people, and has given hundreds of thousands of dollars to educate the public on the horrors of drug abuse, could be a major trafficker? And of course they are heavy contributors to politicians, so they end up with some of the most powerful friends in the nation. It sounds like something from a novel. But it's real, I know it. I could give you a list of names that would shake this entire country. But try to prove it. For instance, the Bank of Bangkok, the biggest in the country, was founded on opium. But try to prove it."

"To what extent do you think corruption has allowed these people to gain such power?"

"Oh sure, there is a lot of corruption at the lowest levels. The Chinese have been very effective at buying compliance through the low levels of Thai society. But at the highest levels, on some of the big cases, the problem may not always be corruption.

"I personally think that in many cases when the case is thrown out of court and everyone cries 'corruption,' it is often the poor trial preparation in the outer districts. In some of the districts outside of Bangkok the local police are not very good at keeping detailed records or following the technical rules set down by the Thai courts. For instance, even if you have a search warrant from a court, you cannot use it after ten at night unless there are certain specific narcotic situations. But the local police don't pay any attention, they just get the warrant and go into the house at midnight and then everything is thrown out of court. Or sometimes it is just bad preparation. The excitement for a young policeman is to be on the investigation and then to make the arrest. The most boring part of police work is the paperwork. So it is the part of the job that the cops do the worst work on. They can't wait to be on to the next case and they keep putting the paperwork off, figuring they will get to it next week, but next week never comes. Then they get called to court a year later to testify and they can't remember the facts clearly and they make terrible witnesses. Then the trafficker gets off or the case is thrown out of court, and since the cop knows the guy is guilty, he gripes that it can't be his fault so it has to be the problem of 'corrupt' officials like judges or prosecutors. Sometimes it is, make no mistake about it.

"In some big cases there has been corruption. And the traffickers have enough money to buy some very influential friends in any country. But don't think it's always deliberate corruption. Sometimes it's just plain bad police work."

I knew that Colonel Viraj meant that his monologue should emphasize the beleaguered status of Thai police and government officials by arguing that corruption was not as widespread as many claim. But the thought that major heroin traffickers were released even when totally honest people were involved in all aspects of the case, because the police work outside of Bangkok was inept, was not a very comforting thought in the war on drugs and the Triads.

"You have to remember that we have our hands full," Viraj continued. "Heroin is a worldwide problem, not just a Thai problem. And we are no longer a major producer. We have become primarily a transit country. Remember, most of the opium is grown in Burma and most of it is consumed in the West. It's very easy to say that Thailand should do this or Thailand should do that, but we don't have the money or the technology to do as the West would often like us to do. The U.S. gave us seven helicopters, but that was years ago and they are getting old. Just because we are situated as an ideal transit country for opium from the Golden Triangle, we should not be the only ones to bear the responsibility of how the narcotics get around the world."

Viraj vividly recalls that during and after the Vietnam War a number of GIs settled into Thailand and became heroin smugglers. The most notorious of the "serviceman syndicates" was a group of black GIs run by Leslie "Ike" Atkinson, known in the underworld as "Sergeant Smack." The leader of a group called the Black Masonic Club, Atkinson started preying on U.S. servicemen by organizing crap games when he was stationed in Germany. By the time Vietnam rolled around, Atkinson was ready for the big time, and he established a narcotics ring with servicemen in Bangkok. The syndicate's headquarters was a popular Southern funk hangout called Jack's American Style Bar. While it hardly rated a passing glance from the outside, inside it was one of the liveliest places in Bangkok during the 1970s. It was the main stopover for tens of thousands of black GIs eager to rid themselves of wads of dollar bills saved for their five-day "rest and recreation" furloughs.

The first floor was a soul restaurant and a dance floor where

Thai prostitutes crammed together with soldiers and hustled to the rhythms of "Funky Chicken," "Soul Man," and "Rubberlegs." The second floor was reserved for the drug trade, where large amounts of heroin were sold to GIs based in Southeast Asia. Also, more than 1,000 pounds of nearly pure grade number 3 and number 4 heroin found its way to the United States.

The Atkinson syndicate moved heroin from its Chinese sources in Thailand through the U.S. military cargo system, mostly to Fort Bragg and Seymour–Johnson Air Force Base. Atkinson received and distributed it to organized crime figures in New York, Baltimore, Washington, D.C., Philadelphia, and a host of Southern cities. During its heyday the Atkinson organization used U.S. servicemen as couriers and also shipped heroin stuffed inside custom-designed oriental furniture and other goods destined to move from Asia to the states. But the most bizarre and macabre legacy of the Atkinson organization was the "body bag" connection. During its investigation of the syndicate, the DEA gathered evidence that the Atkinson group also sent heroin to the United States concealed in the coffins of returning servicemen's bodies as well as stuffed into some of the corpses. An Atkinson courier accompanied the body bags back to the United States and off-loaded the heroin, usually at an intermediate stop like Travis Air Force Base in California.

Atkinson is serving a forty-year sentence in the State Penitentiary in Atlanta, Georgia. Authorities estimate that he may still have $85 million stashed away in banks in the Grand Caymans and Switzerland. Seven other key members of the group received jail sentences in the United States. In Thailand two of Atkinson's accessories, Jasper Myrick and James Warren Smedley, were arrested, and in a high-profile trial were convicted of being part of the Asian end of the syndicate. Smedley, who directed the Asian operation, received a life sentence, which was overturned on appeal for reasons never made clear by the Thai court. He returned to the United States, where he pleaded guilty to a heroin-smuggling conspiracy charge in a Raleigh, North Carolina, courtroom. Although he was sentenced to eight years in prison, the court determined he was eligible for immediate parole because of the two years he spent in a Thai jail. Myrick, a twenty-three-year-old serviceman who was at the courier level in the organization, did not fare as well. He was sentenced to thirty-three years and is still in Bangkok's forbidding Bang Kwang maximum-security prison.

There were a series of smaller cases involving heroin smuggling and GI servicemen. "But no one remembers that there were American servicemen doing the smuggling," Colonel Viraj told me. "Everyone just remembers that the heroin was from Thailand. It seems that we are always the ones who are supposedly not doing the job. But on closer inspection I believe you will find the fault can be shared by many parties."

Colonel Viraj spoke at length about Thai efforts to curtail opium production in the country. One method is crop substitution, which is hindered for historical reasons as well as the official Thai policy that hill tribes should not be taught to rely on alternative crops until an active and stable sales market exists for them. To ensure new markets for substitute crops is difficult, and while the Thais are making progress, it is a slow process.

A second method of reducing the amount of opium grown in Thailand is eradication. It is costly and time-consuming. It involves troops in the field and has to be done so as not to incite a rebellion among the northern hill tribes who depend on the crop for their sole livelihood. Yarbrough told me in Chiang Mai that eradication was partially a sham: "The Thais tell us that certain acreage in a certain province has been eradicated. Then we go there and take pictures and show them the goddamn pictures of the fields filled with opium, and they say, 'Oh, we must have missed that one.' It's a lot of crap. They should be spraying D-24 if they are serious about getting rid of opium."

D-24 is a broadleaf herbicide that the Drug Enforcement Administration is pushing heavily as a panacea for opium-producing countries. It has been used effectively in Mexico. It kills any and all vegetation it comes in contact with. U.S. authorities claim that valuable lessons were learned from Agent Orange. As a DEA agent in Bangkok told me, "This one's safe, and anyway, they are supposed to spray it on opium poppies, not people."

Burma is the first Southeast Asian opium producer to use D-24 as part of its eradication efforts. By accepting the chemical, which the United States provides free of charge, together with the planes to drop it, Burma has also received a tie-in of additional U.S. economic aid. The same financial carrot is held out to Thailand—accept D-24 and more money will come through the aid pipeline. But so far the Thais have remained adamantly opposed to the spraying. Colonel Viraj does not think spraying is a good idea. "One of the problems is that the hill tribe farmers do not just grow opium. They grow opium on one part of their land and then they grow some food to eat on the parcel next door. And when the spraying is done, it doesn't differentiate, it kills everything that grows. So not only is the opium gone, but the farmer then has nothing to eat. And then people get sprayed with the chemicals, and it does happen, like in Burma. If the planes come under insurgent fire, they just drop their load of spray and let it fall wherever it goes. There are lots of stories that people are getting sick."

Days later General Chavolit Yodmanee, director of the Thailand Narcotics Control Board, expanded on his country's objection to the spraying program: "For the superstitious hill tribes, seeing this cloud drop out of the sky and then seeing all their crops die and people get sick, it turns them against the central government. It is the seed for rebellion and great resentment. In Burma the insurgent armies tell the hill tribes that the spray comes from America and this builds a resentment among millions of people, a resentment which the Communists will try to exploit. And we just do not think the spray is safe, no matter what is said. Everyone said Agent Orange was safe. I'm sorry, but it's just not for Thailand. We will continue our own eradication programs, which may be slower than some people want, but are undeniably effective."

Not only has the United States failed to convince any other Asian country to adopt the spraying program, but there is evidence that the Burmese are misusing the program. Reports compiled by the Central Intelligence Agency in 1986 indicate the Burmese are extensively spraying insurgent strongholds and not opium fields. The Burmese are using the American aid in the drug war to fight their own battle against ethnic insurgencies. They hope the spray destroys the food crops that are one of the lifelines of the groups fighting Rangoon. Moreover, the CIA reports conclude that some Burmese military units, with the full knowledge of the Rangoon government, have used the threat of spraying as a form of extortion. In government-controlled areas, villagers are told they will be sprayed unless they pay an additional "tax."

How long the DEA will allow its program to be abused is not clear. What is clear is that although Rangoon claims to have destroyed a record number of opium acres in 1986, the warlords increased acreage at a much faster rate and the Burmese opium crop hit a new record, and it is expected to set yet further records in 1987 and 1988.

But even without the spraying program Thailand has managed to reduce its tonnage of opium. From a high of seventy-five tons in the early 1970s, it has now fallen to under thirty. Yarbrough told me, "The State Department wanted the figure put at seventeen. That's crazy. We got them to move it up to twenty-five, but it's actually about thirty-five." Whatever the exact Thai opium tonnage, it is a small amount compared to Burma's. But while the Thai emphasis has been in pleasing the Americans by reducing the amount of opium cultivated in the country, it has failed to curtail either the nation's opium-refining capabilities or its use as a primary transit center.

Thai laws and enforcement efforts in fighting narcotics are weak. Although police surveillance and telephone taps are freely allowed, traffickers have altered their tactics and avoid critical conversations on the phone. The customs service did not have a speedboat until 1986. No seizure of assets is allowed. In tax cases the burden is on the government and not on the taxpayer. Colonel Viraj is still chagrined by the case of a taxi-cab driver who became a multimillionaire department-store owner, friend of politicians, and a contributor to charities and antidrug programs. His entire fortune is built on opium, and he has challenged Viraj to bring him down. He has never even been charged with a crime.

In 1979 the Thais finally banned some of the crucial chemicals used in the heroin refinery process. But instead of the chemicals becoming unavailable, they simply went underground. New black-market suppliers provided the chemicals, and the Sun Yee On Triad from Hong Kong became the largest distributor of the prohibited chemicals in the Golden Triangle. Within two years of the ban the only change in the heroin trade was not that the key chemicals had vanished but rather that the price had increased twentyfold.

Thai intelligence and DEA reports show that a record number of mobile heroin refineries are operating on Thai soil, many of them close to the Burmese border. As soon as one is discovered and destroyed, another has sprung up to take its place. And instead of Thailand losing favor as a transit country, it seems to have solidified that position. Only four routes out of the Golden Triangle bypass Thailand. Since Hong Kong allowed land entry from mainland China several years ago, there has been an increasing amount of heroin that is taken overland through China directly into Hong Kong, thereby missing Thai soil. From Burma some heroin goes directly west to India, where it is rerouted to the Middle East or to Europe. Also from Burma ships laden with narcotics travel through the Andaman Sea to Malaysia and Penang, and then on to the safety of the archipelagic geography of countless miles of the unpatrolled maritime borders of Indonesia. A final drug route that misses Thailand is when Laotian opium and heroin proceed directly to Da Nang and then on to the South China Sea for a drop-off in Hong Kong.

Law-enforcement personnel agree that at least 75 percent of the narcotics exported from the Golden Triangle pass through Thai soil. Most of it heads south to Bangkok and then out on the thousands of independent fishing trawlers or the commercial ships that ply in and out of the Thai capital. "The heroin goes everywhere," a DEA analyst in Bangkok told me. "Some goes to Singapore, some to Taiwan, some to Australia, but most of it still goes to Hong Kong."

In Hong Kong the Triads have their best chance of changing the bill of lading on a commercial shipment so that by the time it arrives in the United States it will not look as if it originated in a drug-producing country like Thailand. And not only can the Triads play with the paperwork that will help the shipment clear U.S. customs, but they sometimes like to do some final refining in their own labs. They still believe they have the best chemists. And a final factor that draws most of the heroin toward Hong Kong at one point or another is that since the bosses there are paying for it, they feel they have better control by putting it in Hong Kong before it goes on to a final destination. This does not mean the heroin is off loaded in Hong Kong. It may just stop there and be transferred onto a different commercial ship and never leave the harbor or the airport.

Colonel Viraj agreed that most of the heroin leaving Thailand passes through the British colony at some point. "They have their own way of doing things in Hong Kong, from selecting their own

couriers to making sure the amount and the quality of the shipment is okay."

From discussions with drug agents in Bangkok it was clear that
the heroin routes out of the Thai capital lead back to Hong Kong,
and along the way the key operators are Chinese. The heroin
warlords in the Golden Triangle, the major ones being part or
all Chinese, cultivate annual opium crops and refine it in jungle
labs staffed by Chinese chemists. Chinese middlemen in the northern Thai cities of Chiang Rai and Chiang Mai negotiate the deals
for the purchase of the crop and arrange for shipment to Bangkok. Triads based both in Bangkok and in Hong Kong arrange
for further transport either to Hong Kong or to another intermediate Asian stopover. The Hong Kong Triads then take over
the business at the stage when the profitability figures start to
zoom.

Honest men like Viraj were risking their lives to wage a losing
crusade to stop the transit of the drug flow out of Thailand. But
even when it flooded past Viraj, the narcotic was a long way from
ending up in small plastic $5 bags on the streets of New York.
The answer to how the Triads accomplished that transition was
to be found only in Hong Kong.

10

"White Powder Ma"

Three police were in front of me and another two stepped in just behind. The police escort was gathered at the opening to an alleyway off a busy street. With the street light illuminating the front of the path, I walked into the place where a Hong Kong police superintendent had told me, "If you go in alone, the chances are you won't be coming back out."

The alley we entered was enclosed like a concrete tunnel. It was dirty. More than a hundred years of neglect had left the stucco walls with inches of grime. The ceiling was low and covered by a bewildering jumble of knotted wires, dangling electric cables, and exposed fuses and sockets, all hanging less than a foot from the tallest cop's head. The floor was a mixture of broken concrete and dirt, which made it difficult to walk. As my police escort led me deeper into the tunnel, an occasional naked bulb providing the barest light, the ceiling and walls closed in. Within a hundred yards the walls had narrowed so that we had to proceed single file, and the ceiling dropped so we could only walk crouched over. Then the tunnel began to widen again, and suddenly we entered a new section that first appeared to be a maze. Other tunnels led off in a half-dozen directions, and some staircases offered dark climbs to unknown overhead locations. One of my police escorts pointed at a wooden sign imprinted with Chinese characters hanging over the second opening on the right. "See that, it says the name of that street is Rats' Piss. That's where we are going." And we entered the underground tube.

The tunnel was filled with a mixture of strong odors, whiffs of ammonia, freshly baked bread, charcoal and burned plastic joining other jolting and indistinguishable smells. It had streaks of light from the side walls shooting into the middle of the pathway. As we walked farther inside the source of the light was revealed. There were small rooms off each side of the walkway. Some were no bigger than six by eight feet, and in each were men and women, jammed in almost on top of one another, manning a wide assortment of antiquated equipment. In some rooms were open-pit fires with short, emaciated men molding sheets of metal that were licked by the flames. There was not a single window in these depths. The fires filled the entire tunnel with an oppressive heat, making it difficult to breathe.

In one room a group of men piled loaves of bread in front of the turn-of-the-century oven that took up most of the available floor space. In another two woman placed handfuls of candies from a large mound into plastic bags and then sealed them shut with a hot iron. I stopped in front of a room no larger than a walk-in closet. Three young women sat next to each other in front of old-fashioned manual sewing machines. They had piles of cloth behind their chairs and stacks of finished men's shirts in front. One weak bulb was their only source of a work light. The rhythm of their whirring machines seemed to overpower the other little factories all around them. They glanced up at our group, and almost in fright put their heads down, and their hands and feet kept busy on the machinery. You had to be inside the tunnels for only ten minutes to understand why these sweatshop workers had an average life expectancy of forty-five. Breathing in noxious chemicals banned by governments around the world, pried into inhuman working conditions, paid under a dollar a day for work that definitely will kill them.

"That's why tourists can buy a shirt on the streets of Hong Kong for two dollars," one of the police said, looking over his shoulder at me. "No one knows that there are thousands of people working in conditions like this so that the bargain center of Asia can flourish. Most people have never heard of this place.

Wealthy visitors arrive on their trips to Hong Kong, and they don't realize as they drive in from the airport that they are passing another world."

I was in the Walled City, only several kilometers from Hong Kong's Kai Tak International Airport. Constructed by the Sung dynasty in 1197 as a military base to manage the salt trade, the Walled City is only one hundred yards wide by two hundred yards in length. Yet this is the densest patch of urban land in the world. On that small space close to 50,000 people are packed in high-rise tenement housing that rivals the worst slums. Little electricity, virtually no running water, and no sewage system in buildings that require elderly residents to climb fifteen floors to get to the one-room apartment that serves as the home for two generations of the same family. The Walled City is filled with more rats than people, and an uncontrollable population of rabid dogs runs the interconnecting alleys. Mounds of garbage rot in decaying corners of the dark stairwells and tunnels.

Although the wall was torn down by the Japanese during their World War II occupation of Hong Kong in order to provide material for new runways at the airport, the City remained a closed and self-sufficient hovel of misery. When China ceded Hong Kong to the British after the First Opium War, it claimed sovereignty over the Walled City. The British decided the City was more trouble than it was worth, and while never acknowledging the Chinese claim, it decided not to police or govern the compound. As a result the Walled City became a haven for drug addicts, a stronghold of gangsters, and a refuge for those fleeing legitimate authorities. It is a center for numerous illicit businesses ranging from snake vendors to counterfeiting shops. At times it was "governed" by a motley crew of adventurers comprised of gunrunners and narcotics smugglers. It was inevitable that it should also become one of the chief breeding grounds for the Triads.

"This is Triad ground," one of the police told me as we walked farther into the City.

All of the tenement high rises and tin shacks that are piled on top of one another are connected by an intricate system of tunnels, some so small that a person must bend in half to walk through. The alley/tunnels all have names, like the Rats' Piss I walked through, a mocking gesture of a normal city existence.

Only those who live there know the nooks and crannies of the tunnels. On the few occasions when the police have tried to pursue a criminal into the City, they have become immediately lost in the maze of dark passageways. It is possible to enter the Walled City and visit all parts of it without ever seeing daylight. Children grow up within these confines. Taught at inside "schools," they become aggressive gang members by the age of ten, all seeking a way out of their natural hell.

"Triad gangs have been known to fight over a single stairwell inside here," one of the police escorts informed me. "They have brutal fights over which gang has the right to control a small part of one of the tunnels. It is their own world in here. They don't like seeing us come in, and they certainly are not used to seeing many white faces inside here."

Some parts of the Walled City have been converted into sweatshops like those I saw. Police estimate that more than ninety illegal dental clinics are scattered within the confines of the City, unlicensed practitioners with primitive equipment. Abortionists abound, their methods so crude that the pregnant girl often dies with her unborn fetus. Old Chinese still pack the remaining dingy opium dens, the only "medicine" that keeps their aging bodies from rebelling against sixty years of addiction and killing them. Veteran prostitutes offer services out of one-room whorehouses.

The mainland Chinese who are taking over Hong Kong in 1997 have told the British that they do not want the colony with the Walled City. They realize it is a haven for criminal activity and is not governable. The British are laboriously trying to build new housing for the 50,000 residents and starting to slowly tear down some of the outer shacks. By 1997 the British and Chinese hope that the Walled City will be only a historical anachronism.

I visited both of the Buddhist temples inside the City, one a simple table altar set up in front of fifty folding metal chairs, the other an elaborate, colorful shrine in red and gold hidden behind a set of solid metal doors, which the temple's guardian reluctantly opened at the police's request. I walked through a converted nunnery that is now a center for the City's oldest residents. "Some of these people have been outside only a couple of times in their lives," one of the police said as he looked at an ancient Chinese sitting hunched in a wicker rocking chair. She was very frail, a wisp of white hair on her almost bald scalp. She did not move when we walked in; her eyes just bored straight into the floor. A lifetime in this hellhole was enough to make anyone seem brain dead.

"This place is self-contained in almost every way," the policeman continued. "It's primitive, but they get along. They have food shops and dentists and doctors and their own herbal pharmacies, and they never need to go anywhere. And it's self-sufficient as far as the Triads are concerned as well. There are gun shops that make little shotgun pistols from scrap metal. If they don't blow up when you use them, they can be handy. There are hiding places in here for narcotics. There are gambling houses, card halls, places to stash jewels after a robbery, doctors who will fix you up if you get hurt, and they know how to keep their mouths shut. As a matter of fact, everyone in the Walled City knows how to keep their mouths shut. They don't trust outsiders. Although some of them work outside of here, they are loyal to where they come from. They do not cooperate with us in any way."

I first heard about the Walled City when I was in Amsterdam. A Dutch policeman, Arie Bax, specializing for fifteen years in Triad crime and drug trafficking, told me it was a must visit. "You have to get the Hong Kong police to take you inside. It's important for you to go. You see, it turns out that many of the Chinese drug couriers we arrest coming into the Netherlands come from the Walled City. These people get paid from $1,000 to $1,200 to risk a long prison sentence. Unless you see it yourself, you will never understand why someone is willing to risk ruining their whole life for what seems like such a small sum of money. But once you see the conditions inside there, then you will understand why someone is willing to risk everything to earn that money. It is like four years of salary to them, and it lets them get themselves and their families out of that slum and maybe on to a better life. You'll never understand it coming from America unless you go inside and see it yourself."

Not only is the Walled City a safe haven and recruiting ground for the Triads, but the poor residents are ideal victims as well. Without any police authority, the City's dwellers are squeezed for whatever extras they have. Sometimes a family's daughter is gang-raped, called "stamping the merchandise" by the Triads. It leaves the girl so ashamed and in such shock that she barely fights when her family is forced to give her up to the porno trade or as a prostitute. The Triads sell the girls to one of the thou-

sands of "fish stalls" that pack Hong Kong, and the price paid
for her becomes her debt to the brothel. But only 10 percent of
what she earns is applied to her debt, and it will take the average
girl at least ten years before she is free. By then her life has been
ravaged by an endless succession of $2 tricks.

Weak young boys are also snatched from their parents and sold
to child pornography rings in Thailand and the Philippines.
Stronger boys, some as young as eight, act as street couriers for
narcotics or pickups for gambling and extortion payoffs. Others
are intimidated into selling drugs at their schools. Last year ninety-
one Hong Kong children between the ages of nine and fourteen
were arrested as drug pushers. With more than 5,000 registered
addicts under the age of fourteen, social workers are no longer
surprised by child junkies. Families are threatened unless they
allow their apartments to be used as hiding places or for safe
storage of illegal goods. The brave but hardy few who try to fight
the Triads are made into public examples so that the majority
realize resistance is futile. Dissenters are attacked by gangs in the
tunnels and "chopped" with long knives, their carcasses left in a
pile of ribboned flesh, waiting to be discovered by some returning schoolchild.

It is a shame that the British will eventually demolish the
Walled City. It should be left as a shrine, a testament to what the
Triads did to 50,000 people. If Western government and law-
enforcement officials toured the Walled City, the stark realiza-
tion of the Triads' ruthlessness might prompt some advance
planning for the criminal influx of secret societies likely to take
place in the United States and Europe within the next ten years.
But no one is coming to the Walled City.

"As a matter of fact, no one is coming to Hong Kong with any
real concern about the Triads," a police superintendent told me
in the British colony. "You don't need to see something as ex-
treme as the Walled City to be afraid of Triads. They own a lot
of this colony, and by looking at what they have accomplished
here in the last twenty years, that should be enough to scare the
living daylights of Western law enforcement. But it's not. I can
only assume that they are all so busy with their own current crime
problems that when they occasionally hear about Triads at law-
enforcement conferences, they hope they end up in someone
else's backyard and not their own."

But this head-in-the-sand attitude will place Western law en-

forcement at a significant disadvantage when large numbers of
Triads transfer their operations out of Hong Kong by 1997. The
types of criminals spawned from places like the Walled City are
unrivaled in crime annals.

It seems like fiction that a semiliterate street porridge vendor
could join the Yee Kwan Triad and become one of the chief
dragon heads in Hong Kong. But that is exactly what happened
to Ng Sik-ho, nicknamed "Limpy" for a battered leg that resulted
from a Triad fight in his youth. In fifteen years he zoomed from
a petty gang member to become the Dragon Head of one of the
colony's most powerful brotherhoods. Directing a $500 million
heroin syndicate based in Hong Kong and Thailand, the then
forty-five-year-old Chinese godfather's empire was broken by the
police in 1974, when Limpy was arrested, tried, and jailed for
thirty years. But what looked like a major police victory in the
war on Triads was actually the behind-the-scenes work of some
of Limpy's most powerful competitors, the Ma brothers.

The Ma brothers, from China's Chiu Chau region, also came
from slum neighborhoods like the Walled City. Ma Sik-yu and
his younger brother, Ma Sik-chun, were penniless street toughs.
They had no formal education. They progressed from restaurant busboys to lookouts at illegal gambling dens to running small
street gangs in the housing resettlements of the British colony.
But the Hong Kong police believe their rise to the top of the
crime world started in earnest when they joined a Chiu Chau
Triad closely allied with both the 14K and the large Sun Yee On
syndicate. The police have reconstructed the Ma brothers' meteoric career.

They started as petty heroin pushers in 1967, and the older
Ma traveled to Thailand and the Golden Triangle to personally
oversee his narcotics purchases. During these expeditions to
northern Thailand he met General Li and the hierarchy of the
Chinese Nationalist opium armies. By 1968, General Li had taken
such a liking to the up-and-coming trafficker that he arranged
for Taiwan intelligence operatives to meet with both the Ma boys.
Li thought the growing Ma business might provide some assistance to Chiang Kai-shek's Nationalist government.

General Li was right. By 1970 Taiwan intelligence decided that

the Ma brothers were on their way to the top of the heroin business and that their Southeast Asian syndicate could double as a
Nationalist Chinese spy network. According to Hong Kong Police files the network was a series of informants in half a dozen
Asian countries reporting on the activities of the local Chinese
community as well as any developments in the host country that
could affect Taiwan. The elder Ma, Ma Sik-yu, directed the spy
network. At its height in the mid-1970s, it employed more than
40 people and cost millions of dollars a year in upkeep. The elder Ma collated information in Hong Kong and then passed it
to Taiwanese military and intelligence officials on his numerous
trips to Taiwan. At the same time that the elder Ma ran the spy
network, his younger brother, Ma Sik-chun, established the *Oriental Daily News*. Soon it became the number one pro-Taiwan
Chinese-language newspaper in Hong Kong.

By 1972 these two slum toughs were key operatives for Taiwan
intelligence. But their work for the Taiwanese was only part-time.
Their main efforts were saved for their exploding heroin business. In return for their service to Taiwan, General Li supplied
the Ma brothers with top-quality opiates at substantial price re-
ductions. The Taiwanese allegedly made up the price difference
to the KMT heroin armies by sending them additional weapons
shipments. With a direct discount pipeline into the Golden Triangle, the Ma syndicate became the largest drug empire in Hong
Kong history by 1974.

A $750 million-a-year business in the mid-1970s gave the Ma
brothers instant respectability. The elder Ma, known to hundreds
of thousands of addicts as "White Powder Ma," turned into a "legitimate" businessman, financing a series of ventures ranging
from restaurants to commodity-trading companies. Hong Kong
is a city where money buys status. And White Powder Ma bought
a lot. He liked betting on horses so much that he bought the
colony's most fabled track, the Chung Fat Pak. This unschooled
street tough was accepted as a member at the prestigious Royal
Hong Kong Jockey Club. In his European-cut suits, he was a regular figure at the casino tables of Macao, regularly winning or
losing more than a million dollars. He entertained lavishly at his
stunning Kowloon home, hosting parties for political leaders, film
stars, business tycoons, intelligence chiefs, and criminals of international fame. He brought his nephew into the Triad, and

soon another Ma, Ma Woon-yin, had become the third most powerful member of the multibillion-dollar business. It was not long
before Ma Woon-yin was seen in jacket and tie leaving White Powder's villa for Kai Tak airport, his arms burdened with heavy suitcases filled with cash.

Meanwhile, White Powder's younger brother, Ma Sik-chun, became a prominent member of neighborhood committees and social organizations like the Boy Scouts. He was also one of the most
flamboyant and popular nightlife figures on the Hong Kong social scene. A familiar figure in his flashy pin-striped suits, he was
known for leaving behind a stream of $100 tips almost every-
where he went. He partied in nightclubs and on yachts and in
private homes on three continents with tables of caviar, cases of
Hennessey XO brandy, and boxes of Havana cigars. He had a
stream of stunning women trailing after him. Swaggering and
flamboyant, he liked gold watches and chains, fast cars and sexual excess. In the Portuguese gambling oasis of Macao he was
called "the Golden Ma."

White Powder Ma and his family revolutionized the heroin
trade for the Triads. Although the Triads had taken advantage
of the large GI influx into Southeast Asia in the late 1960s and
early 1970s, they were unprepared for the U.S. troop withdrawal.
The Triads had expanded their purchases of opiates from the
Golden Triangle and upgraded their refining capabilities, but
they had not developed the overseas contacts that would allow
them to follow the Americans home.

White Powder Ma changed that. When his syndicate was
formed Southeast Asian heroin accounted for slightly more than
5 percent of the U.S. market and almost none of the European
market. By the late 1970s White Powder almost single-handedly
increased the U.S. share to 25 percent and the European share
to nearly 70 percent. He sent his crime lieutenants around the
globe to establish branch offices for the syndicate and make connections with other organized crime figures. White Powder Ma
was one of the first crime chiefs anywhere to understand the international nature of organized crime. Although he ran Hong
Kong as its top heroin trafficker, he knew that he had to cooperate with other bosses in other countries if he was to expand his
business and increase his profits. The foreign crime kingpins were
pleased to welcome White Powder Ma and his seemingly unlimited supply of "China White."

According to a DEA analyst, he was responsible for connections to U.S. crime bosses like Miami's Santo Trafficante, Jr., a successor to Meyer Lansky, and New York's Anthony Turano (later killed by the Triads when they thought he double-crossed them on a heroin shipment to the East Coast of the United States). White Powder Ma allegedly established ties to the former Corsican chief of the French connection, Auguste Ricord. Later he sent an underboss to the Paraguayan jungle to meet with Ricord in order to establish a southern route for heroin into the United States. Drug agents believe he personally traveled to Japan in a failed attempt to establish a partnership with Japanese organized crime groups called the Yakuza. By 1971 he made overtures for cooperation to the Young Turks, a crime organization in Singapore, and developed smuggling ties to the Saigon Cowboys, one of the toughest street syndicates in Vietnam. White Powder Ma had helped the Triads become international.

His high-profile activities attracted the attentions of the United States government and the Drug Enforcement Administration, as well as the Royal Hong Kong Police and Interpol. By the mid-1970s dossiers on the Ma syndicate were bulging in the law-enforcement agencies of half a dozen countries. Urgency was added to the investigations when Limpy was removed from Hong Kong's heroin scene in 1974. A DEA analyst in Hong Kong told me that the best hypothesis was that White Powder Ma had used his extensive police contacts to build an airtight case against his only major rival. The police did the rest for the Ma syndicate by arresting Limpy and successfully prosecuting him. Limpy, who felt to the very end that he could buy his way out of a prison sentence, was shocked when he was given thirty years at hard labor. "The word behind the scenes was that White Powder Ma had outbid Limpy's final offer to the judge," the DEA analyst told me.

With the removal of the former porridge salesman, the heroin business in Southeast Asia belonged to the Ma brothers. They kept peace among the other Triads by cutting them in for segments of the trade. The Wo Shing Wo was responsible for transportation from the trawler-packed waters into Hong Kong, the 14K ran most of the laboratories, and the Sun Yee On oversaw payoffs to the police and customs. The Ma brothers made the Triads realize their potential as their profits doubled and then tripled from the burgeoning narcotics business.

But in 1976 the Hong Kong police were pressured into a large-scale investigation of the Ma syndicate. By the beginning of 1977 there were more than sixty Hong Kong police working full-time on the Ma businesses. The DEA had thrown its full weight into the investigation. Then somebody slipped word to White Powder Ma that the police were about to seek indictments, and in February 1977 he slipped out of Hong Kong and fled to Taiwan. There his intelligence contacts paid off as he was shielded, despite massive international pressure on the island country and on President Chiang Ching-kuo, son of the late Chiang Kai-shek.

In Hong Kong the police issued an arrest warrant for White Powder and arrested nine other men, including two policemen and his brother, Ma Sik-chun, and his nephew, Ma Woon-yin. They were charged with directing the largest narcotics syndicate in Hong Kong history. The arrest warrant for White Powder Ma was served on Interpol's headquarters in Paris, since Taiwan was a member country. Taiwan refused the Interpol request to arrest Ma. The United States and the British government pressured Taiwan through diplomatic channels, but the island country has no extradition treaty with Hong Kong. The Nationalist government was adamant that White Powder Ma would not be disturbed.

Meanwhile in Hong Kong a fifty-man police squad was assigned to keep a strict twenty-four-hour-a-day surveillance on the nine arrested men. Their passports were seized and their names were placed on watch lists at the airport and at all the seaports and train stations. Despite the security, three of the defendants managed to jump bail in July 1978 and made it to the sanctuary of Thailand. Then one week before the trial was to start, the two Mas, uncle and nephew, who had been released on the inadequate bail of $200,000 each, managed to creep out of their houses at midnight. Slipping past the police guard, they went to Hong Kong harbor on the night of the Chinese Moon Festival, when the port is packed with ships and exploding fireworks. They stepped abroad a Panamanian freighter and steamed toward Taiwan.

At first no one knew where the two Mas had fled. An intensive Asia-wide hunt for them was conducted before Taiwan announced that their boat had been intercepted by a coastal patrol in Taiwanese waters. At the time they were detained each of the Mas had a Taiwanese passport without a proper entry visa, and almost $100,000 in cash. Because their passports were not in order, they were arrested for illegally entering Taiwan. Although each was later sentenced to a year in prison for possession of forged documents, they were free only six months after arriving in their new sanctuary.

Again Taiwan ignored the international outburst at providing shelter to the entire hierarchy of the most notorious heroin syndicate in Asia. It did not take the Ma brothers long to set themselves up in great style in their new home country. They purchased luxury mansions in one of the most fashionable and exclusive sections of Taiwan. The younger Ma still had a bevy of beautiful girls visit him on chartered yachts or planes from Hong Kong. Senior executives from the *Oriental Daily News* made regular trips to Taiwan to report to the Ma boys on the progress of their Hong Kong newspaper.

Meanwhile, back in Hong Kong, an embarrassed government refused to establish an official inquiry into the reasons for the Ma escapes. Instead the colony's judiciary placed the remaining four defendants into a public show trial, and the government prosecutors claimed that the remaining men were as important as those who escaped. The chief defendant became a fifty-four-year-old Chinese businessman who acted as a financial advisor to the Mas. The prosecutor, in a bit of double-talk, claimed he was the "top executive responsible for making arrangements." After a two-month trial and twenty prosecution witnesses, a predominantly Chinese jury acquitted him to a rousing chorus of cheers in the packed courtroom. A humiliated government carried on the cases against the three remaining defendants charged in the Ma case, three low-level smuggling managers. At first there was minor cause for celebration when they were convicted by the trial court. But eleven months later a court of appeals overturned the convictions, and the men walked free into a crowd of 300 cheering supporters.

The Ma brothers had not been touched by law enforcement. Not a single member of the syndicate was in jail. The Hong Kong police and U.S. efforts had resulted only in the inconvenience of forcing them to transfer their base of operations from Hong Kong to Taiwan, forty-five minutes away by air. And if there was any doubt that the Ma brothers were still heroin kingpins, it was resolved by mid-1979, almost two years after the syndicate was supposed to have been smashed.

This time a joint DEA–Thai operation resulted in the arrest

of Cheng Ah Kai, one of the three Ma lieutenants who had first jumped bail when awaiting trial in Hong Kong in 1977. He was captured in Bangkok while arranging a multimillion-dollar shipment of heroin to Hong Kong aboard a Panamanian freighter registered to an alleged Ma front company. The arrest of Ah Kai confirmed what many DEA officials feared—that the Mas were still in business. Again the Ma brothers emerged unscathed. Ah Kai was acquitted by a Thai criminal court sixteen months after his arrest. The Mas seemed invulnerable to police action.

"I wish I could tell you something has changed," a Hong Kong police intelligence analyst told me, "but nothing has. The Ma brothers are still the biggest traffickers of Southeast Asian heroin. They have become legends by evading our efforts. Limpy is finished. His jail sentence has made him a loser in the eyes of the underworld. But the Mas are winners. They created an empire, and as far as everyone is concerned, they got away clean. No one can touch them in Taiwan, unless the Americans can eventually exert enough influence, but I seriously doubt it. Ten years ago if you had asked me who the biggest and most successful Chinese heroin dealers were, I would have said immediately it was the Ma brothers. Today my answer would be exactly the same, but even with more conviction."

Other players have entered the Hong Kong narcotics scene and some of the Triads are grumbling for a larger share of the narcotics business. But the longevity and success of the Ma syndicate make it the unquestioned leader of the Triad heroin connection. What Kuhn Sa is to the Golden Triangle, the Ma brothers are to the Hong Kong Triads. Since White Powder Ma has moved to Taiwan, Southeast Asian heroin's share of the United States addict market has more than doubled.

But even though the Mas have moved to Taiwan, the bulk of their heroin and processing continues to take place in Hong Kong. "Do you think they are going to get all their chemists and move all their labs and all their hiding places to Taiwan with them?" the Hong Kong intelligence analyst asked me. "They still have their other Triad businesses like gambling going on here and they still have their legitimate businesses—those can't be seized from them because of their corporate structures.

"Taiwan doesn't mind if they conduct business out of their country, but it better only be telephone calls. Only orders should be given. The Taiwanese never like to get themselves too dirty. That's why they don't mind if the KMT armies organize the opium harvest, but that is because it is a long way from Taiwan. The same with the Mas. It's okay that they do their business, but the Taiwanese prefer that the actual dirty work of the trade be done over here in our city. They don't want to see any heroin or smell any of the refining."

To find out more about how the Ma brothers and other Triads get the heroin from Bangkok into Hong Kong and then on for farther transport, I ended up in the office of the chief of the Royal Hong Kong Customs and Excise Service. K. L. Mak is in his late forties but appears much younger. His neatly pressed navy blue blazer, white shirt, and maroon tie, illustrated with different English coats of arms, made the slender Chinese officer look more like an up-and-coming advertising executive than a cop with twenty-three years of service behind him. I met him at customs headquarters, an antiquated floor of offices on top of a multistory car garage overlooking Hong Kong Harbor.

Mak's office was enormous. Large sheets of plate glass provided a startling view of the harbor, with its acres and acres of rotting junks moored hull to hull. One side of his office was filled with a floor-to-ceiling map of Hong Kong, and another wall was plastered with a blowup of Southeast Asian water routes. It seemed that large maps covering the walls of offices were the de rigueur decoration for drug fighters. You could tell where you were just by the office. The Golden Triangle had filled the DEA conference room in Chiang Mai. Bangkok and the south of Asia took up the wall space in Colonel Viraj's office. And now the British colony loomed over K. L. Mak. The rest of the office was standard government issue, even down to the simple desk and two straight-back wooden chairs for guests. They were the type of chairs that told you Inspector Mak did not want visitors getting too comfortable or staying too long. Along the windowsill looking out to the harbor were varieties of wood, ivory, and jade elephants, symbols of good luck and fortune to the Chinese.

"I'm sure that heroin belonging to the Mas still comes through here," K. L. Mak said without a trace of apology in his voice. "If you want to know how the heroin gets into Hong Kong from

Bangkok, and then how it goes out of here again, you just need to look at what a hub of activity Hong Kong is. I think you have to understand how busy this city is as a commercial and tourist port before you can understand how easy it may be to get narcotics into the colony's territory."

He pressed a buzzer on the underside of his desk. A young, uniformed Chinese customs officer came in and stood at attention at the side of the desk. Mak spoke to him in Chinese. "I want him to get me a file so maybe you can understand this better."

In several minutes Mak was thumbing through a six-inch manila file folder. "The year 1986 was a bad one for us. The number of addicts rose and our seizures of narcotics were at a five-year low. That means there is more heroin on the street. We don't know if it means that more is also getting through to other places."

"Well, what is your emphasis here? Is it to stop just heroin entering Hong Kong or also shipments that are just stopping here in transit?"

"Well, it's not so easy to answer. It's a bit of both actually. Our main concern has to be narcotics destined for our streets. We cannot worry about a shipment destined for another country. That is the responsibility of the customs authorities at the final destination. They must intercept it. I mean, if we are told by an informant that a load of heroin is on a certain ship in the harbor, we will certainly seize it. But our efforts with our intelligence division and with our informants is to find narcotics that are entering Hong Kong to stay here. You have to remember, the DEA has an office here and it is their responsibility to find heroin that may be destined for the U.S.

"If some heroin is destined for another place but is off-loaded into the colony for more refining or whatever, then it is our problem and we want to seize it because a kilo of heroin in a Hong Kong apartment doesn't bear a tag that says 'Final Destination America.' There's no way for us to tell that it isn't here to be used in Hong Kong. So we concentrate on shipments like that. It's just that the shipments that stop here only as a transit stopover, those are a lower priority for us."

It is little wonder that Hong Kong is the shipping capital of the heroin trade. The chief of customs was at least honest enough to acknowledge that the British colony did not have the manpower to worry about shipments of heroin that stopped in Hong Kong only in transit on their way to another destination. What makes Hong Kong crucial to the narcotics trade is the ability of the Triads to alter shipping invoices so that commercial goods hiding heroin do not indicate that their origin is a suspected drug-producing country like Thailand. Instead the crates look as though they had originated in a non-drug-producing, high-export country like South Korea, and the customs official in the United States would likely wave the shipment through, spending most of his time on cargoes from suspect countries. Not only do the Triads provide drug cargoes with innocent shipping documents, but they also change the papers on some legitimate shipments from non-drug-producing countries to read as though they are from suspect countries.

In this way the Triads hope that European or U.S. customs will spend their small amount of search time on the innocent shipments that indicate they are from narcotics centers. This paper camouflage means that heroin could arrive in Hong Kong from Thailand or any other source and, as long as the Triads have a day to switch the paperwork, the heroin is much more likely to pass an inspection at a later port. This was exactly the type of heroin shipment that K. L. Mak and his men were not looking for.

But Mak did say that if the heroin came into Hong Kong territory for further refining in a makeshift lab, then it would receive a high priority for his service and from the police narcotics squad. Mak showed me a number of heroin labs that his force had found and destroyed in Hong Kong. Most of them were kitchens converted to crude labs that could process a couple of kilos a day. Some clever chemists adapted microwave ovens so they could refine ten kilos of heroin a day. The most ambitious labs that have been discovered during the past year are home sauna units outfitted with a sophisticated array of accessories. They have the ability to refine 200 kilos of heroin a day, as much as the average lab in the Golden Triangle. "And since a lot of the heroin needs further refining in Hong Kong, it means the Triads still have to off-load most of their narcotics and then it is at the top of our priority list, Mak concluded.

"That's bullshit," a DEA intelligence analyst told me. "First, a lot of stuff that arrives does not need further refining. The Golden Triangle labs are getting much more professional. And since 1980 some of the big Triads have done away with the mom-and-pop labs you saw. Instead they have set up labs at sea."

During the heroin refining process, when the narcotic starts to boil, it stinks. It smells like a rotten pile of garbage. Caught in a wind, the noxious fumes can drift for some distance. This is no problem in Golden Triangle jungle labs where there are no roofs on the refineries and where no one lives for miles around. But in a kitchen refinery in a city as densely populated as Hong Kong, it is difficult to synthesize heroin without a neighbor complaining to the police. That is why some of the Triads have established laboratories on oceangoing yachts. The odor ceases to be a problem, customs boats can be seen from a great distance, and when the refining is done the load of heroin can be offloaded directly onto an anchored cargo ship.

"K. L. Mak's a good guy," the DEA analyst told me. "He has caught a lot of dope in his day. But customs is just not set up to deal with the loads stopping here on their way to another location, and they haven't made a dent yet in the boat labs."

K. L. Mak was right about one thing. Once the size of Hong Kong's commercial and tourist traffic was revealed, it was little wonder that Hong Kong customs and narcotics police are overwhelmed by the variety of ways in which heroin is smuggled into the British colony.

Hong Kong is a free port. The government has done everything possible to encourage the movement of trade and commercial cargo. Virtually nothing is taxed. Import/export licensing is kept to a minimum. Permits to do business are required only for health or security reasons. The Customs and Excise Service has 2,700 agents to deal with one of the most congested cities in the world. All three entries into Hong Kong are a customs service nightmare.

First is the international airport. Thirty-seven international airlines bring almost 30,000 passengers a day into the colony, some 5,300 potential couriers an hour at peak times. The state-of-the-art air cargo complex handles 670,000 tons of cargo a year—all the opium in the Golden Triangle makes only 100 tons of heroin. Customs is so swamped at the air cargo terminal that only shipments arriving from drug-producing nations are randomly checked. That is exactly why the Triads change the shipping documents.

A second form of entry to Hong Kong is overland from mainland China. On average, 28,600 people cross the border every day, "each one a potential courier," says Mak. On that single crossing at Sha-Tau-Kok, cars bring 1,500,000 tons of cargo into Hong Kong each year, and another 1,600,000 tons of cargo pass by rail. If this is not enough to make the Hong Kong customs job seem impossible, the largest smuggling point into Hong Kong is the harbor.

In 1987 Hong Kong surpassed New York to become the second busiest port in the world behind Rotterdam. Some 27,000 oceangoing vessels and another 16,000 river ships come and go each year. On top of this are an estimated 140,000 junks and small boats that constantly come in and out of the harbor. These junks are the crucial links to the fishing trawlers packed with narcotics chugging up the coast from Thailand. The cargo generated by all these ships is massive. Some 32 million tons of cargo is off-loaded into the computerized terminal at the edge of the port, and another 14 million tons is loaded onto the ships for export. The river ships add another 10 million tons of cargo. On an average day there are 5,000 vessels in Hong Kong Harbor, and the port prides itself on being able to turn around a cargo ship in under thirteen hours. That is one of the reasons that Hong Kong has attracted so much commercial shipping. But it has been at the loss of effective narcotics enforcement. It means that the Hong Kong port is a massive sieve through which heroin flows almost undetected. Not only is the cargo overwhelming, but another 900,000 "potential couriers" arrive each year on the incoming boats and another 10 million come and go between the Portuguese gambling colony of Macao, just forty minutes away.

In 1986 the Hong Kong police and customs service seized about 600 kilos of heroin, slightly over one-half ton. It did not make a dent in the flourishing business. The average price of a fix of heroin dropped to $1.50, the same as the price of a cold beer. And with a steady stream of heroin getting through to Hong Kong's estimated 50,000 addicts, it is little wonder that K. L. Mak can hardly be worried about heroin that does not even come into Hong Kong but just stops there on the way to another country. His attitude is that the customs service of the final-destination country should have the problem, just as he has the problem of heroin entering Hong Kong destined for Chinese addicts.

Heroin kingpins like White Powder Ma must find that moving

heroin through Hong Kong is not difficult. Dozens of front companies in Thailand and Hong Kong serve as sophisticated centers for hiding heroin within commercial shipments. Insurance is bought through millions of dollars of bribes that are spread from the staff sergeants at precincts to customs officers checking boxes loaded on planes bound for the United States. Hong Kong spends almost $40 million a year on narcotics control. White Powder Ma makes that by selling a mere thirty-five pounds of China White on the streets of America. Now with refineries working overtime at sea, the syndicates have been able to take advantage of Hong Kong's location. It has a convoluted coastline of more than a thousand square miles. There are over 250 uninhabited islands where heroin can be stored and lab boats can dock and finish their work. If Bangkok is the first major stop for most of the opium and heroin coming from the Golden Triangle, then Hong Kong is clearly the second stopover. But from here it only leaves as heroin, and with the dominance of the local Triads, it is about to be spread around the globe.

"How much heroin do you think passes through here?" I asked K. L. Mak.

"I have no idea," he said, while gazing out his picture windows at the harbor. "I only know how much we seize, but it's anyone's guess as to how much goes through Hong Kong. How would we know?" It was not reassuring from the chief of the Hong Kong customs service.

Benny, the former gang member who was my guide to the Hong Kong underworld, was not surprised that I was disheartened at the prospects of stopping the heroin flow. To him it was matter-of-fact: "If I could place a wager on it, it's no question, my money would go on White Powder Ma. It's not a fair matchup. All the cops can do is make the Triads be more careful, cost them more in security, and make them lose some shipments. But stop them—never."

11

The Five Dragons

Before leaving Hong Kong I met with Benny once again. I wanted to discover more about the businesses other than heroin that the Triads controlled in Hong Kong. I also wanted to find out to what degree police corruption had allowed the Triads to build their all-encompassing web over the British colony. Benny decided that I should see the gambling casinos in Macao. Although the clubs were legitimate and licensed by the Portuguese government, Triad officials were known to hover about them.

The Chinese have a passion for gambling. Illegal gambling dens are the trademarks of Chinatowns around the world. In the same way that many Westerners consult their horoscopes before starting their day, many Chinese will start their morning at a gambling hall, their luck on several games like fan-tan or *paigow* determining whether the rest of their day will be lucky or not. They are serious and obsessive gamblers. Their faces do not tell whether they are about to beat the bank or whether they have just lost the deed to their home.

"It's some of the same trait that lets the heroin dealers do so well," Benny said as he met me at the ultramodern Ferry Terminal in the Hong Kong port. Benny's large frame was covered in the latest Hong Kong fashion, a pair of black high-waisted jeans and a purple cotton polo shirt, both bleached to make them look faded as if by years of sunshine. He wore a pair of mirrored wrap-around sunglasses, giving his fat face a sinister look.

"Dealing in heroin is gambling in a big way. By extra good security and with the right tea money [bribes], you can alter the odds in your favor. But on the other side, instead of a bank you have the cops and they are playing the other hand. Sometimes the cops get lucky and draw a good hand and they beat you. But you've always got enough chips left to play another hand, and the payoffs are so good when you win a hand that it's worth playing full-time. That's what it's like. Big-time gambling."

We settled into a Boeing jetfoil, a kind of airplane cabin on the hull of a boat powered by jet engines. The seats were exactly like those in the economy section of a plane. The engines kicked on with a steady high-tech whir, and we were soon cutting low across the water, leaving a heavy wake. Then suddenly the engines kicked into high gear and the boat lifted out of the water and skimmed on top of the surface at sixty miles an hour.

Macao, the Portuguese enclave forty miles down the coast, is the Las Vegas of Southeast Asia. A former eighteenth-century haven for pirates, Macao is Hong Kong's seedy cousin. Macao boosters call the decayed elegance "charming," but it is a mean and battered waterfront town. It has all of Hong Kong's dark side without any of its glitter. It is a jumble of narrow alleys traveled mostly by bicycle-powered rickshaws. There is a feeling that trouble is always just around the next corner.

China will retake Macao in 1999, two years after it gains control of the British colony. Until then it will stand as a tribute to the Chinese obsession with gambling as well as to the effectiveness of some Triad operations.

"Macao is a combination of legitimate business and Triad connections," Benny explained to me over the sound of the jet engines. "Remember that a lot of initiation rites for the Triads are done over here. It's just that most people think there's less chance of discovery here. And if the Hong Kong cops are at least pretty sophisticated and good at times, the Portuguese are asleep. It's hard to do something stupid enough in Macao to get the cops to do anything."

But I knew talk of gambling and Macao could wait until we arrived. First I wanted to get Benny's opinion on a recent Hong Kong police report I had seen. It was an intelligence survey of

Hong Kong's thousands of cinemas, restaurants, bars, massage parlors, nightclubs, discotheques, video-game centers, and martial arts schools. The police concluded that 80 percent of those businesses paid the Triads protection money each week. The 20 percent who did not pay money were luxury restaurants and hotels that catered to foreigners. The report concluded that Triads left those establishments alone because they were often backed by foreign investments, and the Triads feared the government and police reaction if they upset the foreign tourist and business climate.

"There's no doubt about it," said Benny. "I don't know of a restaurant that doesn't pay something. Almost everybody in business has to pay something. It depends on what part of Hong Kong you're doing business in—that determines which Triad controls your area and who you have to give money to. It's important for you not to underestimate all the other businesses besides dope. It's big, real big. If there was no dope here at all, there would still be Triads because the other stuff is not just chicken feed.

"Here, I can tell you, Triads are into everything. Counterfeiting. They have some of the best equipment in the world. Top-grade stuff that makes the finest traveler checks, and paper money from British pounds, American dollars, yen, D-marks, Hong Kong dollars. I have even seen Pakistani rupees and Indonesian rupiahs. You don't even know what that money looks like, so how will you know if it's phony? You won't. I tell you they even have machines for coins. No one has that. No one looks at British pound coins to see if they are real or not. That's a multi-million-dollar-a-year business. And it's just one thing.

"The protection is a big sideline for them. They make so much from the protection, you wouldn't believe it. The gangs are useful because they are the enforcer for people who don't want to pay. I tell you they get protection from everyone, from the street hawkers, from snooker saloons, from fish markets, all over the place. I give you an example. When a new building is going up, the contractors are always hit for money on the new job. They are so used to it that they often negotiate a lump-sum payment for the entire job instead of paying each week or every month. But some contractors have such good gang contacts themselves that they get big discounts when moving into another Triad's area. It's never a question of whether the contractor has to pay money, it's just a question of how much and how often.

"Here's how it works. The Triad will send a young kid in and he will offer services as a 'watchman.' If they tell him they don't need one, then he will point around and say this area is real bad, filled with lots of bad kids and you better watch out. If that warning is ignored, then a small fire is usually next. Then a young kid goes and says, 'I would like to borrow' this much money from you. And he comes every week and 'borrows' the same amount from you. Since he is only 'borrowing' the money he can't be arrested for extortion. Meanwhile the contractor knows he is going to have to pay so he includes the price of the payoff figure in the bid for the job. It's everywhere like this. There are millions in this stuff. You can become a very rich dragon head without ever touching dope or having anything to do with it."

As we crossed the imaginary water line that indicated we were in Macao's territory, the cabin hostesses went around selling instant lottery cards and bingo slates. Although the casinos were only twenty minutes away, the hungry gamblers needed to get an early fix as soon as the law allowed. Benny continued talking. His information confirmed a lot of what I had seen and heard in the Royal Hong Kong Police headquarters during the past week.

Triads start recruiting early. Hong Kong police estimate that in the colony's poorer sections, 60 percent of schoolchildren have some gang affiliation. They also recruit professionals in Hong Kong's overcrowded prisons. Foot soldiers are needed to do everything from vandalizing cars at garages in order to force money from the owners to throwing live snakes and rats into crowded restaurants that refuse to pay promptly. Not only do they monopolize gambling and the protection rackets in Hong Kong, but they also thrive on loan-sharking. Interest rates of 700 percent to 1,300 percent are commonplace. The Macao casinos are prime Triad loan-sharking centers, providing more money to the addicted gambler who cannot stop losing. Those who can't pay are offered a way out—usually a trip as a heroin courier. If they get the heroin to its destination successfully, their debt is canceled. If they get caught, the Triad takes care of their family.

The Triad protection rackets have become sophisticated. To avoid police detection the contractors or retailers are often required to hire some extra employees, who are carried on the books as though they actually worked for the victim company. But they never show up for a day's work. Triad bookkeepers show the businesses how to itemize their protection payoffs as a taxation expense in the company's books. The protection rackets alone are estimated to be a multibillion-dollar business. A 1986 police case showed that from a single fish market on the Hong Kong port the 14K was taking $6 million a year in protection fees.

The money rackets of gambling, protection, and loan-sharking are complemented by vice. Triads control almost all of Hong Kong's prostitution and pornography. Their flesh empire includes tacky nightclubs, massage parlors, one-woman brothels, fish-ball stalls (filthy alley stands where a group of cheap prostitutes are kept), porno theaters, and adult bookshops.

A new generation of Triad bosses are increasingly taking their syndicates into legitimate businesses. They have also pushed the secret societies into white-collar crime, including massive credit-card and business fraud, counterfeiting, and pervasive embezzlement.

"They have also become high-tech," Benny assured me as we neared Macao. "A lot of the syndicates are on computers now. And the systems are real clever. If the police ever catch the main computer, it's done so that unless you know the right password to get on the system, then it automatically transfers the files to another computer in another country and destroys whatever it has in its own files. So the police can't follow the information. The computer doesn't tell them where it sent all of the information on the syndicate. It could be sitting in someone's machine in New York or Switzerland or around the corner in Hong Kong. And there is nothing left for the police on the computer they've caught. It makes running the businesses of the Triads much easier.

"And not only at the center of the organization have things gotten so technical. In a lot of the business things have changed. Now bookies use portable telephones and digital beepers to be available any time of the day for business. And when they place a call it can't be traced by the cops. The phones cost almost $4,000 but they are worth it. They automatically reroute a call to a second and sometimes even a third phone. The police just can't follow that. When we get to Macao maybe you'll see some of them standing on the beach. They have powerful portable telephones, and they take bets while they soak up some sunshine. It's the best life."

It was overcast in Macao. No bookies were getting a tan. Law enforcement was trying to enter the twenty-first century, but the Triads were beating them to it.

A five-minute rickshaw ride along the beach and we arrived at the most prominent landmark in Macao, the Lisboa Casino. A multistory circular complex badly in need of renovation, its Moorish-style main building looks like an Arabian turban covered in thousands of light bulbs flashing the casino's name. Wide white steps lead to the main entrance, where Chinese doormen are dressed in sea-green uniforms with velvet trim. It looks as though the Lisboa bought the leftover uniforms from the Havana casino circuit when Castro forced them to close shop in 1959. With a nod the doormen open up to reveal a circular lobby with 1950s-style tile murals of Asia surrounding you like a cheap imitation of the Sistine Chapel. Through the lobby and past a row of arcade shops announcing jewelry and electronics bargains is a neon sign announcing the direction to the casino halls.

After passing through a short, dim hallway, we came to the main gambling center, an enormous circular room packed with Asian men. The noise was terrific. So were the smoke, the heat from the bodies, and the odor of the sweat. This mass of humanity was broken only by the green gambling tables. Baccarat, dice, fan-tan, poker, mah-jongg, *paigow,* every possible game of chance was being played in earnest. Not a smile in the room. Four and five deep around the tables, stacked chest to chest, they pushed and jostled and thrust themselves forward to place their bets. Cigarettes waved in the air, crisp Hong Kong dollars folded in half between the fingers moved back and forth over the bobbing heads, the jostling stopping only for a moment while the winning hand or dice roll was revealed at each table. The gaming attendants were middle-aged men in frayed tuxedos. Fluorescent light fixtures attached to the side walls cast an eerie glow over the entire room.

This was far removed from American casinos in spirit as well as in style. No extravagant floor shows with dancing girls kept the casino crowded. None were needed. These gamblers were not here to have a good time. They were here to win money. It did not matter to them if the pressure started an ulcer, the cigarette cloud contributed to cancer, and the din gave a migraine— they merely wanted to walk out with more money than they came in with. Few did.

Off of the main hall were annexes to the casino. The room of slot machines, with its polyester-clad tourists intently dropping five- and ten-cent coins into the one-armed bandits, contrasted sharply with the main hall. Another room had large wheels of chance, and a small private room in the rear was "reserved for the big-time players," according to Benny. "If you're going to lose a lot, they let you do it in privacy. It's still as crazy back there and as crowded, but at least you know that you're not going to get your $10,000 bet fucked up by some grandmother placing a two-dollar bet and screwing up your cards with some bad play. Back there they are all professional."

The Lisboa is a cash machine. It might as well print money. The Portuguese government grants a monopoly license for the exclusive right to control the Lisboa and the other casinos on Macao. In 1962 a tough battle was waged for the right to the lucrative licenses between the megarich Fu family, owner of the Furama Hotel in Hong Kong, and a group called STDM (Portuguese initials for Macao Tourism and Entertainment Company). STDM was represented by a smooth-talking Macao business trader, Stanley Ho. Today, Ho owns 25 percent of STDM and it is his empire. He has investments in property and shipping and casinos in Asia, Europe, and Australia. The sixty-five-year-old gambling czar has become one of the wealthiest men in Southeast Asia. He is Hong Kong's Donald Trump.

In order to keep the exclusive gambling rights on Macao, Ho pays a substantial surcharge tax that provides 45 percent of Macao's annual budget. Yet despite providing half the budget for the entire colony, Ho's group turns an enormous profit. Although its finances are shrouded in secrecy, STDM is valued at $1 billion by Asian financial experts. Ho and one of his partners, the New World Group in Hong Kong, have recently offered $417 million to obtain the exclusive rights to develop the largest casino project ever proposed in Australia.

Stanley Ho thinks big. No one denies it. But the rumors abound on Ho. His associations are questioned. Hong Kong police have an extensive file on the chief of security at the Lisboa, Lau Wing-kuei, indicating possible criminal connections. Yip Hon, a professional gambler who worked as a croupier for the Fu family, had become one of Ho's four partners in STDM. They had a terrible falling-out, and according to a DEA analyst, Yip Hon ac-

tually put a murder contract out on Ho. Intervention by key
Hong Kong society figures supposedly saved Ho's life. Yip Hon
now owns the lucrative Macao Trotting, the colony's biggest race-
track, and his chief of security is a former Hong Kong cop,
Charlie Lee.

Also according to the DEA, when one of Hong Kong's biggest
Kungfu screen stars, Chan Wai-man, a Triad member, was arrested in a narcotics case, Stanley Ho reportedly came to his assistance. Members of Hong Kong intelligence and the Drug
Enforcement Administration will talk about Ho, but only under
the strictest assurance that they not be identified. The Hong Kong
police say he is a Triad member. Confidential files on the Lisboa
claim that the club's eighth floor is where the Triad loan-shark
operations are headquartered. "It's very convenient," one DEA
agent told me. "If you are in deep over your head at the casino,
they just zip you right upstairs in the elevator and you can get a
loan that you'll regret for years." The fourth floor is where the
enforcers supposedly hang out waiting for any trouble. The DEA
claims that questionable characters are frequent Lisboa visitors,
including a 14K overlord from Taiwan, Fung Sui-may, as well as
Hong Kong's number one moneyman, Li Ka-shing. As far as the
law-enforcement personnel are concerned, if Stanley Ho is not
involved with the Triads, he may tolerate their use of his club
because he realizes it is a necessary evil of being in the gambling
business.

Stanley Ho has never been indicted. No investigation is ongoing. He is a respected and upstanding figure in the Hong Kong
social and business scene. But his business may have been used,
very possibly without his knowledge, as a recruiting ground for
heroin couriers, loan-shark operations, and laundering of money.
According to DEA sources, many of the drug couriers are paid
in gambling chips so they can spend them at the Macao casinos.
That type of payment is harder to trace. It also encourages the
same behavior, compulsive gambling, that led some of the men
and women into becoming couriers in the first place.

"Young gang members hang out here," said Benny, looking
around the casino. "They like to come here to show how much
money they can play. It shows how much they are making."

Stanley Ho's empire is legitimate. The Triads are simply so
close that long shadows are being cast over his enterprises. I was

learning that maybe no one in Hong Kong was powerful enough to shake off the Triad cloak. Details had emerged on the central criminal enterprises that kept money rolling in whether there was a good or bad crop in the Golden Triangle. For vice, gambling, protection and loan-sharking, business was always booming.

If the Lisboa was an example of how much money a single casino could take with only several thousand players, then what about the hundreds of illegal gambling clubs in Hong Kong where hundreds of thousands of intent gamblers spend their days? In those alley clubs, shut off from the outside by a steel door, an oriental face is the passport for entrance. White faces are not trusted. Inside those basement rooms, eight-by-four wooden planks are covered with green cloths nailed to the sides of the planks. They serve as gaming tables, with the colors of chips indicating the betting limits. These illegal gambling halls operate twenty-four hours a day. Their overhead is negligible. They take 10 percent of every winning hand. They pay no taxes and do not worry about gaming licenses like those in Macao. If Stanley Ho's legitimate casinos in Macao made him a billionaire in twenty-five years, there is little reason to doubt that the far more numerous underground gambling dens in Hong Kong have done the same for some of the Triad bosses.

"You needed to see this," a sweating Benny told me. "They wouldn't have liked to have seen you in a club in Hong Kong, so it's best you see it this way. If you understand how much the Chinese like to gamble, then you will understand how crucial a place like this is. And how important it is to have gambling in Hong Kong. Millions of people come here every year, but far more stay on the other side in Hong Kong. It's like a license to print money, huh?"

After an afternoon in the Portuguese colony, we headed back to Hong Kong on the jetfoil. As Stanley Ho's tacky Lisboa faded into the background, our discussion turned to the question of corruption in the police department and how important that was to the Triads' stranglehold. With more than 36,000 police, Hong Kong has the fifteenth largest police force in the world. But a crime is committed every six minutes in the British colony. Those are only the reported crimes, the majority remaining a secret in the tight-lipped Chinese community.

Although most Hong Kong police are honest and hardworking, receiving low pay and earning little respect from the community, the celebrated past cases of pervasive corruption have forever tarnished the force's image. In 1969 the mere hint of an anticorruption campaign produced a wave of resignations by senior Chinese detectives and sergeants. By 1973 the first British police commander, Peter Godber, fled to England to avoid an investigation into how he accumulated $880,000 in a bank account when his police salary had paid him only $180,000 over twenty years. Godber was eventually brought back to Hong Kong, tried, and convicted of corruption charges.

The case so embarrassed the British administration that a special commission was formed to permanently investigate police corruption, the ICAC (Independent Commission Against Corruption). Six hundred full-time staffers had more than 500 major corruption investigations under way within one year. The ICAC concluded by the end of its first year of operation that "narcotics has become a tremendously lucrative source of corruption in the police force."

But what the ICAC stumbled across forever changed the public's perception of the Royal Hong Kong Police. It discovered that five key Chinese staff sergeants inside the Triad Bureau, the police department responsible for investigating and prosecuting Triad crimes, were themselves Triad members. The very people expected to protect the public against organized crime were in fact criminals. The ringleader of the group was Sergeant Lui Lok, a highly decorated policeman with an excellent arrest history. Junior policemen referred to him as "Tai Lo," the Chinese equivalent of the Mafia's godfather. Lui Lok, a 14K member, and his four associates were on Triad payrolls, receiving a percentage of the gambling, vice, and drug operations to which they turned a blind eye. The rampant payoffs amounted to hundreds of millions of dollars.

As the ICAC intensified its investigation of the five masterminds, they received advance warning of the commission's interest in their affairs. Fleeing Hong Kong, they settled in Vancouver, Canada, in November 1974. They formed a company called The Five Dragons Corporation and spent money at a staggering rate. A downtown Vancouver office building was purchased for $60 million in cash. Lui Lok became known as the "600-million-dollar man," the police estimate of his illegal fortune. But their free-spending habits attracted the attention of Canadian authorities, and the "Five Dragons" were stunned when Vancouver police arrested one of the group and threatened extradition proceedings to Hong Kong. The Five Dragons received the message. They packed up their Canadian operations and quickly headed for the sanctuary of Taiwan.

By 1977 when the Five Dragons arrived in the capital of Taipei, they joined more than forty millionaire ex-Hong Kong police officers who had fled ICAC investigations. Other millionaire police fled to the United States, where one of them, Eddie Chan, became the dragon head of New York's Chinatown well into the 1980s (see Chapter 15). Some of those who fled Hong Kong were among the most decorated and respected officers in the police force. One of them, a soft-spoken crime buster who had the department's most enviable arrest record, martial arts expert Sergeant Tang Sang, forfeited a $330,000 bail to arrive safely in Taiwan. The colony was crowded with similar startling stories. But in Taiwan the policemen's past was unimportant. What mattered was the amount of their wealth. It commanded respect from the local authorities. And since there was no threat of extradition, the police lived flamboyant and extravagant life-styles.

The Five Dragons embarked on a long celebration of their Canadian escape. They spent thousands of dollars nightly hopping from club to club in the company of starlets, fashion models, and Mandarin opera singers. By day they invested their millions in dozens of Taiwan businesses. The Five Dragons shocked local businessmen when they forfeited a $1 million deposit on a landmark restaurant rather than involve themselves in a lawsuit over disputed ownership. Money was like water to them—plentiful and easy to waste.

The Taiwan government finally asked the high-profile ex-policemen to tone down their life-styles, and most complied. Sanctuary in Taiwan was too important to risk by living in a way that aggravated the authorities. The Five Dragons helped purchase a series of restaurants, clubs, and brothels where the crooked police could party in privacy.

When White Powder Ma arrived in February 1977, he found some old friends among the fugitive policemen. Some owed their wealth to him. When White Powder was indicted later that year, one of the charges included a conspiracy to deal in narcotics with none other than the chief of the Five Dragons, Lui Lok. On September 18, 1978, only two days after Ma Sik-chun and his nephew successfully fled Hong Kong, the Ma brothers were seen dining in a Taipei restaurant with two ex-Hong Kong detectives. One of them was Lui Lok. The Mas had been reunited with the key policeman who had helped them form the largest heroin-trading syndicate in Asia. Lui Lok, the Five Dragons, and all of the millionaire ex-policemen are untouchable in the "Isle of Fugitives," Taiwan.

"Not much has changed now," Benny said to me as he sipped a Coke he had bought from the jetfoil's trolley. "The ICAC announces every so often that it has some more cases of corruption under way. But if you look at what has happened since the Five Dragons, it's all small-scale. It's against some cop for accepting a couple of cases of whiskey at Christmas. It's all real low-level. They are not touching any of the big police syndicates."

"Look, there are still police that are Triads, the ICAC hasn't changed that. And the ICAC hasn't changed human nature. Some guys join the police just to make it into a business. If some guy is earning $6,000 a year, and somebody offers him $50,000 to just look the other way one time, it's hard for most people to say no. Especially when everyone knows about the Five Dragons. The young cops almost expect an envelope with cash to be in their desk drawer when they get out of training school. They think that everyone on top of me does it, all the senior guys are making a fortune, so why shouldn't I? The ICAC can't do a fucking thing about that. All the ICAC has done is make everyone be a lot more careful about how they get the payoffs and also real careful about not showing too much money. I mean no one is crazy enough nowadays to put all the money into their bank account. But they used to do that because they thought no one could touch them. But that made it too easy for the ICAC."

Today, police taking significant bribes have to launder their funds just like the Triads launder their illegal profits. The Triads pay the bribes, and then offer a side service to launder it in return for a small handling fee. It helps serve the Triad interest of ensuring that the police on their payroll are not easy targets for the anticorruption commission.

The corruption system is well entrenched. It is organized and operates like any efficient business. If a Triad wants to start a new illegal enterprise in part of Hong Kong, it first has to obtain an unofficial license from the district sergeant at the precinct responsible for that part of the city. Not only is a single "license fee" paid, but a weekly "maintenance" fee is also paid. The chief collector in the police districts is usually a civilian Triad member. The policeman who comes to inspect the books and collect the payoff money is called the "caterer." He is responsible for distribution to all other police.

Corrupt staff sergeants receive $50,000 a month from just one large operation, with smaller payoffs filtering down the police pipeline. The lucrative staff sergeant ranks are among some of the most coveted in the department. To mask the extent of police corruption, the Triads feed them information on expendable members and certain crimes so that the police appear diligent in the war on crime. The most corrupt ex-policemen usually have some of the best arrest records in the department.

The Hong Kong police force offers additional incentives for widespread bribery not present in other law enforcement agencies. At least 75 percent of the officer rank, made up mostly of British career police officers, speak hardly a word of Chinese. They never deal with the rank-and-file Chinese, who comprise the backbone of the force and who are responsible for the street investigations in the war on Triads. Many rank-and-file officers resent what they see as a nasty vestige of the colonial British mentality—the British run the show, and the natives do the dirty work. Sometimes the only satisfaction the Chinese patrolman can extract is accepting a payoff from a Triad. That payoff, from another Chinese, lets him not only make a better life for his family but is taken without any feeling of guilt toward a hierarchy that is not respected and is generally disliked.

Another unusual factor that is currently laying the groundwork for increased bribery is the 1997 deadline for the colony's return to China. "With only ten years left, many police feel they should get as much as they can while they still can," a DEA analyst told me. Uncertain of what the Chinese Comunists will do to the police force, few police think of a long-term career. Recruiting good men is proving difficult. Coupled with the traditional Chinese lack of respect for police work, few young Chinese want to embark on a poor-paying police career that may have a ten-year time limit on it. The British allow new recruits to join the force for two-year increments. At the end of two years, young policemen can either retire and receive a cash payoff or re-sign for two more. Many are leaving and taking the money. The police force is constantly training new contractees. Building consistency and long-term dedication is impossible.

"Some of those guys joining now are clearly doing it to make a business out of it," Benny told me as the ferry pulled into Hong Kong Harbor. "They know the Triads are going to try to squeeze the last drop out of Hong Kong and they know the Triads need police help in doing it. So they are going to make as much money as they can before it's all over."

The situation in Hong Kong seemed as desperate as that in Thailand. Corruption may not be worse, but since the Triad's profits are greater in the British colony, the payoffs are bigger, and the corrupt police who surface seem almost bigger than life. A Hong Kong DEA analyst told me that even the next scheduled chief of the Hong Kong police was himself a Triad member. The flamboyance of the Five Dragons is over, but the extensive police–Triad cooperation is far from finished. Places like the Walled City continue to fester and provide not only the expendable cannon fodder of the drug trade but also the next Triad dragon heads. Men like White Powder Ma and the "600-million-dollar" Lui Lok continue their businesses with impunity just across a strait of water from Hong Kong. The Triads have extended their control over the Hong Kong underworld by adopting state-of-the-art technology. They have entered a new age of computer crime, and law enforcement is trailing far behind. Hong Kong police and customs service are overwhelmed by the massive amounts of cargo and the large numbers of visitors each year. Somewhere in the midst of the tourist and trade boom most of the heroin of the Golden Triangle slips through on its way to Triads around the world.

To understand what Triads did abroad I needed to visit the first place they successfully invaded outside of the Orient. I was leaving behind Benny and his gang friends, the opium dens on Ladder Street, the Red Pole in the Canton Disco, the sweatshops of the Walled City, and Stanley Ho's gambling empire. The trail of China White had moved out of the Orient. Its next major stop was Amsterdam.

12

The Unicorn

The cafe looks like dozens of trendy new coffee shops in Europe. It is black and white, sporting lacquered walls, chrome and glass tables, and leather chairs. A few scattered ferns provide the only warmth. A couple of young girls move to the curved bar to order espressos and a thick wedge of chocolate "spacecake." A group of middle-aged men, looking like university professors, are having an intense conversation at a corner table. They are drinking fresh-squeezed orange juice and smoking cigarettes. At the table closest to me is a fashionably dressed woman eating a plate of biscuits and sipping an herbal tea.

But this is not a normal coffee shop. Its walls are decorated with illustrations of the marijuana plant. It is one of Amsterdam's 200 "cannabis cafes." The spacecake, the cigarettes, and the biscuits are all made with marijuana and hashish. These cafes sell those drugs over the counter, and the air is filled with the pungent odor of the pipes and cigarettes of dozens of stoned customers. The cannabis cafes are scattered around the Dutch capital, some of the most famous set along the Leidseplein, the city's busiest square. The customers seem ordinary. The long-haired and grubby men often standing in front of the cafes are the ones you would expect to find inside. But they are in uniform—they are the Amsterdam police, and they look like no other force in the world.

The Bulldog cafe occupies a former police headquarters and

also features a foreign-exchange counter for tourists and a small clothing boutique. The neon menu behind the counter lists the "fare": the red side lists hashish from various countries, while the green side lists different marijuana. Twenty dollars buys a mixed sampling, varying in weight from 1.5 grams to 5 grams, all neatly packed in plastic bags imprinted with the popular bull-dog logo. These shops, filled with sedate customers enjoying their drug-induced highs, are the modern-day equivalent of opium dens.

An industry association publishes a *Golden Blow Guide,* which lists all of Amsterdam's cannabis cafes in addition to those in six other Dutch cities. Service and atmosphere are rated in the guide, but the most important attributes are the quality of the drugs and the competitiveness of the prices. On Saturday afternoons a leading Amsterdam radio station broadcasts the current prices of imported marijuana and hashish: "Thailand 21.90 [Guilders], Morocco 13.50, Nepal 16.10..." For years the voice belonged to Koos Zwart, son of the Dutch Minister of Health and a leading proponent of legalizing so-called soft drugs. By the spring of 1987, when other countries were concerned about drug-abuse epidemics, the Dutch capital dedicated a museum to the lore and enjoyment of marijuana.

But Europe's drug capital, where "flower power" flourished in the 1960s, and which became a sanctuary for drug users and Bohemian squatters in the 1970s, is faced with its own "hard" drug epidemic. Cocaine, hallucinogens, and barbiturates are common-place on the streets. And heroin has more than 20,000 estimated loyal customers among the small Dutch population.

Not only has the Dutch laissez-faire approach to drugs created a domestic addiction problem, but it has also encouraged for-eign narcotics merchants to move into the Netherlands. Most of those who came were Chinese. "Today the only organized crime we have in our country is Chinese crime," a Dutch police super-intendent told me over coffee at the Interpol center in The Hague. The Chinese realized that the law-enforcement policies toward "soft" and "hard" drugs could not be divorced. They rea-soned that if the Dutch were easy on one, they would be easy on both. The Chinese were right.

Obstacles to effective law enforcement abound. The Dutch "conspiracy" law is as good as not having one. It is almost im-possible for the police to prosecute anybody not physically in possession of the illegal drugs. Moreover, the police are forbidden by law to act as "provocative agents," so undercover work is handicapped because the police can never suggest any criminal activity or lead the criminals into a crime. Wiretaps, a major aid in U.S. law enforcement's battle against drug traffickers and organized criminals, cannot be used as direct evidence. The Dutch police must independently confirm the information they obtain from the wiretaps, a laborious and often impossible task. Another restraint on Dutch law enforcement is that government prosecutors cannot offer an arrested drug dealer a reduced sentence in return for testimony on his accessories and the rest of the syndicate. Although the Dutch system does authorize payments to confidential informants, a DEA agent posted in The Hague told me, "They have no money to spend. Any drug dealer worth his weight in salt could outbid the Dutch with his spare pocket change. They don't get anyone worthwhile to talk to them. No self-respecting informant would go to the Dutch police."

Until 1977 the maximum sentence for drug trafficking was four years. With time off for good behavior, that meant that a trafficker was back on the streets in a little over two years. It did not matter if you were a heroin kingpin responsible for supplying most of Europe's addicts—there was no provision under the law for a longer sentence.

The DEA still bristles at the case of a Chinese trafficker who was so contemptuous of Dutch laws that he dismissed his couriers and personally brought thirteen kilos of heroin into Amsterdam. Although he was arrested at the airport, his contempt for the Dutch system was justified. He was given a three-month suspended sentence. The judge was sympathetic to his incredulous contention that the heroin was medicinal and wherever he went he carried a supply for the rest of his life. In most other countries he would have been sentenced to life, and in eight countries he would have been executed. But in Holland, although he was found guilty, he walked free. No one suggests that the Dutch system is riddled with corruption. It does not have to be. It is just so lax that the criminals fare as well as they would when they pay large bribes in other countries.

In 1977 the law changed to provide a maximum sentence of twelve years. The maximum is seldom given by trial courts. And with time off for good behavior, a major trafficker can still be back in business in eight years. But in reality he is never out of business because the Dutch jails are more like hotels where most traffickers continue their narcotics businesses. "Dutch prisons have a reputation for being as nice as the Hilton Hotel," an Amsterdam policeman told me. "It's a bad problem for us. We are so human to the criminals that we have made it better for many of them than if they were still free. Their sentences become like long vacations."

Jails are not overcrowded. Only one prisoner per cell. The cells have televisions, radios, a fresh stock of magazines and books. Video machines can be brought from home to use the video collections at the prison libraries. There are no watchtowers with armed guards, no barbed-wire fences, no guard dogs. The prisons look like college campuses. Some offer first-run movies, health-conscious menus, weight-training gymnasiums, and exercise classes. Conjugal visits are encouraged, and prisoners have full access to the telephone. The number of visitors is not limited, and packages can be brought in and out of the prisons with few restrictions.

The lax Dutch laws and the comfortable prisons encouraged the Triads to select the Netherlands as their European base of operations. Amsterdam has Europe's largest Chinese community. Initially it was encouraged by the continent's most liberal immigration laws. Amsterdam's Chinatown has increased from 1,500 Chinese in 1970 to 10,000 in 1980 to almost 20,000 today. They are crammed into a small and mean community with no charm. The luxury Chinese and European restaurants have closed their doors. In their place along the main thoroughfares are ramshackle cafes and bars, many with blacked-out windows. Topless clubs and seedy discotheques spill over to the side streets along the canals, where prostitutes lounge behind lit windows. So much heroin has flooded into Amsterdam that young Chinese will sometimes offer passersby a free sniff of granular powder on a piece of paper.

In addition to the growing Chinese population and lax drug laws, Holland offers additional advantages for Hong Kong's heroin kingpins. It has the world's largest and busiest port in Rotterdam, with a volume of commercial traffic that makes even Hong Kong pale in comparison. Not only does Rotterdam provide unlimited smuggling opportunities, but the entire country is a trafficker's paradise. It has a long and uncontrollable rugged coastline in the north and west and an open southern border with Belgium. Holland is ideally located to take advantage of the significant drug traffic to nearby Germany, France, and England, as well as providing easy transport to the most lucrative market, the United States.

The Triads also gambled that Western law enforcement was unprepared for the heroin flood. The Hong Kong bosses were right. The Dutch police had no special branch to deal with heroin, there was virtually no international police cooperation on the drug, and there was not a single Chinese officer on the entire Dutch police force. The first heroin seized in the Netherlands was a mere two ounces found in the pocket of a Chinese man in an illegal Chinatown gambling den in 1971. By that time China White had already addicted tens of thousands of GIs in Southeast Asia, but the Dutch authorities had never seen it.

Richard Weijenburg, the chief of the Dutch criminal intelligence division on Chinese crime and heroin trafficking, told me, "We were very unprepared in those days. We didn't even know what heroin looked like. A couple of police went to a Chinese restaurant in the early 1970s and did an inspection. In the kitchen they saw a large wicker basket with plastic bags stamped with a tiger on the front. The bags were filled with a white powder and there must have been 100 large bags there. The police asked the chef what the bags contained and were told it was a common Chinese spice used in the restaurant's cooking. When one of the police asked if he could have some for his wife, an avid cooker, he was politely refused because it was very expensive and hard to get.

"When they returned to the station house they were looking through some information files on the Chinese and one of the officers saw a picture of the same exact plastic bag he had just seen at the restaurant. We now know it was Double U-O Globe, one of the most famous brands of heroin ever made. The police went right back to the restaurant but the basket was gone, and despite persistent questioning, everybody at the restaurant said that no such basket or spice existed and that the police must have confused their restaurant with another one in Chinatown. We were real naive then."

While the Dutch police were just beginning to learn what her-

oin looked like in the early 1970s, the Triads were starting to
expand the trade. They had moved into Holland before World
War II. The 14K was the first Triad in Amsterdam's Chinatown,
setting up two illegal gambling dens and a prostitution service
for the small prewar community. The front for the 14K operations became the Amsterdam headquarters of the Overseas Chinese Association. From this small turn-of-the-century building
in the center of Chinatown, the Chinese community was directed
with little interference from the Dutch authorities.

By the 1950s the 14K operations in the Netherlands had been
taken over by a thirty-year-old Triad member. Only five feet six
with slick black hair set against a high forehead, the fat gangster
was Chung Mon. The Chinese underworld nicknamed him "the
Unicorn," a symbol of strength and magic to the Chinese, a com-
pliment to his criminal talents. The Unicorn reorganized the
gambling and opium trade, and by 1960 had made the small
Amsterdam Chinatown one of the most profitable 14K operations outside of the Orient. Although in 1968 he tried to extend
the 14K influence to Düsseldorf, Germany, the home of another
small Chinese community, he did not match his Amsterdam success story. By 1969 the Hong Kong 14K directed him to concentrate his efforts solely on the Netherlands, and they gave him
substantial infusions of cash to expand the Triad's influence.

By 1969 the Hong Kong Triads had been shown the international profit potential in heroin by Limpy and White Powder Ma,
and the 14K decided to use the Unicorn to form their European
heroin base. The Unicorn had several legitimate businesses by
that time, including restaurants, a travel agency, and a casino.
He was also the president of the Overseas Chinese Association
and became a frequent traveler to Hong Kong and Taiwan. By
1970 he had developed a profitable friendship with the Ma brothers. Through their influence, whenever he visited Taiwan he received a hero's welcome and was feted by government officials
and even the Vice President. The reception in Hong Kong was
not so warm. There police intelligence had a file on him by 1970,
and during his visits to the British colony his meetings with crime
figures were monitored. On several occasions he was detained
by the Hong Kong police and questioned about the drug trade,
but his silence, coupled with his friendship with the Ma boys, ensured that no charges were brought against him.

By 1970 the Unicorn oversaw a distribution network that flew dozens of couriers into Amsterdam and sent loads of heroin hidden inside cargo shipments through Rotterdam. He spread smokable number 3 heroin among Chinese and Dutch addicts and concentrated on injectable number 4 heroin for the large GI population in Germany and the French and British addict populations. By 1973 he organized his first heroin shipments to New York by ship from Rotterdam. He also organized an armed gang of shotgun-wielding young Chinese hoods that became one of his trademarks. Traveling around the Dutch capital in a bulletproof Mercedes 600 limousine, he was the undisputed godfather of Amsterdam.

While his efforts greatly increased the 14K profits in the Netherlands, they also earned him the attention of the DEA and the envy of other ambitious oriental traffickers. By 1973 the DEA started a full-time investigation of the Unicorn and concluded in an internal report that the Netherlands had become Europe's number one distribution point for Asian heroin. In that same year the DEA broke its first successful heroin case in Holland. The two undercover agents were Hong Kong-born Stephen Tse, posing as a Chinese middleman, and Ben Yarbrough, the former station chief in northern Thailand, posing as an American mobster in search of China White.

"The Dutch were nice guys but they didn't know what the hell was going on," Yarbrough told me over a beer in Thailand. "We set up a time with these Chinese traffickers to actually get the delivery of dope. We had only enough flash money to get them to bring thirty pounds of heroin, but if we had had more money we could have gotten as much as we wanted. These guys were swimming in dope and were anxious to sell it to anyone who had the money. They had so much dope that they were willing to break their normal rule of never dealing with a white guy. And with all that heroin around the Dutch had seized less than a pound before we went there.

"Well, the night comes for the Chinese to come and give us the dope. The Dutch police are in the next-door apartment, and when we give them a signal, two knocks on the wall, that means the deal is done and they should come in and make the arrest and get the credit for it. Because you have to understand we weren't even supposed to be operational in Holland then—we were supposed to be just advisory.

"So the Chinese traffickers show up and they have the dope

and I give the big knock on the wall and we all just stand around smiling at each other. Then I knock again and we all just are waiting like horses' asses. The fucking Dutch have fallen asleep. Suddenly the Chinese realize it's a setup and the next thing I know Steve is wrestling with one of the traffickers on the floor and I have two of them on top of me. The three of us crashed through a window and rolled onto the roof of the next building. When we finally get them under control, the Dutch finally run in. Well, they were so nervous about us making the arrest that they had us run across the adjoining roofs and they shot their pistols into the air. The next day the headlines announced the Dutch police had made a major arrest of Chinese heroin traffickers but that the U.S. Mafia buyers escaped in a blazing gun battle over the rooftops of Amsterdam. Ha. They wouldn't have had thirty pounds by 1980 without us."

Although the public did not know the DEA was involved, the word spread quickly in the Chinese community that the Americans had joined the war on Triads in Holland. The Unicorn was recalled to Hong Kong, where he underwent an intensive "course" in ways to deal with the DEA, including the standard precaution of always taking money up front, since the American agents could almost never part with their funds without possession of the narcotics. The 14K central committee also taught the Unicorn the importance of community public relations.

Returning to Holland, he established a number of valuable welfare organizations for the local Chinese community. His secret efforts provided loan sharks and heroin and gambling dens for Chinatown, and his public persona provided hot meals for the hungry and free medical care for the poor. The Dutch government was so impressed that it decorated the Unicorn for his public service. The Hong Kong 14K had taught him well. Even as an increasing number of couriers were intercepted with documents listing his business addresses, he summarily dismissed the implications. He merely said that in his role as chairman of the Overseas Chinese Association he had to meet newcomers to the Chinese community. In that capacity it was not surprising that incoming Chinese, even a "few crooked ones," would have his address.

In 1972 two separate events helped to catapult the Unicorn into one of the most influential heroin roles in the West. First, in

Southeast Asia the hastened American withdrawal from Vietnam left the opium armies in the Golden Triangle and the Hong Kong Triads holding excess heroin stocks. While General Li and the KMT sold twenty-six tons of opium to the United States for $1 million, the Triads wanted to dump their extra capacity at higher profits. The opportunity presented itself when Turkey agreed, after intense U.S. pressure, to eliminate its massive 1972 opium crop. The United States already had a bulging addict population, and Nixon had declared heroin "public enemy number one." Europe had a rapidly growing number of addicts. Most of the Western addicts were traditionally supplied by the so-called French connection, Turkey to Marseilles and then to Europe's and America's junkies. But in 1972, with a sudden and complete cutoff of the narcotic from Turkey, the French connection was unable to meet the addict demand. The Mediterranean's loss was Southeast Asia's gain.

The Hong Kong Triads sent record numbers of couriers and heroin shipments to the Unicorn. The results were impressive. The purity of street-level heroin in Europe and the United States rose sharply and the prices plummeted, a sure sign of oversupply. Addicts liked the new, purer, Southeast Asian heroin, and by 1973 the Unicorn was distributing large loads of street-level heroin to organized crime figures in the United States, England, France, Germany, Italy, and Spain. The Triads had found hundreds of thousands of new, satisfied customers. The Unicorn had become the White Powder Ma of Europe.

While he developed a crime empire he also followed the established Triad maxim of developing key contacts within the local police. The Unicorn became a personal "informer" to Amsterdam's Police Commissioner Gerard Toorenaar. He fed Toorenaar information on competitors' operations and also swore to keep peace in the Chinese community. In return, the Dutch police did not disturb him.

He was constantly in the commissioner's office. In the Chinese community and among the Hong Kong 14K, this easy access to the highest-ranking policeman in the Dutch capital gave the Unicorn "great face," as the Chinese describe great prestige or honor. When the Unicorn's Mercedes was confiscated in a Belgian heroin investigation, Toorenaar personally intervened to recover the car. This was the same car that DEA internal reports concluded was regularly picking up couriers at Schiphol, Amsterdam's international airport. In addition to helping retrieve the limousine, Toorenaar gave the Unicorn a letter that is supposed to have cleared him of any involvement in the heroin trade. Senior Dutch policemen knew the letter existed, and to their embarrassment it was flashed around Chinatown. In 1974, when the Hong Kong police detained the Unicorn once again on suspicion of narcotics trafficking, he showed them Police Commissioner Toorenaar's letter and was set free.

Scenting the heady perfume of easy money, other Hong Kong Triads, particularly the Wo syndicate, poured into Amsterdam. Even an ambitious Triad from Singapore, the Ah Kong, set up operations in the Dutch capital. Triad rivals established headquarters in Rotterdam, in Antwerp in Belgium, and in Koblenz in West Germany. As competition for the lucrative trade heightened in the early 1970s, the quiet, law-abiding Chinese community erupted in a savage series of street fights called "the shotgun wars," as rival gangs lined up on opposite sides of the narrow Chinatown streets and opened fire on each other in a roar of shotgun blasts. But the Unicorn had no intention of allowing competing Triads to get a foothold in the heroin trade he had almost single-handedly developed.

The Dutch police, who were totally perplexed by the sudden outbreak of violence centered in Amsterdam's Chinatown, went to the Unicorn for help in quelling the disturbances. He gave them a list of names, the supposed masterminds behind the violence. The list was false. It was a way of getting rid of most of his competitors. Many of those confronted by the police admitted their "guilt" even though they were innocent. They knew they had been outfoxed by the Unicorn. Since the maximum sentence for murder at the time was six years in a comfortable Dutch prison, many of them figured that was preferable to death at the hands of the 14K shotgun gangs.

The Unicorn seemed at the height of his power. He was the leader of an exploding heroin syndicate, had the strength of one of the most powerful Triads behind him, and had selected as his base of operations a country with an uninformed police force and lax and ineffective laws. The Dutch godfather took no chances. He traveled everywhere in his bulletproof limousine and had a massive bodyguard always near him. He carried a fully loaded Baretta automatic 9-mm pistol under his baggy blazers.

By early 1975 the Unicorn learned that the Dutch police were starting to change their opinion about him. A growing dossier was sprinkled with accusations by the Hong Kong police of narcotics involvement. Acting on a tip from the British colony, the Dutch customs even seized a food cargo in Rotterdam destined for the Unicorn. Although they did not find any heroin, it served as a warning that the police intended to get tough.

On March 3, 1975, the Unicorn left an old Dutch-style building on a canal waterfront. He had finished a late night meeting and had let his bodyguards go home early. He was walking briskly toward his limousine when suddenly three young Chinese gunmen ran out of the dock's shadows and opened fire on him just steps from the safety of his bulletproof car. He reached for his Baretta, but before he could withdraw it the assassins' bullets had found their target. Ten bullets hit him in rapid succession. They tore into his face, chest, back, and legs. He was dead by the time he hit the ground, his fat body sprawled next to the side of his Mercedes. At the age of fifty-five the Unicorn's rise to the top had come to a sudden halt.

But even though the Unicorn was out of the picture, the organization he had established had revolutionized the importation and distribution of Southeast Asian heroin into Europe and across the Atlantic to the East Coast of the United States. The Triads still consider him the founding father of the Chinese connection outside of the Orient.

The Unicorn's killers were never found. Interpol believes they were three professional hit men hired by his rivals. The killers were from Hong Kong and flown in just for the contract on the godfather. But the Hong Kong 14K refused to allow their profitable heroin business to be carved up by other Triads just because their chief kingpin had been killed. Within a month of the Unicorn's murder, his replacement flew in from Hong Kong. The 14K had selected a rising star in the Hong Kong underworld, Chan Yuen-muk, to become the next godfather of Amsterdam.

But Chan had none of the Unicorn's finesse. The Chinese community dubbed him "Mao Tse-tung" because of his physical resemblance as well as for his authoritarian ways. While the Unicorn had claimed adamantly that he was a mere businessman and arguably owned some legitimate businesses, Chan boasted that he was a "486," almost a dragon head in the 14K. He made no pretense about being a businessman—he was a gangster and proud of it. He demanded increased protection money from many businesses and tried to levy substantial surcharges on the illegal gambling dens. He also tried to get rival gangs to pay the 14K a percentage of all of the heroin deals passing through Holland. They balked. Chan was so brutal in trying to enforce compliance with his harsh demands that the general Chinese population turned against him within months of his arrival from Hong Kong.

Rival Triads did not overlook the growing popular dissatisfaction with the 14K. As the one-year anniversary of the Unicorn's murder approached, the Ah Kong Triad decided to move against Chan. The Ah Kong is a Chinese Triad based in Singapore's large Chinese community. It was one of the first Triads to move into Amsterdam shortly after the Unicorn started expanding the trade. Although the Ah Kong initially was at odds with the 14K, the Unicorn had bought compliance by allowing them to do their own heroin deals, as long as it did not affect 14K business and the 14K received 5 percent of the moneys. Chan tried to change that. He banned Ah Kong heroin sales unless 14K middlemen were involved for a much larger percentage of the overall deal. Ah Kong decided that Chan must go.

An Ah Kong hit man was flown in from Singapore. On March 3, 1976, the anniversary of the Unicorn's death, Chan spent most of the day gambling at the Yowlee casino in Amsterdam. When he finally came into the street, with all his bodyguards in attendance, a young Chinese man ran up to him, put a pistol to his head, and blew his brains onto the street. The second 14K godfather was dead in as many years.

This time the 14K could not spare another leading crime figure to run the European end of the business. It had its hands full in Hong Kong. The Ma syndicate was dominating an ever-increasing share of the colony's underworld, and 14K profits had been cut. But more important, the top 14K police link, Lui Lok, the 600-million-dollar man, had fled a corruption investigation and was in Canada. Without Lok and the Five Dragons, the 14K was having a difficult time retaining its share of the crime business.

Consumed with its own Hong Kong problems, the 14K grudgingly accepted a balance-of-power arrangement with the increasingly powerful Ah Kong. "The Singapore Triad kept control of Amsterdam and the 14K got The Hague and Rotterdam," a DEA analyst told me in The Hague. "The 14K also got London and

Paris while the Ah Kong got Germany." Just as the colonial powers had carved up Asia in the nineteenth century, Chinese Triad
bosses from the former colonies were now carving Europe into
modern-day colonial crime spheres.

"The arrangement lasted for almost five years," Richard Weijenburg, chief of the Dutch police intelligence unit on Triads and
Southeast Asian heroin, told me. "I wish today it would be so
easy. Just the 14K and the Ah Kong and we only had to look at
one or two Triads. Since 1980 the business has become so big
and the money to be made is so large that it is split between many
different Triads. The days of Chung Mon [the Unicorn] are over.
Amsterdam won't know a single godfather again. Today the
Chinese controlling the heroin trade in Holland belong to the
same groups you hear about in Hong Kong. It sounds like a part
of Hong Kong has just moved here. We have the Wo Triads, the
14K, the Big Circle, the Chiu Chau groups, the Sun Yee On, you
can go down the list. And because it's so much more spread
around, it makes our job more difficult also."

I was sitting with Weijenburg at Interpol headquarters in The
Hague, where a giant wall tapestry of a fingerprint greets you at
the armed entrance. We were in an ultramodern, long gray caf-
eteria on the building's third floor. One side of the room was
lined with new vending machines promising everything from
freshly brewed cappuccino to microwaved omelets. The opposite wall consisted of large plate-glass windows covered in thin
gray metal blinds. Through the slats I could see the motorway
that connected The Hague and Amsterdam. It was an overcast
miserable winter day in Holland. Looking at a soda machine was
preferable to watching the sheets of rain pound the windows.

Around the table joining Weijenburg and me were five of
Interpol's "Chinese specialists" from other countries, all in The
Hague for a meeting on Triads. There were police from England,
France, West Germany, Italy, and Spain. The eighth person at
the table was Arie Bax, an Amsterdam policeman who special-
izes in Chinese crime and heroin smuggling.

"They've brought us a real problem, the Chinese have," the
Spanish delegate said between sips of his espresso. "I think I
speak for all of the European countries when I say that until 1970
heroin was a very small drug problem on the Continent. And as
far as the Chinese were concerned, if they brought any opium

or heroin into the country, it was always for addicts inside the Chinatowns. They never sold outside to nationals of the country they lived in. Now that has all changed. The bulk of their business is selling to white customers. And the number of heroin addicts in all the countries has gone up a lot. It is running about two percent of the population in Spain, and I believe more here in Holland, right?"

"About three percent in Amsterdam could be right," said Bax. "There are 8,000 registered with the government and who knows how many unregistered."

"But the Chinese are not just bringing in heroin to sell to people who live in the European countries," the German representative broke in. "At least in our country a lot of their initial interest was in the large number of American soldiers stationed there as part of NATO. They were used to selling to the American soldiers during the Vietnam War, and they thought that Germany could provide the same type of customers. I think they have had some success in selling to U.S. soldiers, but not nearly as much as they hoped for. In a place like Vietnam, in the middle of a war and all, it is much easier to get a front-line soldier to take a powerful drug like heroin. You actually want to try and cut out as much of the war as you can. So heroin takes you away from your problems. So it was easier to addict soldiers in Vietnam.

"But in Germany, being a U.S. soldier is not too much stress. It's a nice place and everyone likes you and no one is shooting at you. So there is not the same pressure to take hard drugs and I would bet the percentage of heroin users is much lower than in Vietnam. So the Chinese were coming at first for the GIs, but when the Americans did not buy as much heroin as expected, then the Chinese sold it to the local residents. That's when our addict numbers started to go up."

"And the amounts seized also started to increase," the English delegate added. He never even looked up while he intently cleaned his pipe. "It seemed that during the past ten years all of us were involved in record seizures of narcotics almost every six months. It was a combination of becoming more aware of the problem and focusing on it, and also since more heroin was coming into Europe it would be logical that more would be turned up through good law-enforcement efforts. Today seizures are near record levels. But I do not believe any of my colleagues would venture to say that the amount of heroin being imported has been reduced. The volumes are probably larger today than ever before—"

The Italian policeman interrupted. "Not only is more heroin coming into Europe, but we never know whether the heroin is coming in for the addicts in our own countries or we are only being used as a shipment stopover for shipping the heroin somewhere else."

Evidently K. L. Mak and the Hong Kong Customs Service were not the only ones confronted with the problem of heroin transit shipments.

The Englishman finally looked up. "Well, this is exactly what is happening with us in London. We see that some of the Chinese smugglers from here in Holland make regular trips to London. And Hong Kong tells us that they have intercepted shipments of narcotics bound for London. And although we have seized some Southeast Asian [heroin] at Heathrow, we are not finding it on our streets. That means that today London is being used only as a transit center by the Chinese. The only reason that would make any sense is that there must be more profit to make in other countries and that the Chinese cannot keep up with the demand for their product. So they have to allocate it to the countries where the most money can be made."

"It's certainly true that a lot of the heroin passing through is only for transit," the French policeman added. "We started to see Southeast Asian heroin for the first time among Parisian addicts around 1979 or 1980. Then a special task force was formed to combat the Chinese problem and within a couple of years the Chinese heroin had disappeared. We thought we had beat the Chinese and the task force was disbanded. Today the Chinese heroin is back and it is a real problem. We are also finding some small Chinese laboratories for refining some of the shipments. I think all they did when we formed the task force was to take a low profile. They never disappeared. We just thought they did. They just passed heroin through France instead of selling it to our addicts. Once the pressure was off, they returned to a full-time narcotics business in France. They are really quite clever."

Weijenburg turned around in his seat toward me. "The Chinese started here but now they are everywhere. You can no longer say the Dutch Chinese or the French Chinese or the English Chinese. They are international. We find that the Chinese here who are involved in heroin, they move back and forth and visit each other all the time. Because of the European Economic Community, passport checks and cargo inspections are kept to a minimum. This helps the Chinese traffickers. They think of Europe as one large market, and they are not concerned where one boundary starts and another ends. They just worry about the price they are getting for their goods. They are very international, just like the heroin business."

The Interpol representatives told remarkably similar stories. Amsterdam is no longer the first stopover for drug couriers from Asia. Just as shipments from Thailand or Hong Kong are subject to more detailed customs inspections, Asians traveling into Amsterdam are subject to closer scrutiny. Especially if they fit the courier's "profile," or if their passports show they are frequent travelers between Europe and Asia. Today the Triads often employ American and European couriers, usually teenagers stranded flat broke on long Asian vacations. The chance of getting a free ticket home plus $1,000 in cash is too tempting for some reckless travelers to pass up. The Triads also have couriers reroute their trip so that they spend at least a night in India or Egypt or Morocco. By the time they arrive in Europe they do not show they originated at the Golden Triangle or Hong Kong. Moreover, many couriers now first arrive in Europe through Portugal, Italy, England, or Switzerland and then travel to Amsterdam by car or rail.

But while the courier traffic has become more sophisticated, as in Hong Kong, most of the heroin coming into Europe arrives buried inside tons of commercial shipments. Probably more than half of the China White entering Europe comes straight into Rotterdam. But aside from a 220-kilo seizure in mid-1986, the police have been notoriously ineffective there.

"The Dutch customs and police have the government all over their backs when it comes to Rotterdam," a DEA agent in The Hague told me. "The Dutch government tells the customs and narcotics police that Rotterdam is the number one port in the world because companies enjoy doing business there. It has a computerized cargo system and everyone is friendly and everything gets done quickly. So if the cops have a tip on a load of heroin arriving in a ship, they can go ahead and search it. And they can also do their random searches just like any customs service. But if the government starts to hear complaints from businessmen about a lot of slow-ups or ships being searched, and the police do not have kilos of heroin to show for it, somebody's ass is going to be in the ringer." As long as the Dutch government is more concerned about the business climate than in stopping the flow of heroin, Rotterdam will continue to receive most of the Chinese heroin. It serves a role similar to that played by Hong Kong in Southeast Asia.

In addition to the uninterrupted flow of heroin, one of the most disturbing developments in the Netherlands is the surprising number of heroin labs police have recently discovered. The labs, mostly located in Amsterdam's suburbs, vary in size and sophistication but are always manned by Chinese chemists. "They have expanded their operations since Chung Mon's days. Now they have set Holland up as a processing and refining center for heroin," Arie Bax said as he rolled some black tobacco into a filterless cigarette. It smelled like a stale cigar. "They are importing the stuff as heroin base and then, depending on the market conditions in Europe or the U.S., they are refining how much they need of each variety. Here in Europe most of the addicts smoke their heroin, so number 3 is the heroin of choice. But we also have needle addicts here, so they need some number 4. But since the United States is almost totally a needle population, most of the number 4 goes there.

"I think the trend of the future is that the Chinese will market more and more number 3. They read the papers and they know about AIDS. It's no good to them to have their clients dying from dirty needles. So eventually in the U.S. I think the Chinese will introduce number 3 and you will get a smoking problem there. Remember, when American soldiers were addicted in Vietnam, many were hooked on number 3. They all smoked it. It's just when they got back to the States they couldn't find any number 3, so they either kicked the habit or moved to number 4 and a needle.

"But the strange part of the labs in Holland is that we are not finding any of the variety of heroin we discover in the labs on our streets. It's a strange refinement of heroin they are making here. It's almost a mixture between number 3 and 4. While it can be smoked, it can also be heated up and injected. Old number 3 could never be dissolved, you would just destroy it. But this new stuff, we only find it in the labs and not among the addicts. That tells us that heroin base is being brought into the Netherlands, refined here into this new type of heroin, and then exported elsewhere. We think it's going to most of Europe and to the United States, where bigger money is to be made."

All of the Interpol representatives spoke about Triad organized crime within their Chinese populations. Each admitted that the Triads ran illegal gambling dens and also collected protection money and engaged in loan-sharking. Prostitution was present but no one thought it was a major business. So far none of them had seen signs of white-collar crime or extensions of the organized crime enterprises into the local populations. Only the heroin business had expanded to strike at Europeans and Americans. "And that was the result of the Unicorn's efforts," the Spanish representative added. "He was the one who showed the Chinese that they needed to sell heroin to non-Chinese if they wanted to make billions, not just millions."

For most of the European countries represented at that table in The Hague, their governments had failed to recognize the amount of heroin the Chinese were pushing into and through Europe. Although Sweden, England, West Germany, Holland, and France had narcotics officers in Bangkok, it was strictly an advisory and intelligence-gathering role. Budgets to fight Triads were almost nonexistent. The Dutch, who acknowledge that Triads form their only organized crime problem, have only three police officers full-time on the Chinese connection. None of the countries have Chinese police officers working on the Triad and heroin problem. The addict populations have swelled during the past ten years, and the amount of heroin coming into Europe may have doubled or tripled, but not a single major Chinese trafficker has been arrested. Not one Triad boss has been deported back to Hong Kong. The flow of Chinese heroin from Europe into the United States is increasing, and the eastern seaboard is particularly hard hit by the Chinese–European connection.

While London, Paris, Rome, and Frankfurt have grown as Chinese crime centers, Amsterdam remains the Triad's European headquarters. The permissive Dutch atmosphere and its lax judicial system have made the Netherlands the Triad's first choice. Unless the Dutch suddenly undergo a mighty metamorphosis, the Triads will continue to use it to import heroin, to refine it, distribute and export it.

The major Hong Kong Triads have established secondary offices throughout Europe. More of the best Chinese criminal talent will arrive before Hong Kong reverts to mainland China. If Europe expects to cope with the growing Chinese connection and the future influx of Triads in the same way they are currently treating the problem, then European law enforcement is bound to fall further and further behind. Unless the European governments and law-enforcement agencies make Triads a top priority, there will certainly be more Unicorns in Europe's future. And unfortunately, as the trail of China White shows, Europe's problems soon become America's problems.

13

The Invasion

The Golden Dragon is a San Francisco Chinatown landmark. An ornate, sprawling, two-level restaurant, its rococo details are set against walls of gold-leaf paper. Dragons in bronze and gilt curve over the doorways and around the red-lacquered plaster columns. Situated in the middle of America's largest Chinese community, with low prices and good food, it is a popular late-night gathering spot for both Chinese and whites. It is also a favorite of tourists hoping to catch a glimpse of Chinatown.

In the autumn of 1977 the Golden Dragon earned a gruesome place in the developing history of Chinese Triads in the United States. On that evening members of two Chinese gangs had gone there for beers and snacks. Some of the Wah Ching boys, California's largest Chinese youth gang, were at a large red banquet booth in the mezzanine. The Hip Sing boys, one of San Francisco's most violent gangs, were at a long, low table in the rear of the main floor. At 2:40 in the early morning hours of September 4, two nondescript, black, American mid-sized cars pulled up to the Golden Dragon. They were illuminated by dozens of multi-colored neon signs jutting across the confined Chinatown streets. Except for the English street signs, the scene could have been Central Hong Kong.

One of the cars stopped in front of the restaurant while the other stopped at the beginning of the narrow Chinatown street, blocking the road. They kept their engines running. The streets were still crowded with tourists and local residents. Inside the two idling cars were members of the Joe Boys, another Chinatown street gang, at "war" with the Wah Ching over control of the lucrative fireworks business. They had come to kill Michael "Hot Dog" Louie, a leader of the Wah Ching.

Inside the front car were three boys. Two were seventeen years old and one had just turned eighteen. Each weighed only slightly more than one hundred pounds. They reached for satchels resting at their feet and pulled from the darkness two shotguns, one sawed-off, a .38-caliber chrome-plated revolver, and a black .45-caliber assault rifle. The semiautomatic Double "O" Buck 12-gauge shotgun was powerful enough at point-blank range to lift a 500-pound refrigerator into the air. They checked that the guns' magazines were full, stuffed extra bullets and shells into their jeans, and then almost in unison they clicked bullets into the chambers of each of the weapons. The three young hoods then pulled stocking masks over their faces and threw the car doors open. They sprinted across the pavement in a blur. The drivers of the cars waited, slung low in their seats, the engines barely audible.

The three gunmen ran to the Golden Dragon's street-level entrance. It was locked, but at an inside table one of the Wah Ching gang members looked up at the rattling door and saw the tip of a gun and a masked face. In Cantonese he yelled, "Men with guns," and the Wah Ching boys hit the floor and started crawling toward the back of the restaurant. Meanwhile, the tourists and local residents had not seen any sign of danger. They looked bewildered at the apparent antics of the Wah Ching boys, but no one knew they were trying to save their lives.

The three Joe Boy gunmen ran twenty feet down the street and burst through the Golden Dragon's front entrance. The two with shotguns started walking toward the mezzanine, where their information had placed the Wah Ching gang. The clatter of dishes and the din of the conversation stopped as if a television set had been suddenly switched off. The sight of three small boys carrying jackhammer-sized weapons had immobilized the restaurant in terror and disbelief.

At a rear table, next to a red column with an enormous gold dragon, sat four Japanese students. They were celebrating the graduation of one of them from law school. Unfortunately, the graduate resembled Hot Dog Louie, the Wah Ching leader. The smallest of the gunmen, "Crazy" Melvin Yu, turned his heavy assault rifle toward them and started emptying his banana clip of .45 slugs. The first bullets struck just in front of the four horrified students, tearing into the white plastic tablecloth, hitting the plates of food and sending them flying like Frisbees smashing against the wall. The young gunman seemed to have difficulty controlling the heavy, kicking rifle. He yanked the barrel downward to control it, but more than forty bullets crashed into the floor, shattered the chandeliers, and cut up the ceiling. The next burst hit the student who resembled the wanted gang leader. A .45 bullet tore off the top of his head and his body spun out of the chair. He slumped against the bullet-ridden wall.

The killer boy ran over and fired extra rounds into the corpse. By now the restaurant had erupted in pandemonium. People screamed and cowered under tables as chips of plaster flew about. The bullets were invisible, but the smoke and the flames from the barrel and the crashing noise filled the Golden Dragon. The young killer turned on the three girls left at the table where he stood. He pumped the first bullets into the girl on his right, severing the artery in her leg, leaving her to bleed to death. Then he spun the heavy weapon around and aimed at one of the girls, who was curled in fear on the floor. He spat eleven bullets into her. He grabbed the fourth screaming girl, lifted her off the floor, and threw her into a chair. Then he fired a bullet that shattered her face. Crazy Melvin then started firing the assault rifle in a sweeping motion. The first shots demolished an entire wall of mirrors, sending splinters of glass flying around the restaurant. A Filipino airline stewardess went down with a bullet in the thigh. A UCLA student had his elbow shot off. Another slug split a doctor's foot in two.

At the moment that Crazy Melvin started shooting at the table of Japanese students, the two shotgun-wielding killers were climbing the stairs to the mezzanine. An elderly waiter, the father of six children, was in their way. He did not even hear them coming. One of the killers pulled out a .38-caliber revolver and placed the barrel against the waiter's neck before pulling the trigger. The bullet severed his spine and flung him onto the second-floor landing, a jet of blood shooting back down the stairs. The two gunmen then ran to the top of the mezzanine landing and emptied their shotguns in a deafening thunder. The guns kicked so much that the two tiny shooters almost seemed ready to fall back down the stairs. But they held their ground and their uncontrolled shooting hit everything from the floor to ceiling to tables to people. Two high school students at a nearby table caught the bulk of the shotgun blasts. Their torsos were splattered against the wall where they had been sitting. Their faces looked like raw, red masks.

The shooting lasted only a minute. The three boys had emptied their weapons and exhausted their ammunition. They were in the getaway cars and gone before the first police sirens could even be heard. Inside the Golden Dragon it looked like a battle scene. Widening pools of blood, the glistening evidence of death, spread around splintered tables and shattered glass. Some bodies lay contorted over chairs hastily piled up as ineffective barricades. The screams of the terrified and the moans of the injured filled the rooms. Five people were dead and eleven hurt. All were innocent bystanders. Not one Wah Ching gang member was hurt. Hot Dog Louie had locked himself into a back-room closet. The other Wah Ching members had taken refuge behind a rear table, the shotgun pellets striking only around them.

San Francisco was outraged. The mayor and police chief held a news conference. A new police task force was formed to deal with Chinese gang violence. Police Sergeant John McKenna, later the chief of the gang task force, had been one of the first on the scene the night of the Golden Dragon shooting. "I had been in homicide for fourteen years, but I had never seen anything like that. It was a massacre. I knew this was warfare. We badly wanted the people who were responsible for this." It took nearly two years before the murderers were caught. The driver of the backup car was never found. Reports have placed him at different times in places as diverse as Utah, Mexico, and Hong Kong.

It was the first time the modern American public had seen such a violent explosion in a Chinatown. And the mayor's office was quick to react because this time the victims were not just quiet Chinese but tourists and non-Chinese who were dead. A senior San Francisco police officer told me, "I hate to say it, but although we had some fifty gang murders before the Golden Dragon, they were all Chinese-to-Chinese. The moment the violence spread beyond the Chinese, the politicians were jumping on camera and into the fight." The public assumed that something was wrong in normally peaceful Chinatown, and they blamed the hooligan youth gangs. What few realized at the time was that the youth gangs were the lowest-level foot soldiers for powerful criminal syndicates. "As a matter of fact, no one had heard of Triads in San Francisco back then," Sergeant McKenna told me.

The problem from the start was that police departments and local governments had no idea of the international scope of the violence that erupted for a brief moment in San Francisco. What was commonplace in Hong Kong or Bangkok was new and unexplainable in the United States. There was no knowledge of the backgrounds of the Triads or their extensive control of the Chinese underworld. There was not even a fundamental understanding of the sordid history of the American Chinese community. It is a history marked by exploitation and discrimination that helped lay the groundwork for the invasion of the Triads. Officially, the Chinese are the only minority ever declared undesirable by the U.S. government, and for many years they suffered more as an ethnic group than any other non-white segment of the population.

Tens of thousands of Chinese had fled the slaughter of the Taiping Rebellion against the Manchu dynasty, which began in 1851. The United States promptly established immigration laws prohibiting incoming Chinese laborers from bringing any women with them. Wives and daughters had to be left in China. Sons could come in only if they were strong enough to work on the railroads or in the gold mines. The first immigrants arrived with the promise of high pay, and they thought of making fortunes in and around San Francisco, a name that in Chinese means "Golden Mountain." Instead they found backbreaking work, restricted and squalid living conditions, and constant abuse directed at their different dress and customs. Yet without the hardworking Chinese laborers, there is little doubt that the great railroads that linked the East and West Coasts would have been delayed at least another generation.

However, when the Chinese work force finished working on a network of minor railways in the West, Congress decided they had served their usefulness and legislated against them. In May 1882, Congress passed the Chinese Exclusion Act. It banned all further immigration of Chinese laborers and decreed that no Chinese residents already in the United States were eligible for citizenship. Within seven years an attempt to repeal the racist act was rejected by the United States Supreme Court. The highest court upheld the law, stating that Congress had an inherent power to exclude "foreigners of a different race who will not assimilate with us."

While laborers were banned outright, an exception was created for Chinese merchants. They were granted entry to the United States and also allowed to bring their wives. But in 1924 Congress decided to restrict the Chinese once again. This time the law banned any Chinese woman from gaining permanent residence, no matter what the professional status of her husband. Even as late as World War II, when the United States responded to the Japanese attack on Pearl Harbor by allying itself with Chiang Kai-shek's Nationalist Chinese armies, Chinese immigrants were still legally regarded as unworthy for U.S. citizenship. It was not until 1943, under growing pressure from Chiang Kai-shek and Triad financier Charlie Soong, that President Roosevelt signed a law repealing the Chinese Exclusion Act, and for the first time Chinese were regarded as fit for naturalization.

Yet, the new law allowed only 105 Chinese to immigrate annually to the United States. Moreover, individual states had wide latitude in determining how they were to be treated. California, with the largest Chinese population, legally prohibited even native-born Chinese from marrying white women. Large surcharges were placed on traditional Chinese businesses such as laundries, and special taxes were levied on Chinese money transactions. For many years Chinese, including even native-born American citizens, could not legally testify in court, their testimony considered unreliable. A law banned any corporation from employing them.

It was in this background of official undesirability that the Chinatowns formed and flourished. With the first wave of immigrants in the mid-1800s, Triad members also arrived. Since the Chinese were objects of well-conducted campaigns of hatred and vilification, the Triads established American branches called "Tongs." *Tong* means "town hall," and based on the principles of the Triads, they were established as safe havens for the battered Chinese. These benevolent societies took care of everything from food to rent to the enforcement of the local laws. The

Chinese who immigrated to America brought with them their traditional fear and mistrust of outsiders and authorities, and they considered whites to be demons. The crude treatment they received at the hands of drunken bands of white hoods did little to dismiss the historical fear. Chinese shunned any contact with local police and civil authorities, and as a result the Tongs became unofficial local governments. They exerted strong influence on the social life of the Chinatowns. And, most important, they controlled the vice and opium trades, which became the hallmarks of America's Chinatowns.

Since the original Chinese laborers were not allowed to bring women into the states, prostitution and gambling supplied the entertainment. The other vices were only a step behind. Opium use became widespread. Many things that the Chinese considered acceptable were illegal in the United States. To the Chinese gambling was a legitimate social game. Opium use was ingrained from persistent British efforts and was socially sanctioned. Loan-sharking, a natural outgrowth of the gambling halls, was not considered wrong. The Chinese considered that if they were in debt, and someone was willing to lend them money at a high interest rate, it was the decision of the two parties and no law should restrict it. The new immigrants also expected they would have to pay someone to do business in the new country, so when the Tongs collected protection money disguised as "dues," the money was willingly paid. The Tongs handled the bribes to white officials so that a blind eye was turned to the Chinatown crimes. This allowed the Tongs to quickly expand their power. It also made the Chinatowns sordid neighborhoods that served as examples for proponents of anti-Chinese sentiment.

By the turn of the century the Chinatowns had accumulated such a depraved reputation that middle-class whites with morbid curiosities had tours, complete with armed guards, to catch a firsthand glimpse of the filth and violence they hoped to find. These Chinatowns had been used for thirty years by numerous whites who had become regular customers of gambling halls, whorehouses, and opium dens. Hundreds of gambling dens were crammed into rat-infested basements and tenement apartments throughout the Chinatowns. While many refused to admit whites, enough did so that rowdy and drunken groups of whites were commonplace in fan-tan parlors from San Francisco's Grant Avenue to New York's Bowery.

Although the gambling halls attracted a fair number of white customers, the whorehouses attracted enormous numbers. The Tongs operated numerous bordellos employing Chinese and other Asian women. The "better class" of Chinese prostitutes catered only to Chinese men, while the seedier whores serviced the white clientele. The prostitution trade flourished. A Chinese girl could be bought for a quarter at the turn of the century, whereas white prostitutes in other sections of New York or San Francisco cost more than one dollar. Because of the low prices, many white customers felt free to engage the Chinese slave girls in aberrant sexual behavior they would have blushed to even mention to the most jaded white prostitute.

In addition to the gambling halls and whorehouses, whites came to Chinatown to smoke opium. By 1900 it was estimated that 40 percent of San Francisco's Chinese community were regular opium users. Anti-Chinese propagandists cast all Chinese as "opium fiends" or "hopheads." But by that time dozens of Chinatown opium dens were catering to white "hopheads." Eventually white girls fell prey to opium addiction and often turned to prostitution to finance their expensive habits. By the early 1900s the Tongs were operating white whorehouses filled with opium-stupefied girls.

The white patronage allowed Chinese vice to expand much faster than it would have with just Chinese customers. The anonymity provided by the closed Chinatowns increasingly attracted the dregs of white society. But the Chinese saw only the worst examples of white society, the drunken and drugged flotsam who came to relieve their taste for cheap women, gambling, and narcotics. Into the 1930s many Chinese who stayed strictly within the borders of the Chinatowns thought all whites were gamblers, thugs, and shady characters.

The vice businesses became so profitable that in New York, Irish mobsters and Sicilian hoods unsuccessfully tried to move into the Chinese rackets in the early 1900s. But the fact that the Chinatowns had degenerated into giant vice centers fanned the flames of the anti-Chinese movement that viewed the "pagan Chinese" as a menace to Christianity and Western civilization. A turn-of-the-century popular guide to New York City observed that "Mott, Pell and Doyer streets and vicinity are now given over to the Chinese....The district is a veritable 'Chinatown' with all the filth, immorality, and picturesque foreignness which that name implies." Lurid accounts of disease, opium, white slavery, and gambling were used in anti-Chinese publications. Pictures of afflicted beggars on street corners and piles of decaying garbage swarming with flies and overrun by rats and cockroaches were widely distributed. White rowdies who operated escorted tours of the Chinatowns sometimes hired Chinese to put on shows for the tourists. A favorite was a sudden street knife fight between two opium-crazed Chinese over a slave girl. The horrified tourists never knew the scene was staged for their benefit.

This view of the Chinese as a depraved society led to increased racist abuse. Disorderly whites caused numerous problems. Groups of hoodlums often went into the Chinatowns for a night of beating the "slanty eyes." White toughs treated the Chinese contemptuously. When two white pleasure seekers were accidentally wounded in a Tong war in Los Angeles in 1871, gangs of whites invaded Chinatown, hanged fifteen Chinese from lampposts, shot four others, and looted dozens of homes and businesses. The Tongs decided that only by paying white security to provide protection could the Chinese alleviate the problems caused by white thugs. Special white bodyguards started appearing in Chinatowns by the turn of the century. Also, handsome payoffs to municipal police ensured that the lawmen arrested dangerous white visitors while protecting the lucrative flow to the illegal resorts.

The combination of the booming vice rackets and lax and corrupt police enforcement led to a volatile climate in the Chinatowns. For instance, in San Francisco's streets after dark so many men thronged the narrow alleys that prostitutes had to travel in the company of armed guards. By the turn of the century the Tongs began employing young street toughs, called the *"boo how doy"* (literally "hatchet boys"), as lookouts and extra security for their vice rackets. These street toughs were the first Chinese youth gangs in America. They served under the strict direction of the neighborhood Tongs.

The Chinese underworld had a vested interest in perpetuating and expanding the vice rackets. Also, the political establishments in Los Angeles, San Francisco, Chicago, Sacramento, and New York had many white leaders who enjoyed a financial interest in ensuring a flourishing Chinatown underworld. As long as the Chinese Tongs kept crime out of the headlines, many white politicians were content to allow the Chinatowns to do as they pleased. Since the Chinese almost never reported crimes, they usually had the lowest official crime rate. As long as it continued to be statistically impressive, the white establishment was willing to allow the Tongs to control the community. These decisions eventually allowed Triads to gain an unprecedented control over every aspect of Chinatown life.

As the Tongs grew more powerful they vied for larger segments of the profitable vice trade. The result was a series of brutal Tong wars. Since the major Tongs had branch offices in each American city, when competing Tongs in one city went to war, the same war was fought in every major Chinatown. They were dubbed the "hatchet wars" after their favorite killing instrument and were marked by assassination, vendetta, and mayhem. The last great Tong war raged during the mid-1920s, and open bloodshed on the streets left seventy dead gangland Chinese.

The Tong violence kept many whites out of the Chinatowns. Rudyard Kipling was almost killed in a gunfight in a San Francisco Chinatown gambling hall. Later he advised others not to go into Chinatown after dark. The San Francisco police stated that every day someone was killed in gang violence. Los Angeles established a separate commission to investigate street violence in their Chinatown. Even as late as 1940 guidebooks to New York and San Francisco had to assure the wary tourist that the Chinatown streets were safe to walk during daylight hours.

Several factors changed the face of the American Chinatowns. By the 1930s an influx of Chinese women helped balance the sex ratios. As normal husband-wife families started, the local Chinese mania for vice subsided. Also, World War II was responsible for a tremendous shift in American attitudes toward the Chinese. After the Japanese attack on Pearl Harbor, the ferocious American anti-Asian sentiment was directed against Japanese-Americans. A contrasting and favorable image of the Chinese developed. Chiang Kai-shek and his Nationalist armies were allied with the United States in a joint effort against Japan, and Chinese-Americans benefited. World War II provided a singular opportunity to upgrade the status of Chinese-Americans and eliminate most of the discriminatory and racist images. The Chinese were suddenly portrayed as sympathetic victims of Japanese aggression and as heroic soldiers and courageous citizens. In addition to changing the American perceptions of the Chinese, World War II took away most of the young white male trade that had kept many of the vices booming.

The Tongs, under strong pressure from the merchant classes, decided that the wave of the future was tourism. By the end of World War II there had been a tremendous transformation in many American Chinatowns. Vice rackets existed in the Chinatowns only for the Chinese residents. For whites they were no longer a haven of gambling, prostitution, and opium. Increasingly they became filled with restaurants offering food invented for the white palate, like chop suey, as well as numerous grocery stores, butcher shops, and fish markets. By the early 1950s, San Francisco's Chinatown had been transformed from an enclave of crime to a "must" tourist stop. Many Tongs had become "merchants' associations." Images of "opium-fiend" Chinese were replaced with admiring stories of Chinese family loyalty. Lurid exposés of immorality were replaced with tales of Chinese culture and examples of their hardworking nature.

In 1965 the U.S. government opened up Chinese immigration. Thousands fled Hong Kong's slums. They came to overcrowded Chinatowns and sweatshop jobs. The Tongs found new recruits in the mass influx. In 1960 there were 20,000 Chinese in New York. By 1985 there were 300,000, and 1,400 more are arriving each day. (More than 50 percent of all new American immigrants are Asian, and most of those are Chinese.) They faced language and cultural barriers, and as a result more than 95 percent of them moved into a Chinatown. The Tongs expanded the vice rackets to satisfy the new residents. In the early 1970s the number of illegal gambling halls in New York almost doubled. But while the Tongs grew to meet the new wave of Chinese, law enforcement fell behind. Even today, of 26,300 police in New York, there are only 117 Asian officers and only thirty-seven speak Chinese. For the Tongs it is like having a small Hong Kong in the middle of America, but law enforcement is left to a foreign police force that does not understand the language or the customs and therefore leaves the Chinatowns alone.

Today five major Tongs extend across the United States. The largest is the On Leong Tong, based in a small headquarters building at 83 Mott Street in New York City. The second-largest nationwide Tong is the Hip Sing, based in San Francisco. The third brotherhood is the affluent Ying On Tong, which controls the southwest United States, including Los Angeles. The last two large Tongs are based on the Pacific coast and have extended branch offices to the East. They are the Hop Sing and the Suey Sing.

No one knows how many members they count. To join an applicant must be sponsored by an active member. Then the applicant's name is posted in the Tong and if there is no objection to his membership within three weeks, he can begin the initiation rites. The traditional Tong ceremonies are clones of the Triads'. Inductees often kneel before a shrine and, with crossed swords, take a series of oaths vowing loyalty or death. But the Tongs are involved with many useful and charitable enterprises in the Chinese community, and it is difficult to establish whether some of them are ongoing criminal enterprises. As a result Tong membership is legal in the United States. Although U.S. law enforcement has compiled extensive evidence that some of the Tongs are heavily infiltrated with Triad members, they cannot establish that the Tongs are merely covers for Triads, just operating under a different name. A Hong Kong police superintendent had no doubt:

"Look, the United States has given the Triads a tremendous advantage. These Tongs are organized on the same structure of the Hong Kong Triads and they communicate on a regular basis with each other and with Triad figures in Asia. If you think that the Tongs are anything but public Triads, you are seriously mistaken. They may do a lot of good things in the Chinese community, but rest assured that some members are criminal and are using the Tong's apparatus to control everything from gambling to narcotics."

Sergeant McKenna of San Francisco was not as sure the situation was so clear cut. "I don't think you can say that Tongs equal Triads. It's not quite that simple. Some Tongs have criminals in high positions and they use the Tong apparatus to further their criminal aims. But while that is happening a lot of the other Tong members may be legitimate and have nothing to do with crime. In a Triad everyone is there for criminal purposes. Not necessarily the same with the Tongs. I don't think it is fair to say Tongs are automatically criminal enterprises, only that some of their members are criminal."

The FBI compiled a 1985 report on organized Chinese crime. The report stated, "While the FBI recognizes that the majority of members of the various Tongs in cities throughout the United States today are law-abiding citizens who are exemplary assets to their communities, the presence of Triad influence, control or manipulation is evident in certain Tongs in major cities." The report concluded that the major Triads operating in the United States were hidden behind Tongs. "These groups are believed to be the '14-K,' 'Wo Shing Wo,' 'Wo On Lok,' 'Kung Lik,' as well as the traditional 'Hung Mun.'" The FBI had zeroed in on many of Hong Kong's major Triads. According to the FBI, the Tongs employ youth gangs for "street muscle," and each Tong has its own enforcement thugs. For instance, New York's On Leong uses "the Ghost Shadows." The Hip Sing Tong has "the Flying Dragons." These archrival gangs have a "shoot-on-sight" policy.

Even the Tongs have trouble in controlling new, unruly gangs like the Asian Invasion and Local Motion. Often fourteen- and fifteen-year-old kids straight off the boat from Hong Kong, they have little respect for authority, even for Chinese Tong elders. While the street gangs provide important protection for the Chinatown vice trades, the Tongs also allow them to have their own side businesses—fireworks sales, for example. Sometimes the street gangs have "wars" over the side businesses, and until the Tongs stop them, blood flows. Sometimes the gangs go too far. The Golden Dragon massacre in San Francisco was one such case. By shooting up an entire restaurant and killing innocent people, they stimulated the police response of a special task force, and the government started to look much closer at organized Chinese crime. That type of scrutiny is bad for business, and the Tongs discourage open gang fights for that very reason.

Yet gang wars are still what most people think of as Chinatown's only crime problem. Nicky Louie, the head of New York's Ghost Shadows, had had thirteen publicized attempts on his life by the age of twenty-one. He is now in jail for his gang activities. San Francisco's Golden Dragon massacre was repeated in New York in 1983 when eleven people were shot in a war between the White Tigers and the Freemasons. A Tong dispute in Seattle left eleven executed at an illegal gambling club. In Boston rival Tongs conducted a gambling war with raids on each other's clubs that left behind innocent bodies.

Yet, despite the visible problems caused by the gangs, the Tongs still exert great influence in America's Chinatowns. Part of the reason for their power is that many of them are supported by the Chinese Nationalist government in Taiwan. Although Taiwan officially denies it supports the Tongs and youth gangs, evidence gathered in confidential government files indicates otherwise. In return for the KMT's financial and political backing, the Tongs ensure that the local Chinese communities support the KMT and that no leftist groups get a toehold in Chinatown. The end result is that some key Tongs have the instrumental assistance of a foreign government to run the Chinatowns as though they were separate small countries within the United States. For the KMT it is merely part of the same chain of control that starts in the hills of the Golden Triangle. Its opium army is one of the largest in Asia. The Taiwanese government provides sanctuary to leading heroin kingpins like White Powder Ma and corrupt ex-police like the Five Dragons. And the KMT supports the Tongs.

The KMT and its associated Tongs and Triads protect their interests around the world. In October 1984, San Francisco journalist Henry Liu was gunned down in front of his suburban house. He was a vocal critic of the Taiwan government and had just finished a stinging article on President Chiang Ching-kuo, the son of Chiang Kai-shek. The eventual investigations in California and New York, coupled with unprecedented pressure from the U.S. government, revealed the extent of the official Taiwan–criminal partnership.

Mr. Liu was killed by assassins dispatched from Taiwan by the United Bamboo Triad. The murder was personally ordered by the Triad's dragon head, forty-one-year-old Chen Chi-Li, nicknamed "Dry Duck." Although Taiwan refused to extradite Dry Duck for trial in the United States, it reluctantly placed him in the court docket in Taiwan. There he shocked the court by implicating the chief of Taiwan's version of the CIA, Admiral Weng Hsi-Ling. Admiral Ling hired the United Bamboo Triad for a political murder. Both Dry Duck and Admiral Weng were given life sentences. Two of the admiral's top intelligence aides were also convicted as part of the murder conspiracy. But only one year later the FBI complained that Dry Duck was still directing the United Bamboo Triad from prison. The Taiwanese ignored the complaint.

During the course of the investigation into the Liu murder and the United Bamboo–KMT partnership, a massive heroin network was uncovered. By 1985 undercover officers had been "inducted" into American branches of the United Bamboo. They soon broke the case with the arrests of thirteen Triad members preparing to import billions of dollars of Golden Triangle heroin.

The United Bamboo is now reorganizing in the United States, still recovering from its legal setbacks. But the KMT-backed Tongs have not suffered any similar law-enforcement defeats. They continue as public Chinese brotherhoods, and they have a lock grip on an exploding illegal empire.

"Every top Chinese criminal in the United States is a Tong member, so you can draw your own conclusions." I was sitting across from Mike Yamaguchi, an assistant United States Attorney in San Francisco. He is an expert on Chinese organized crime. I sought him out to get a better idea of how the Triads and Tongs worked together. I met him on the sixteenth floor of the Federal Building. We sat in his large, windowed office, crammed with government-issue furniture and file cabinets, looking out onto Golden Gate Avenue and the deteriorating state office building directly across the street. Behind the desk, sitting in a high-backed, brown leather chair, was Mike Yamaguchi, a short, wiry man of thirty-six. He wears wire-rimmed glasses and is neatly outfitted in a dark gray suit with a white button-down oxford shirt and a yellow tie. There are no maps on the wall. This is the judicial part of the war on Triads.

Yamaguchi is serious, bright, and articulate. He is one of a new breed of prosecutors who understand the importance of Chinese organized crime. He is surrounded by piles of paper detailing an extensive investigation into the Hop Sing Tong and a heroin distribution network.

"The Chinese are smart, patient, and extremely bright criminals," he said as he leaned back in his leather chair. "Heroin and gambling are their backbones. They have excellent sources for heroin, but their distribution is not great so they are working with traditional organized crime. They are also getting into cocaine. They used to deal only in heroin, and that is still the vast bulk of their business. But now the Chinese community has its own yuppies and some are moving out of Chinatown, and just like yuppies all over the country, they have discovered cocaine. So the Chinese criminal groups have started to make source contacts with anyone they can and they have started dealing in coke to the up-and-coming Chinese professionals. But heroin is still dealt to the inner-city American addicts.

"I have a confidential informant who tells me that a commission, similar to that of traditional organized crime's ruling council, runs nationwide Chinese crime out of New York." Yamaguchi's confidential informant was sent back to New York to study under the commission. He has broken major ground in his investigation. He is the first law-enforcement fighter to discover the existence of a ruling council for organized Chinese crime. It is a degree of sophisticated control that few American law-enforcement experts thought the Chinese possessed. Some still disagree with Yamaguchi's intelligence information.

"Look, a lot of law enforcement used to believe there was no such thing as the Sicilian Mafia or that a council controlled Italian organized crime in the U.S. No one will dispute that today. But until they are forced to see it in the Chinese area, some may still doubt it. But I tell you my information is solid. There are five commission members. They do not all have criminal records, but they are all Tong members. As for their Triad affiliation, I couldn't say. Membership is so secretive with the Triads that it's difficult to say."

When I pressed Yamaguchi on the existence of the central commission, he stood his ground. "Look, it's silly to think that the Chinese syndicates are so formally organized in the Orient that they wouldn't take that structure with them here to the U.S. You underestimate criminal societies that have flourished for hundreds of years. If you think they are intimidated by opening up operations here in America, when they have already clearly established extensive operations in Europe, I don't think that's right. It's almost an advantage for them here, with the problems that law enforcement has in penetrating the Chinese community.

"Look, it's very scary sometimes in this area. Some of the Chinese leaders that come into the civic and political scene come out of nowhere. Suddenly they appear with the entire support of Chinatown and they have political clout and we know nothing about them. It's like the Tongs have selected somebody and thrust them into the limelight. Remember, they have ultimate control over Chinatown, and now they want more political power in the city as a whole."

"What if you were faced with a situation where a Chinese per-

son made inroads into government or political circles and you
had evidence that his associations were questionable?"

"That's what we are faced with right now. A prominent person with some very questionable contacts. But not enough proof
for an indictment and conviction, so we are forced to sit quietly
with our suspicions. It can be very frustrating."

Later, over a few beers at a nearby bar, Yamaguchi told me
more about the Tongs and their role in the United States. "All
major crime is Tong oriented. Tongs set the tone. Gangs enforce
everything for the Tongs, but gangs also carry on their own side
businesses such as extortion, robberies, and the like. Tongs steer
clear of a lot of the petty crime. But Triad involvement is harder
to figure. But if you're asking me if there are 'made members'of
Chinese crime just like there are in the traditional organized
crime families, the answer is yes. They go through initiation rites,
very traditional rites, carried out and based on lots of history.
Not just anyone can join, it's a very formal process."

I asked Yamaguchi what traits he thought made the Chinese
different from other criminals.

"Well, there are a lot. Say you look at the differences between
the Chinese and the Colombians, as an example. A comparison
like that shows you how good the Chinese are. The Colombians
are the nouveau riche of the criminal world. They have no patience, they just want to do it, score big, and get the money. That's
why you read about massive busts with 100, 500, or 1,000 kilos
of cocaine with the Colombians. They get together, they are not
very sophisticated, they know they may or may not get arrested,
but they decide that if they are going to risk it, then they will do
it big and try to make a killing. So they will ship hundreds of
kilos hoping to make a big hit. This may succeed a couple of times
and then they may be busted by law enforcement. Meanwhile,
they are ostentatious, loud, visible, partying on their own stash.

"But the Chinese are quiet, avoid the limelight, and are happy
to ship just five kilos of heroin each and every week year after
year. Nothing flashy, nothing to increase the risk. It's a real business. So if they get busted on one shipment, it seems like only a
five-kilo bust, but the overall significance may not be immediately apparent. In the long term, the Chinese route can be much
bigger than the flashier Colombian routes. But cops always like
to bust the Colombians with their red Ferraris and a big table

stacked with cocaine, cash, and guns. That will get them on the
evening news and a citation in the department. But arresting a
fifty-year-old Chinese accountant in a suit and tie, driving his
Datsun to work with half a pound of heroin under the hood,
that's just not glamorous enough."

Yamaguchi pointed out that during the past several years law
enforcement has been faced with a new problem. Tongs are employing newly formed Vietnamese gangs for some of their most
violent and dangerous work. This adds yet another dimension
to the already complex organized-Chinese-crime picture. With
Vietnamese immigration soaring since 1980, brutal youth gangs
have sprouted across the United States. Nationwide gangs include
the Black Eagles, the Pink Knights, the Thunder Tigers, and the
Viet Ching. They are financed through petty extortion as well as
an elaborate system of collecting "dues" for anti-Communist fronts
like the "National United Front for the Liberation of Vietnam."
Gangs like the Frogmen are composed of former Special Forces
soldiers from the South Vietnamese navy and are trained in assassination and the sophisticated use of explosives. Before the
President's Commission on Organized Crime in 1984, a hooded
witness told the panel that the godfather of the Vietnamese gangs
in the United States was none other than former South Vietnamese Air Marshal Nguyen Cao Ky. He denied the charges from
his California residence.

"The Tongs have been quick to see an advantage in using the
Vietnamese gangs," Yamaguchi told me. "By using these gangs,
some of whom were in the war and therefore are very tough and
ruthless, they take the pressure off the Chinese community. They
use the Vietnamese gangs for the worst jobs, and then if they
get caught, the blame goes on the violent new Vietnamese immigrants and not on the Chinese Tongs that have hired them.
And the Vietnamese are all too happy to do work for the Tongs
because it means they are getting cut into a much larger crime
picture. It's just another wrinkle that's going to create some additional law-enforcement headaches."

I asked Yamaguchi if his intelligence work had uncovered any
evidence that the Triads were looking to the United States as a
safe haven once Hong Kong reverted to mainland China.

"Everyone talks about Hong Kong going back to the Chinese
in 1997 and that the criminal syndicates are fleeing to Taiwan

and Canada and elsewhere. I can't speak for everyone, but I know that a lot of it, most of it in my opinion, is coming into the U.S.and straight into San Francisco. There has been an incredible surge in banking activity and a giant surge in cash among a growing number of independent Chinese banks. I can tell you the incoming cash is staggering. Prime property all over San Francisco is being bought in cash and at big prices. They are getting ready here. They are preparing for moving here. It's already happening and there's little to do about it. If you want to see what's happening in America with the Hong Kong syndicates, follow the money. Look at what is coming out of Hong Kong and where it is going and you'll get a good idea of what the future holds. It's not all good news."

14

The Chinese Laundry

Small advertisements in *The Wall Street Journal,* the *International Herald Tribune,* and the Miami *Herald* proclaimed, "Many multinational corporations know the benefits of confidential banking outside of North America. No reporting requirements. Total secrecy. Guaranteed results." Those interested were told to contact the Canada–Asia Finance Group of North America, headquartered in Vancouver. An assortment of motley characters, involved in a wide range of businesses that could not use public banking services, responded to the ads. Inquiries were eventually reviewed by Aaron Lee, a twenty-seven-year-old Hong Kong-born financier. Raised in Canada, he was chief of the Canada–Asia Finance Group.

In 1983 two men approached Lee. They were cocaine smugglers from Florida, Fran Dyer and Darryl Whitehead. When Lee met the two smugglers they looked like typical new narcotics millionaires—gold watches, silk suits, thousand-dollar silver belt buckles, and the baggy eyes that were the giveaway sign of too many all-night parties.

The two dealers, Dyer and Whitehead, wanted what every other dope dealer wants—an easy way to turn staggering narcotics dollars into legitimate money that can be publicly consumed.

The drug business generates enormous amounts of money, more than $100 billion a year just in the United States. That is more money than the profits of the combined Fortune 500 companies. And the drug business generates only cash. International criminal syndicates take in so much money so fast that sophisticated microchip scales weigh sacks of different denominations and let the traffickers know how much they have. For instance, 107.4 pounds in $20 bills equals $1 million. Traditional money-counting machines are just too slow.

Chartered Lear jets leave the United States from major airports and fly the money in cardboard boxes directly to offshore banks in the Bahamas or the Dominican Republic. Sometimes so many cartons of cash arrive that the banks need trucks to transport the shipment from the airport. U.S. banks are more difficult to use because of a law mandating that every cash transaction over $10,000 be reported to the Federal government. In a multi-billion-dollar cash business, the $10,000-dollar limit is like having the average worker report each $1.00 banking transaction.

So much money is flooding through the narcotics business that even low-level operators are making the kind of money that used to be reserved for the kingpins. When New York police investigated the case of a thirty-seven-year-old murdered courier, they discovered that he owned two twin-engine Cessnas, a $300,000 helicopter, a $90,000 Rolls-Royce, a Mercedes convertible, a twenty-four-foot stretch limousine, a forty-one-foot luxury yacht, and had just bought a neighborhood discotheque for $1.5 million in cash because he did not like the service he received and on an impulse decided to fire the staff. The money at the top of the business is staggering. Some, like major heroin dealer Frank Lucas, can drop $15 million at the blackjack and dice tables of Las Vegas without any worry. Others invest their megadollars to become some of the land's most prominent businessmen. Instead of buying personal luxuries, billions of dollars are recycled as clean money into skyscraper office buildings, multistory luxury condominiums, flashy nightclubs, shopping centers in rural America, new casinos and hotels, expensive European clothing boutiques, deluxe health spas, silver and gold mines, horse farms, and even banks, among an entire assortment of businesses.

Dyer and Whitehead were moving up the drug ladder. As they told Lee in Vancouver, they had a growing business and were already sending so much money through Miami banks that they needed to put their cash through another part of the country. Lee told the aspiring drug kingpins that he was the solution to their problems. He assured them the best laundering center in the world was Hong Kong, and that he had connections with important banks in the British colony. His fee was a flat $10,000 plus 5 percent of all the money that passed. Dyer and Whitehead agreed.

Within a couple of months the two Florida drug dealers sent $150,000 in small bills through Lee and his Canadian company. Lee sent the money to the Liu Chong Hing Bank. It is one of Asia's largest family-run banks. Although it has twenty-seven branches scattered around Hong Kong, its only foreign branch is a small nondescript office in the heart of San Francisco's financial district. That branch is not licensed for customers to open accounts, serving instead as a liaison office for clients with business in its Hong Kong branches. Yet that legal limitation did not stop it from handling the questionable Dyer and Whitehead deposits.

But the Florida pair wanted Lee out of the way. They thought the 5 percent handling fee was onerous. Deciding to do away with their Canadian middleman, they approached the Liu Chong Hing Bank directly. The vice president for North American operations, Kwong Shing So, invited the ambitious pair to discuss their business in Hong Kong. During Thanksgiving, Dyer and Whitehead settled into the British colony. They met So at a Hong Kong nightclub, a suitcase crammed with cash resting next to Dyer's leg.

Over a series of drinks, Dyer told So that he owned an aviation leasing company in Miami and also represented numerous business interests in Atlantic City. "But there is something I want to discuss with you," Dyer told So. "The type of people we deal with, they deal in currency. And very often, because of the nature of their business and where they take the aircraft and what they do with them, sometimes we...have had the aircraft seized."

So looked impassively at the two Miami "entrepreneurs." There was no reaction. Dyer pushed on. "Well, do you care how we make our money?"

So shrugged his shoulders. "I don't care. We are a bank. Since it's real money, we cannot refuse deposits."

Dyer looked relieved. He told So that they needed to move

$1 million through immediately. So did not flinch. Again, Dyer wanted to be sure that So was their type of banker.

"Do you care whether our money is legal or illegal?" he asked.

Lifting his glass in a toast to the two Americans, So shook his head and firmly said, "I don't care." He told them not to be so nervous. He assured them he had customers in Taiwan and Bangkok involved in smuggling and black-market enterprises and they had the same problems as Dyer and Whitehead.

The two Americans relaxed. So was finished baby-sitting his guests. It was time to get to the business details.

"Which one of you makes the business decisions?" he asked them.

Whitehead spoke up for the first time. "Well, we are partners ....It's fifty-fifty."

So paused for a moment. "Okay then, I will handle your business for one percent."

It was a much better deal than they had with their Canadian middleman. On their million-dollar investment, that would save Dyer and Whitehead $40,000 over Lee's fee.

Dyer looked relieved and spoke for the pair. "Well, that's fine with me."

"Let's shake on this," So suggested as he stretched his hand across the table. They all gave hearty handshakes, smiling and leaning back to order another round of drinks. So lifted his glass in the air for another toast. "Gentlemen, you have just bought yourself a Chinese laundry."

During the coming months the Liu Chong Hing Bank officials plugged Dyer and Whitehead into a sophisticated money-laundering operation. The bank customized eleven separate accounts, all under the names of dummy corporations bought from the shelves of Hong Kong lawyers for $1,000 each. Money was transferred in increments of $9,000 so as not to trigger the United States reporting requirement. In a series of computer-generated currency movements, the Liu Chong Hing Bank moved Dyer and Whitehead's money through the dummy companies and secrecy-shrouded bank accounts. Detailed schematics were produced to show the Florida dealers where their money was at any given time. The Hong Kong handlers wired the money through a maze of accounts and companies running from San Francisco to Vancouver back to Hong Kong, over to Seattle, and then making the penultimate stopover in Zurich before coming back to the United States. It arrived in America as "clean money," ready for investments in real estate or business ventures or whatever Dyer and Whitehead desired.

Liu Chong Hing officials even bragged that their computer programs were capable of foiling the United States' "spectrum system." The spectrum computer analysis is an advanced mathematical technique applied by the government to notice disturbances and significant variations in the normal volume of a bank's cash flow. It is designed to notice laundering in bank transfers of less than $10,000. The Hong Kong bank officials claimed their computers knew the limits of the spectrum system, and therefore their laundering operation was foolproof for the United States.

Dyer and Whitehead were so impressed with the laundering operation that they invited So to the United States. They told him that they had numerous friends "in related businesses," and if he came to America, he could leave with many new and profitable clients. So arrived brimming with expectations for expanding the bank's laundering services. He stepped off a plane right into the arms of federal agents. Dyer and Whitehead were not drug smugglers. Instead they were veteran IRS undercover agents. They had posed as drug dealers, passing more than $1.3 million through the Hong Kong laundering system, discovering important aspects of a top-to-bottom Chinese laundry. So was tried on a number of felony charges, including currency violations, making false statements, and conspiracy. He was convicted by a San Francisco federal court but sentenced to only six months in prison. He was back in Hong Kong by 1985.

"The Liu Chong Hing case was just the tip of the iceberg," Assistant U.S. Attorney Mike Yamaguchi told me. "There are a lot of operations like that, many better and bigger. It's just that this was the first Chinese one that we got to see from the inside. It was a how-to case, and hopefully it will help in future investigations."

It had better help, because the United States is faced with massive illegal profits from two Chinese sources. One is the Hong Kong-based Triads preparing for their departure from the British colony by 1997. They are concerned with laundering money from foreign accounts into the United States. The second concern is illegal Chinese syndicates already in the United States.

Their problem is taking billions of dollars earned in this country and laundering it so that it appears legitimate.

As for the money coming from Hong Kong, statistics show that large amounts are coming into the United States. Ever since the British decided that Hong Kong would revert to mainland China in 1997, the flow of money has been spiraling. While much of it may be legitimate, earned in honest endeavors in Hong Kong's booming financial climate, a fair percentage is undoubtedly "dirty money." Yamaguchi explained. "Make no mistake: a lot of dirty money is coming straight out of Hong Kong into the United States. Money from narcotics, from gambling, from all of the organized crime activities."

More than $2 billion a year comes into the United States from Hong Kong banks. Only $250 million flows back across the Pacific. Two-thirds of all the money coming in from Hong Kong is in denominations of $100 or less. The volume of small bills sent between Hong Kong and the United States exceeds the volume of such denominations with all the countries in Europe. The fact that so much of the currency traffic with the British colony is in small amounts is a "telltale sign of drug trafficking and money laundering," according to the U.S. Treasury Department. Hong Kong annually sends nearly another billion in U.S. currency, also in small bills, to Switzerland. The amount of U.S. dollars handled by Hong Kong has doubled almost every year since 1982, paralleling the growth of Southeast Asian heroin's share of the United States market.

Dozens of Asian banks have established U.S. branches to help with the flow of money. The Southern California community of Monterey Park, with 58,000 residents and a large Chinese community, boasts twenty-eight Asian banks. The chief of the Monterey Park police, Jon Elder, has little doubt about their role: "It is suspected that money-laundering is a featured specialty of these banks. The growth of these banks has been so fast that it is very difficult to keep track of them, let alone monitor any illegal activity in which they engage. Banks have sprouted up to replace gas stations, veterinary hospitals, hardware stores, restaurants, and all other variety of businesses." Elder fears that $1.5 to $2 million a day is laundered through his town. Chinese money has found its way into popular hostess clubs and card clubs, both legal in California. A group of investors with no visible assets has made a multimillion-dollar bid for a Las Vegas casino. Elder is worried that the investors are a front for a Hong Kong Triad.

Hong Kong makes money-laundering easy for the Triads. The banking system in the British colony is unfettered by government restrictions. There are no reporting requirements for cash transactions. The British administration does not even keep track of how much cash leaves the colony. There is no central bank and no currency exchange controls. This makes Hong Kong a launderer's dream. Without central regulation, commercial banks and currency dealers operate as they deem fit. While the laws governing the actions of banks are few and far between, some of the strictest are reserved for regulations guaranteeing the absolute privacy and confidentiality of bank deposits and records. Hong Kong courts are legally barred from issuing subpoenas for bank records unless the individual depositor has been indicted. By the time any major criminal figure is indicted, his money has long since been removed from the colony.

"We do not even investigate money-laundering," Brian Merritt, a senior Hong Kong police superintendent, admitted to me. "It's too new and it's very difficult to prove currency transaction cases. There are no IRS-type investigations for people living above their means, and there is no law that allows us to seize assets of known criminals or drug dealers. So without those tools not many people are concerned about who brings what through the banks here."

Tony Lee, a superintendent in the criminal intelligence division of the Hong Kong police, acknowledged the futility of searching for dirty money in Hong Kong. "Money-laundering is just too hard to follow. Once a half million was taken in a bank robbery. A CI* told us that the money was going to be changed into German Deutschmarks. We even knew the day it was going to be done. But still we could not find it. We did computer analyses on the flow of money into the more than 3,000 foreign exchange stores to see if there was a blip anywhere. Nothing. We later found out that the money was changed on the day it was supposed to be. It's just that half a million got lost in the sea of changed money. I think you would need five to ten million changed at the same time for us to be able to find it.

"Another time I was told by a CI that $400,000 was leaving

---

*Confidential informant.

Kai Tak Airport in a suitcase. I had extra police and customs stop almost everybody. We found forty-eight people with at least $250,000 in suitcases or bags. There was almost $15 million in cash leaving. That's just one day of checking. It's too much for us to try to deal with."

The flow into the United States is also more than American law enforcement can deal with. Geoffrey Anderson, chief of the Federal Organized Crime Task Force in San Francisco, admits, "I don't know how to do it with the system we have. The money brought in can barely be measured."

Rollin Klink, the chief U.S. customs agent in San Francisco, points out an additional obstacle for law enforcement: "If the money is laundered abroad, then we can't do anything about it here in the U.S. If dirty money is laundered in Hong Kong and it's clean by the time it comes to this country, then there is no law broken."

A lot of that money is arriving on the Pacific coast. One indicator of where laundered money ends up is the Federal Reserve's figures for cash surpluses and deficits for regions of the country. The Federal Reserve system suspects money-laundering when its banks receive more cash than they send to commercial banks. From 1975 to 1983 the only Federal Reserve bank that showed a cash surplus was the one in Miami, a sure sign of the booming cocaine business. But in 1985 both San Francisco and Los Angeles had cash surpluses. At the end of 1986, while Miami's surplus had stabilized, Los Angeles' had increased tenfold to $1.2 billion and San Francisco had $150 million in extra funds.

These figures show the extent to which the West Coast has become a haven for dirty cash. The Treasury Department says that banks, real estate agents, car dealers, and lawyers are taking cash in record amounts. The advance teams for the Triads are already arriving on the Pacific coast. One of the first to come is Wai Man Lee, fifty-six, reportedly a prominent Triad boss, who had controlled Hong Kong's illegal gambling halls. A confidential Hong Kong police report pinpoints Lee as a "most wealthy and influential criminal currently residing in the United States." The police files list him as a member of the Kwong Luen Shing Triad, controlling six major casinos in Hong Kong during the mid-1970s, and the largest bookmaker at the Royal Hong Kong Jockey Club. Despite the damning case against him by the Hong Kong police, he has never even been arrested.

Born on a junk in Hong Kong Harbor, Lee moved from a fisherman to a hawker to the bookie business. As he built his gambling empire he served as a member of Hong Kong's auxiliary police force. From 1972 to 1976 he passed almost $40 million through bank accounts that Hong Kong police have identified as his. They do not know how many other accounts he may have controlled under different names or dummy corporations. By mid-1976, together with his wife, Lee fled a growing Hong Kong investigation and arrived in California. Since then he has been buying and selling property in San Francisco as though it was a game, often in conjunction with some of San Francisco's most prominent Chinese businessmen. In 1979 the Hong Kong police intelligence division concluded in a confidential report that "it is probable that Lee is using his position in the United States to act as a broker for other vice crime personalities in Hong Kong who wish to transfer their earnings overseas without having them recorded by bank transactions."

That report prompted the United States Organized Crime Strike Force to kick off an overdue investigation. Four years later, despite the help of the IRS, Customs Service, the DEA, and Immigration and Naturalization, the investigation ended in failure. The government could prove some $12 million in San Francisco property had been bought and sold, but it could not prove that U.S. laws had been broken. Lee was not indicted. He now moves back and forth between Taiwan and San Francisco, apparently untouchable, despite the bulging Hong Kong dossiers.

The Chinese money flood is not only washing onto the West Coast. New York is also unable to cope with the Hong Kong cash flow. The rapid money infusion has caused commercial rents in New York's Chinatown to soar. Some fruit stands at Pell Street and other main Chinatown thoroughfares cost as much to rent per square foot as Tiffany's at Fifth Avenue and Fifty-seventh Street. "It's pure hysteria," according to Michael Dirzulaitis, the assistant commissioner in the Division of Real Property for New York City. "Every time you turn around the prices have shot up. It's hard to believe that there is enough money to keep it going, but there is." City officials cite numerous examples of property and buildings transferred in multimillion-dollar transactions— all cash. They almost uniformly put the blame on the 1997 deadline and the growing Hong Kong exodus. But officials also believe that the major Hong Kong money has not yet started to leave the British colony. What has rocked the Federal Reserve system and skyrocketed Chinatown property prices is just "nest-egg" money. No one wants to think of what will happen as 1997 draws near.

While the Hong Kong Triads are moving tens of millions of dollars into the United States, Chinese syndicates already established here must still worry about cleaning their illegal profits. The money from the heroin trade, the gambling halls on Mott Street in New York and Grant Avenue in San Francisco, the extortion, loan-sharking, prostitution, and the rest of their illegal enterprises generate sizable fortunes. Because the federal government has strict laws allowing the seizure of criminal assets and the subpoena of banking and financial records, underworld figures are especially careful with moneys earned in America. For the Chinese syndicates in the United States, laundering is simply the process of getting illegitimate money out of their hands and then back into them again in a form that can be safely spent. The trick is to do it without leaving an incriminating trail. That is why secretive banks in countries like the Bahamas, Switzerland, Luxembourg, Panama, and other havens are often employed. Twenty-five countries aside from Hong Kong have banking secrecy laws. Many of them, like Panama and the Dominican Republic, refuse to disclose customer information even for an international narcotics or terrorist investigation. Major U.S. banks like Chase Manhattan, Bank of America, and Citibank have branches in the twenty-five money-haven countries. It facilitates the flow of funds into the United States.

The process used is marked by complexity in order to mask the trail. Criminals usually establish several dummy corporations in different countries under the names of local agents and attorneys. Then up to half a dozen numbered and secret accounts are established in as many banking havens. The accounts never list the real owner's name but always a "beneficial representative," usually a local lawyer specializing in laundering. Many of the haven countries offer layers of names on an account. For instance, the name of the account can be in one corporate name, the name of the depositor can be another dummy company, and the investment certificate can be held by yet a third shelf corporation. With local lawyers acting as the board of directors, coupled with no reporting requirements and guarantees of absolute secrecy, it is almost impossible to discover the actual owners of multi-million-dollar accounts. The criminals then transfer the illegal moneys back and forth between the corporations and bank accounts in a myriad transactions that are impossible to trace.

Once the money is sitting "clean" in the foreign account of a dummy corporation, the criminal will then bring it back to the United States by either "borrowing" the money from the dummy company or by getting the front business to "invest" in a project in the United States. If he "borrows" the money (actually borrowing his own laundered funds), he will continue the charade by paying interest on the loan and thereby earn himself a sizable tax deduction. Once the money has been invested into a legitimate U.S. business, the criminal can launder even more funds by creating double invoices or billing the business for nonexistent property or merchandise. In 1983 the Senate estimated that more than $45 billion a year in illegal money was permanently "cleaned" in this manner.

At New York City's most expensive luxury condominium building, Trump Tower, where apartments start at $1 million, fully one-third are owned by foreign corporations, most from the banking havens of Panama and the Netherlands Antilles. Their real owners are hidden behind the dummy companies. No one suggests that these apartments are owned by drug dealers. But that is the point. Since no one knows, there is nothing the authorities can do.

In many cases the criminals do not even have to go to the expense and difficulty of dealing with foreign banking havens. It is often not difficult to launder money in the United States. More than $225 billion in currency is moved every day between international banks and U.S. banks. Another $100 billion a day is moved between privately owned security companies. Trying to find the illegal moneys, hidden behind a dazzling array of companies, bank accounts, and a shelter of sophisticated lawyers and accountants, is virtually impossible.

In spite of a $10,000-cash-transaction reporting requirement, intended to highlight the movement of illegal money, U.S. banks often assist criminals in hiding their profits. The United States has required since 1972 that banks report such cash transactions, but the penalties under the original law were only $1,000 fines and a possible five years in prison. No one went to jail. The law

was generally ignored. By 1983 a Senate investigating committee reported that "the federal law designed to halt the flow of
illegally earned dollars...is a monumental failure....For most of
the decade after passage...its reporting provisions were rarely
invoked. Some banks, especially small banks, have willingly par-
ticipated in schemes to circumvent or evade the requirement....
[E]ven large domestic banks prefer to close their eyes to the
source of their deposits and thus accept dirty money."

If a U.S. bank does not report cash transactions over $10,000,
then it provides almost the same security to underworld figures
as that provided by banking-haven countries. Many criminals feel
secure in America. In 1984 the Bank of America was fined $4.75
million for failing to report 17,000 cash transactions over $10,000.
The Treasury Department concluded that Bank of America's actions hindered timely investigations in a number of drug cases.
Later that same year Crocker Bank, also in California, was fined
$2.25 million for failing to report 7,900 cash transactions totaling
nearly $4 billion. In the Crocker case, Hong Kong banks shipped
millions of dollars in air freight crates directly to the Crocker
headquarters in San Francisco. Two of the Hong Kong banks
involved were out of business by 1985. The president of one of
the closed banks was arrested trying to leave the colony with a
suitcase filled with $154,000 in cash and $1.4 million in negotia-
ble securities. Crocker and Bank of America are not unique on
the Pacific coast. It is estimated that San Francisco banks fail to
report one of every four cash transactions over $10,000. This is
the highest failure rate for a banking system in the United States
and conservatively allows a billion dollars a year to move undetected.

The problems with U.S. banks are not only on the West Coast.
In 1985 the First National Bank of Boston was caught failing to
report brown-paper-bag cash deposits. A total of $1.2 billion went
unreported. Some of the New York giants—Chase Manhattan,
Chemical Bank, Irving Trust, and Manufacturers Hanover—
have all admitted cash-reporting violations. In 1987 the Hong
Kong–Shanghai Bank bought controlling interest in Marine Mid-
land Bank, despite complaints from New York State banking authorities that the Hong Kong bank did not disclose the source of
all its hidden profits.

If the laundering problem with banks seems almost insurmountable, the situation becomes worse when other currency-intensive businesses are included. Security companies dealing in stocks and bonds are not subject to any reporting requirements, and they move more than $100 billion a day worldwide. Commodity companies also move billions a day and are not subject to any cash-reporting rules.

One of the major suspected laundering outlets for the Triads is a series of worldwide companies called King Lung Commodities Limited. Although based in Hong Kong, it has numerous foreign offices, all independently incorporated, so that if one office has criminal problems, it will not affect the entire company. In Vancouver and Seattle, King Lung has been investigated for stealing customers' money. In Amsterdam and Singapore, King Lung is considered a primary launderer for the Triads. The scheme used is simple but effective. The criminal buys $1 million in gold contracts betting that the price of gold will go up. At the same time the criminal buys $1 million in gold contracts hoping the price will go down. Since money is highly leveraged in commodity transactions, a $1 million investment can often return $30 to $40 million within six months if the investor has chosen the right direction for the commodity's price. When the market moves in one direction, King Lung rips up the losing tickets, alters the books, and leaves the criminal with a massive money profit that is then legitimate. For this service King Lung charges between 2 and 6 percent of the clean money generated, depending on the amount involved.

In addition to security companies and commodity companies like King Lung, casinos are also exempt from reporting requirements. From Stanley Ho's casinos in Macao to those in Las Vegas or Atlantic City, millions of dollars in cash can be wired in or exchanged for gambling chips and no government authority is informed. Suspected Chinese Triad figures have bought a major casino in the Dominican Republic, a country with bank secrecy laws and without an extradition treaty with Hong Kong. Government files indicate that Triad representatives enter the Santo Domingo casino with satchels of cash that are turned into gambling chips and then later exchanged for U.S. dollars. The criminals merely pay taxes on large "gambling profits" instead of going to jail for having illegal funds.

While the international banking system, security companies,

commodity firms, and casinos would seem enough to hide the Triad's billions, the secret societies have yet one further advantage that is unknown to other ethnic criminal groups. It is the underground Chinese banking system. Not only do the Chinese have a historical distrust for banks, but the system also grew out of political turmoil, Communist takeovers in many countries where the Chinese reside, and constant harassment of expatriate Chinese in nearly all countries where they have settled. It is operated through money changers, gold shops, trading companies, and other small businesses throughout Asia. Through these shops smugglers establish letters of credit that seem magically to appear in similar stores across the world. The underground banking system employs scrambled telephone lines, couriers, and a clandestine radio network to transfer funds. The system has the ability to move funds from one country to another in a matter of hours, provide complete anonymity for the customer, total security for the money, and can convert currency into gold or diamonds or convert one currency into any other.

The record-keeping procedures of the underground banking system are nearly nonexistent. Coded messages given on chits authorize pickup and delivery of tens of millions of dollars. The Hong Kong police recently discovered a small piece of paper with an elephant on it. That paper represented a collection receipt for $3 million at a Hong Kong gold shop. Upon presentation of the chit, money is paid, no questions asked. The system is based on ethnic and historical trust as well as kinship ties to the Chinese-dominated heroin production business and to an intricate web of other Chinese commercial interests. No white man has even seen the inside of the system. It is impenetrable.

The National Intelligence Council, together with the assistance of the DEA, CIA, and National Security Agency, studied the underground system in 1983 and concluded:

"While commercial banking centers are instrumental in the movement of drug money between Asia and its U.S. and European markets, the lion's share of heroin money probably is handled within Asia by the Chinese underground banking system."

So aside from the billions that are being tracked from Hong Kong into the United States through banks, law enforcement fears that billions more are coming into the United States through brokerage houses, investment houses, import–export companies, and travel agencies. These are all high cash-turnover businesses, exempt from bank regulations and considered an integral part of the Chinese underground banking system.

"They have made a fortune in Asia and now they want to get it here before the Communists take over in 1997," a senior DEA official in Washington told me. "There's no way we are going to spot it all coming in. And before we know it, they are going to own a lot of important businesses and property and they are going to be here to stay. It's coming out of Hong Kong right now and it's coming right here to the U.S. of A. We're going to be swimming in money soon, and a lot of it will be dirty. It's only going to get worse."

15

The Dragon Heads

It is February, the middle of winter in New York. By 5:30 in the evening it is already pitch black. I am sitting in a sprawling, disheveled suite in the corner of a federal office building located at the southern tip of Manhattan. Fabric screens create small patches of privacy around large wooden desks piled high with papers. Maps of Southeast Asia, posters from Chinatown, and oriental scrolls are the only decorations. Half a dozen men are reviewing papers in front of tall metal file cabinets packed with dossiers. The crackling sound of walkie-talkies fills the room. This is the nerve center for the DEA's Chinese Crime Task Force, Group 41. Based out of New York, Group 41's sole mission is to develop cases against major Chinese heroin traffickers. Nearly a dozen investigations are under way at any time.

Sitting in front of me is a middle-aged man, Richard, his neatly trimmed goatee making him seem more like a professor than a federal drug agent. But he is the chief of the Chinese Crime Task Force, and he is probably the federal government's most knowledgeable man regarding Triads. Fluent in Cantonese and Mandarin, he has fought Triads in Bangkok, Amsterdam, Paris, and now New York. Because of the sensitive nature of Group 41's pending investigations, the DEA does not want his last name used.

"This, New York, is one of the places to be right now," Richard says as he slips his glasses into his pocket. "There is a lot of activity here and we are in the middle of some major cases."

Prior to forming Group 41, Richard was assigned to Paris, where he helped French law enforcement organize their first response to Triads. But when the DEA realized it had a more pressing problem in the United States, Richard was brought back to New York. Without his guidance the French program sputtered and then fell apart.

"It's a real shame," he says while looking out the window to the empty Federal Plaza. "We were starting to make some progress in France, but now I think things may have gone back to where they were. That would be too bad."

But he has no doubt that his move to New York was necessary. The 1997 exodus from Hong Kong, the increasing number of immigrating Triads, the skyrocketing Chinese control of the heroin trade have all helped convince Richard that he is at the center of the war on Triads. He views his group of specialized agents as a commando force trained to carry out complex operations to cripple the enemy. The legal system is their weapon, and their battles are won by courtroom verdicts and long jail sentences.

"C'mon, I've got to go to a meeting and you might as well come with me." Richard reaches into his drawer for his .38-caliber snubnosed revolver. He straps the gun, nestled into a leather ankle holster, onto his left leg under his navy-blue suit.

The traffic is light for rush-hour Manhattan. In less than twenty minutes we have arrived at a seedy Howard Johnson's Inn near the Hudson River. We walk through a stark lobby into a Formica- and plastic-covered blue barroom. Two men are waiting for the chief of Group 41. One is Captain Wipon, having flown in from Chiang Mai for an undercover case he is working on. The other is an Israeli narcotics agent. Burly, in his mid-forties, he is working on his fourth beer.

Captain Wipon looks half his size out of uniform. He is wearing an oversized corduroy jacket. "Excuse me for the coat, but I am so cold I cannot stand it here. I don't know how anyone can take this cold. It's much worse than I thought."

Richard orders him another beer, hoping it may warm him. Richard and the Israeli are quiet but Wipon is talkative. "The only thing that must make the cold more bearable for some of the criminals that have come from Thailand is how much money they are going to make here. In New York, anywhere in America, it is possible to make ten times in one deal what you can make in Thailand. Much more than that sometimes. I guess you don't feel the cold so much in that case."

"Do you see a lot of differences between the Chinese criminals here and those in Thailand?"

"Sure. Here it is harder to spot them unless you know something. I mean in Thailand they are often the wealthiest person in the town. You can see them straightaway. But here there is a lot more money and many people have their money honestly. It is not so easy to just say, 'They are dope dealers because they have wealth.' The Chinatown here is very tight, very closed to the outside. It appears that the people who run the dope business here are sometimes very respected in the community. It seems to me that these criminals have made a success of the American dream."

"That's the problem," the Israeli cut in. "In the U.S. you're fighting the establishment when you go after the major Chinese criminals. You just have to look at what happened in New York in the past decade to get an idea of what can happen when a Chinese gangster also becomes a respected member of the New York scene."

That night our conversations were cut short when Captain Wipon and the Israeli had to leave for a rendezvous with suspected Chinese heroin suppliers. I did not have a chance to find out what they meant when they spoke about "respected members of the New York scene" becoming crime overlords. A New York police detective filled me in later.

"We may make cases against major Chinese criminals in the next few years. But the hardest part of our work will be to get to the people at the very top, the godfathers of Chinese crime. In some instances we know who they are. Some are old-timers who have been around for a while. They are a problem, but the real pains in the ass are the new guys, the Young Turks. There are a lot of them just itching to move to the top. One of these guys is going to become the next Eddie Chan, that's what worries me. That's what they were talking to you about. The Feds are worried about it as well."

Tse-Chiu "Fast Eddie" Chan was a Hong Kong police staff sergeant who had served under the Five Dragons. During the height of the investigation into Lui Lok and his partners, Chan was pinpointed as a junior part of the corrupt police network. He did not stay in Hong Kong to await the investigation's outcome, instead fleeing to Taiwan in 1975. There Chan encountered too much underworld competition, ranging from Triads such as the United Bamboo to more than forty millionaire ex-Hong Kong police fugitives. He decided his future prosperity lay in America, and in late 1975 Chan arrived in New York.

Of average height, stockily built, the balding Chan was then in his mid-forties. He sported a Fu Manchu mustache that gave him a sinister look. His first decision was which Tong to join. Although he was a Hong Kong Triad member, he knew that in New York, Tong membership was essential for his plans. Control of Chinatown had traditionally been through either the Hip Sing or the On Leong Tong. The Hip Sing, founded as a laborers' protective association, has about 60,000 members. It is headquartered in a decaying brownstone that originally housed a grocery store and an illegal gambling den. Situated on Pell Street, the Hip Sing and its affiliated youth gang, the Flying Dragons, run Pell as though it owned the street's fifteen restaurants, seven shops, three travel agencies, and ice-cream parlor.

Nearby, on Mott Street, the On Leong Tong originally opened as a merchants' association. The On Leong runs Mott as its own empire and employs the Ghost Shadows gang as enforcement. Since their foundings in the mid-1800s, the two rival Tongs have often been at war. Hundreds have died in gang skirmishes. Doyer Street, which separates the two Tongs, was supposed to be neutral territory. But that did not stop the gangs from piling corpses in the V-shaped alley. It became known as "Blood Angle," reportedly the site of more murders than any place in America.

At the time that Chan arrived in New York, the Hip Sing was under the iron-fisted rule of sixty-six-year-old Benny Ong. Ong, codenamed "Uncle 7" by law-enforcement agencies, has been convicted in a murder case and for immigration fraud. In 1975 he had just taken over the Hip Sing from his brother, Sam, who had run the Tong since 1960. The Ong brothers were a Chinatown institution. Benny Ong was the unofficial mayor of New York's Chinatown and the senior Tong chairman in the United States. Chan felt that Ong could not be intimidated and decided he was too powerful to challenge. Chan instead joined the On Leong.

Chan was ambitious and aggressive. First he put his corrupt

Hong Kong profits into a jewelry store. Then he opened a funeral home. Within a couple of years he had expanded his business interests to include several restaurants. Chan adopted the
American first name of Edward as his career started to zoom.
Police investigators dubbed him "Fast Eddie" Chan. He made important alliances with some of the most violent members in the
Ghost Shadows, including its reckless teenage chief, Nicky Louie.
He reestablished his contacts with Hong Kong Triads. Under the
direction of the 14K and Wo syndicates, Chan was flush with new
funds and access to large amounts of Southeast Asian heroin.

By the late 1970s, Fast Eddie had muscled himself to the national presidency of the On Leong Tong. He had taken control
of the Tong faster than anyone in its history. A new dragon head
had arrived in New York and was challenging Benny Ong and
the Hip Sing, and he was twenty years Ong's junior. Fast Eddie
became chairman of the National Chinese Welfare Council, a nationwide group that lists its mission as "solely for the promotion
of the well-being of Chinese-Americans and Chinese nationals
in the United States." In that role he lobbied for less restrictive
quotas for Asian-Americans. He often traveled to Washington,
and his restaurants were filled with pictures of himself with congressional leaders.

He followed the Triads' rule of ingratiating himself with local
government and police officials. He was a contributor to political campaigns on the state and local level. Fast Eddie gave $1,000
to Geraldine Ferraro's 1982 reelection campaign to the House
of Representatives, and he attended her fund-raising parties in
Queens. Donald Manes, the Queens borough president who later
stabbed himself to death during a pending investigation into widespread borough corruption, counted the former Hong Kong policeman as a "very friendly acquaintance." Manes was seen with
Fast Eddie at political and civic functions.

Chan hired Michael Nussbaum, a leading New York political
and public relations consultant, to enhance his image. Nussbaum,
unaware of Chan's criminal activities, introduced Fast Eddie to
important political figures. He became an American citizen. Chan
ran Chinatown through the On Leong Tong and intended to
expand his influence far beyond the confines of southern Manhattan.

Chan's influence began to reach inside the police force. In 1982 a New York City police captain and an assistant director of the FBI's New York office took a vacation to Hong Kong. There they were met by associates of Fast Eddie who picked them up from the airport and entertained them during their vacation. By 1983 the New York police had launched an investigation, trying to stop Eddie Chan's corruption from spreading inside the department. The Fifth Precinct, responsible for Chinatown, was swept clean of a number of officers accepting payoffs for ignoring the gambling dens and the youth gangs.

But Fast Eddie was more than just the unofficial mayor of Chinatown and a growing Chinese political force. According to Drug Enforcement Administration files, he had become one of the kingpins for Southeast Asian heroin on the East Coast. As a front man for the Hong Kong Triads, he helped crime figures move illegal profits from the British colony and place them into legitimate New York businesses. He was on his way to becoming the White Powder Ma of America.

When some dissident members of the Ghost Shadows tried to break away from Chan's On Leong Tong, Fast Eddie dispatched loyal Ghost Shadows to Chicago, where they ambushed the rebels. In a shoot-out in front of Chicago's On Leong headquarters, the threat to the Tong was violently neutralized. Fast Eddie did not tolerate any dissension within his ranks.

As his political and crime power grew, he expanded his business interests. He bought an interest in a chain of movie theaters. He became the chief executive officer of Continental King Lung Commodities Group, already discussed in Chapter 14 as a key Triad money-laundering front. He also became the vice-chairman of the board of directors for the United Orient Bank in New York's Chinatown. Law-enforcement officials believe the bank played a central role in cleaning illegal funds for the Tong and for Chan's Hong Kong friends.

While Chan's empire grew, challenging the Hip Sing and Benny Ong's domination, other ambitious Chinese were encouraged to stage rebellions against the Ong regime. In 1980, Herbert Liu, then a forty-year-old real estate and travel agent, became head of the Chinese Freemasons, a new and expanding Tong. Liu is a former Hong Kong auxiliary policeman and a Triad member. He established his headquarters on East Broadway and tried to ride Chan's coattails to the top of Chinatown. But Benny Ong was patient. Forty years of Tong politics and intrigue had taught him not to panic. To Benny "Uncle 7" Ong, Chan and Liu were just *fan gud rai* (young rebels). When talking once to Herbert Liu, Ong told him "When you go up stairs, you walk little by little. You go up too fast, you fall down." His competitors did not listen to his advice.

By 1983, Chan's rise to the top was attracting attention from a number of law-enforcement agencies. That year a high-level Triad officer in Hong Kong pinpointed Eddie Chan as the key new crime figure in the United States. By that time the Drug Enforcement Administration had a growing dossier on Fast Eddie. Police contacts informed Benny Ong and the Hip Sing that Chan was under investigation. Ong decided to let the legal case against his rival gain momentum. Meanwhile, no one waited for Herbert Liu to have legal problems. Masked Flying Dragon gang members raided the Golden Star bar, a Freemason hideout, and shot eleven of Liu's followers in a one-minute assault. Herbert Liu claimed the shooting was the work of then seventy-four-year-old Ong. Uncle 7 denied everything, but he did ask rhetorically, "Sixty years I build up respect, and he thinks he knock me down in one day?"

Liu was finished as a major Chinatown power broker. His forces were too weak to respond to the Hip Sing offensive. It was a significant loss of face. Ong had eliminated the Freemasons as competitors. American law enforcement was about to do Ong another favor by finishing off Fast Eddie Chan.

In October 1984 the President's Commission on Organized Crime heard public testimony that named Chan as the chief of organized crime in Chinatown. In one hour of testimony, Chan's carefully constructed cover life as a prosperous Chinatown businessman, whose generosity in campaign contributions and lobbying efforts on behalf of Chinese-Americans had propelled him into the company of leading New York and national public figures, was shattered. He refused to answer subpoenas to appear before the investigating commission. The public started a panic run on his bank, and the police had to close its doors permanently to stop a near riot. Rumors abounded that Chan was resigning from his businesses and abandoning his social positions. The President's Commission put a warrant out compelling his testimony before the panel. For the hierarchy of Chinatown, men who lived in and relished anonymous shadows, the media's glare of publicity was unwelcome. Chan was publicly accused and had lost face in the Chinese community. No shots had to be fired. No threats were made against him. It was a matter of honor—he had to leave.

By November 1984, Fast Eddie Chan was missing in New York. He had left the United States for an undisclosed location. His restaurants and jewelry store and funeral home are still open and operating under the same names, but no one claims to know Chan's name. Sightings reported in law-enforcement files have placed him at numerous locations around the world. The Dutch believe he is safely operating a crime empire in Malaysia. The Hong Kong police believe he splits his time between Canada and Taiwan. The New York police believe he is in the Dominican Republic, still monitoring the remnants of his crime empire on the eastern seaboard. Some DEA intelligence analysts think he has established a new heroin network in France, with access to the lucrative Dutch market.

Wherever Fast Eddie Chan is today, his departure from New York left Benny "Uncle 7" Ong as the chief statesman and elder of Chinatown. Now retired as chief of the Hip Sing Tong, the seventy-eight-year-old Ong still wields the most power in the American Chinese community.

A DEA analyst told me, "If there is a godfather in Chinatown, it's Benny Ong. You'll never prove it, but everyone knows it. Eddie Chan was big news until he left New York. And Herbert Liu made some noise for a while. But Benny survived them all and is still there. He is from the old school, where you still respect your elders. And in his way of thinking, that means everyone has to follow his orders since he is the main elder left."

Intelligence files gathered by the federal investigators in San Francisco pinpoint Benny Ong as the most likely chairman of a national commission controlling Tong activities. Benny Ong's loyal service has earned him a preeminent position in the Chinese-American community.

"But what we are worried about is not Benny Ong," a DEA agent told me in Washington. "Benny knows how to keep things within control in the Chinatowns. The guys you have to worry about are the Eddie Chans. The young fellows who want everything and want it right away. They don't respect any of the old-timers and they want to expand all the criminal businesses. They aren't content with a few gambling halls in Chinatown. They want to be the godfathers of America. It's the Young Turks who are going to be real troublesome."

The Young Turks prepared for their future drive in a 1983 summit meeting called by the Hong Kong Triads. The dragon head of the Luen Kung Lok Triad, Lau Wing-kui, summoned a conference of the up-and-coming Chinese talent in the United States. Lau was a notorious Hong Kong casino operator before he fled a growing criminal investigation in the mid-1970s. He settled in Canada where he realized the potential of the North American market. But a 1979 magazine exposé pinpointed him as a Triad boss and a drug trafficker, and he fled to the Dominican Republic. In his Dominican sanctuary he controlled a casino in Santo Domingo and became friends with Fast Eddie Chan in New York. By 1981 he had returned to Hong Kong and was pleased to discover that the investigation that had caused him to flee had been forgotten. While settling back into the British colony, he decided to expand Triad influence in his old home, North America. He called the summit meeting to coordinate policies in the United States and Canada and enhance cooperation between the Hong Kong syndicates and the American bosses.

In January 1983 five young Chinese checked into the ultramodern Miramar Hotel on the Kowloon side of Hong Kong territory. Confidential Hong Kong police reports identify the five and describe their roles in the Chinese-American community. The most promising of the group was Vincent Jew, thirty-one years old, an American citizen who was reportedly the chief of the largest Chinese youth gang in North America, the Wah Ching. A second arrival at the Miramar was Danny Mo, alleged dragon head of the Kung Lok Triad in Canada, and the North American middleman for arranging the summit. The third man to enter the British colony was Pai Shing Ping, a nightclub owner from the California sanctuary of Monterey Park. Lee Yoo Ting took a suite at the hotel. He is a prominent actor in Taiwan, with reputed ties to the United Bamboo Triad. Peter Man was the fifth attendee, a San Francisco restaurant owner and major money man in California. Tony Young, the Toronto Wah Ching leader, had been at the hotel but left before the summit. Tin Lung, chief of Boston's Ping On gang, was due to attend but canceled at the last moment. New York was not represented because there was open warfare on the streets between Benny Ong's Hip Sing Tong and Herbert Liu's Freemasons.

The Hong Kong police intelligence division, tipped off by Canadian authorities about the meeting, monitored the group at the Miramar's restaurant. They discovered the meeting was called as part of a general trend by the Triads to enforce a more tightly controlled and traditional criminal structure. The Hong Kong summit involved discussions of territorial rights and ways to enhance cooperation between the Hong Kong syndicates and the new American leaders. The Hong Kong police raided the meeting and arrested and questioned all those present. Although Hong Kong police believe that all of the meeting's attendees were Triad members, a criminal offense in Hong Kong, they were all subsequently released without any charges. The exception was Peter Man, who was carrying small amounts of cocaine and marijuana.

The new Chinese who will eventually replace the aging figures like Benny Ong are a young and ruthless class. Many of them received their education on the streets in youth gangs. They moved to the top of the gangs and now have turned themselves into legitimate businessmen. A few fell along the way. Nicky Louie, the rising twenty-one-year-old star of New York's Ghost Shadows, had survived thirteen assassination attempts. But he was arrested and convicted under racketeering laws by the U.S. Attorney's Office in New York and is serving a long prison sentence. One of the other rising stars in the New York gangs scene, Peter Chin, was also arrested, tried, and convicted, and jail has stopped his career. But other young Chinese-Americans seem unstoppable.

The Hong Kong police files claim that Danny Mo is still a Triad boss in Canada. He has not been arrested. American and Hong Kong records allege William Tse is chief of the Luen Kung Lok Triad in Los Angeles, and Stephen Tse is a Triad member and gang boss in Boston. They have yet to be charged with crimes. Tony Young has been identified in Hong Kong papers as the chief of the Wah Ching in San Francisco and Toronto, but no law-enforcement agency has moved against him. And the most powerful of the new group may be Vincent Jew, now thirty-four. Jew runs a legitimate entertainment company in San Francisco and effectively represents all Asian entertainers performing in the United States. Sergeant John McKenna, the former chief of the San Francisco gang task force, told me, "Vincent is the best of the new generation. The movie role in *The Year of the Dragon*, the young good-looking guy in a white suit—that's Vincent Jew. And no one can prove anything on him."

A senior police intelligence officer in San Francisco told me, "Jew is smooth, real smooth. He could talk his way out of anything. He's very impressive. Suave, handsome, very sophisticated. He has a nice suburban house, a wife, a luxury car, a nice watch, all the signs of a good young businessman. There are files on him in a half-dozen law-enforcement agencies but no one can prove enough even for an indictment."

A 1983 confidential Hong Kong police report states, "Information on Jew from the Americans and Canadians is scant. The FBI considers him to be ARMED AND DANGEROUS, while the RCMP [Royal Canadian Mounted Police] believe him to be the leader of the Wah Ching in San Francisco and to be involved with Toronto, New York, and Boston in the videotape business and Hong Kong performers." A New York policeman with more than ten years of service on Chinese gangs and organized crime believes that Jew is a new kingpin: "I think he is one of the best coming up. He may never be charged with anything because I think he is just too smart to get caught at anything illegal. But one day he may have the same control and influence over the Chinese-American community as Benny Ong does now."

Jackie Chan, a well-known Hong Kong actor who claimed to have been threatened by Vincent Jew, told the Hong Kong police, "Vincent Jew told me he was chairman of the Wah Ching, and when asked what the Wah Ching was, he said it's the same as the 14K. If you come from the Hong Kong 14K, you join the Wah Ching and vice versa."

Hong Kong police monitor Jew on his visits to Southeast Asia. The FBI had an intelligence tip in January 1986 that Jew was about to rendezvous in Hong Kong with a pair of Chinese brothers involved in Atlantic City crime. The three arrived in Hong Kong in December 1985, but no meeting took place.

Vincent Jew was also subpoenaed by the President's Commission on Organized Crime, but he fled the country at the time so that he was unavailable to testify. His absence made him impervious to a bench warrant for his arrest seeking to force his testimony. After the government inquiry disbanded, he returned peacefully to the United States. While Eddie Chan fled the country, Vincent Jew returned to a peaceful and comfortable life in northern California.

"Some of the Triads may be coming here in 1997," a DEA agent in San Francisco told me. "But they aren't going to find it all that easy to take over here. They are going to have a lot of troubles with the Tongs and with the new Young Turks who think this is their country. They aren't going to take kindly to new syndicates trying to run the businesses. The new guys here are every bit as good as anyone in Hong Kong. It's not going to be a cakewalk for the Hong Kong boys. There's a lot of top talent already here and developing in America. We've already got our hands full."

16

The Challenge

The war against Triads cannot be waged effectively by any one country. It is an international problem—from Kuhn Sa and General Li, with their Golden Triangle opium armies, to the Bangkok syndicates that serve as the first stopover for tons of heroin, to White Powder Ma and the Five Dragons in the sanctuary of Taiwan and the Unicorn's successors in Europe, to the Tong bosses in the United States. The Chinese crime dragon has systematically spread its tentacles around the world. Unfortunately, law-enforcement efforts are disjointed and seriously flawed.

There is little international police cooperation. Interpol, the only worldwide police effort, is a mere data bank. It is not active in narcotics suppression. Interpol earmarks less than one-third of its budget to combat drugs and Triads. It has little control over member countries. For instance, when Hong Kong served an arrest warrant for White Powder Ma through Interpol, it hoped to force Taiwan, then a member country, to extradite the Triad dragon head. Taiwan merely refused, and Interpol was powerless to enforce the warrant.

Little better than Interpol is the United Nations. The U.N. invests $20 million a year in combating drug abuse at the user level. Its efforts are marked by a lack of success, as the number of addicts continues to climb in almost all countries. The U.N. makes no effort to encourage eradication or suppression efforts, and most of the teeth are taken out of the toughest antidrug proposals by squabbling among nations.

Aside from Interpol and the United Nations, the fight against Triads and the heroin kingpins is left to the private law-enforcement agencies of various countries. The largest single effort is mounted by the U.S. Drug Enforcement Administration. It has more than 2,500 agents, with 250 concentrated in Southeast Asia and Latin America. The DEA benefits from a large budget, including a $25 million fund with which to buy tips from informants. The agency is also assisted by the largest computer data bank on narcotics traffickers in the world, containing more than 1.6 million records. Yet the DEA has had limited success in its foreign efforts.

In almost every country in which it operates, the Drug Enforcement Administration serves only as a liaison and advisory office, and is prohibited from becoming operational. Thailand and Mexico are exceptions. Yet even there only a handful of agents must work within the restrictions of the host country's laws. Weak statutes and corrupt local police often wreak havoc with DEA efforts. Most countries do not allow the seizure of assets, a crucial tool in fighting money-laden drug dealers. Many of the key producing and transshipment countries do not have effective conspiracy laws. Others restrict wiretaps, police surveillance, and the scope of undercover operations. Some have lenient sentencing that allows major criminals to go free within a few years.

Within the DEA there are only a handful of Triad "experts" who understand the nature of Chinese organized crime and the narcotics threat. Ben Yarbrough and his dedicated team did their best at the mouth of the Golden Triangle. But they were admittedly only a "finger in the dike." The DEA limits foreign tours of duty to a maximum of six years. A Hong Kong-born agent told me that when he was stationed in the British colony, just at the point he felt he had made sufficient high-level contacts to develop major cases, he was transferred to another country. All of his preparatory work was lost. Moreover, the agency does not automatically send Chinese or Thai agents to Southeast Asia, nor does it assign agents with knowledge and interest in a subject to work in the area of their expertise. So it is possible to be an expert on Triads and Chinese traffickers but to end up in Turkey fighting Southwest Asian heroin. The DEA hierarchy believes the limits on tours of duty and the random placements make it difficult for criminals to establish ongoing corrupt relationships with agents.

The DEA has some excellent agents to engage in the fight against Triads. The chief of a special New York City task force on Chinese traffickers speaks fluent Mandarin and Cantonese and is acknowledged as one of the leading Triad experts in America. The intelligence analysts in both Hong Kong and Chiang Mai are walking encyclopedias on the inside of the Chinese crime business. But unfortunately these experts are the exception. Until Chinese traffickers and Southeast Asian heroin are targeted as higher priorities, the DEA enforcement efforts will continue to lag.

The DEA promotes agents based on a point system that forces them to focus on crime groups that receive the most media attention. An agent posted to a U.S. city must prioritize the trafficking groups in his jurisdiction, and then show that he has made progress against those groups. If Chicago newspapers and television shows highlight only a Mexican heroin connection, there are few agents who will concentrate on the Chinese connection. Arresting a group of Mexican traffickers may not be as important as breaking a Tong network, but for the Chicago agent it will guarantee media coverage, points for a promotion, and commendations from the Washington headquarters.

Also, aside from the promotion system, there is a natural tendency for agents to concentrate on the flashiest traffickers. Those arrests receive the most press coverage and result in official commendations. Evening news clips are often filled with groups of Colombians or Bolivians carted off in front of the cameras with a jacket or sweater hiding their faces. Then the next television pictures are invariably of the successful agents in front of a table stacked with bags of cocaine, piles of cash, and an assortment of high-tech automatic weapons. This is the press relations battle waged by law enforcement. Although the media-intensive war has little effect on the drug warlords, it is unfortunately the focus of Washington politicians when it comes time for annual budget discussions. The DEA hierarchy understands that no congressional budget committee will take the time to listen to a group of agents explain how important it was to arrest two elderly Chinese Tong members and their half kilo of heroin.

"Instead, the politicians just want to know how much dope you have seized and how many people you've arrested," a DEA agent told me in Washington. "You better be able to tell them that the figures are going up each year. They understand seizures and arrests, but they'll never take the time to understand the inside of an international network you have just busted. They want it simple. No complexities. Just who's the good guy and who's the bad guy, and if you can't give it to them real simple, then their eyes glaze over.

"So what do you think the average [DEA] supervisor is going to spend his time on? Trying to get inside a culture that no one understands and a language no one speaks, in the hope that we may be able to break a foreign connection that no one cares about? Or do you think he might concentrate on the young Spanish kids with flashy sports cars and gold chains, importing 500 kilos from Colombia every other month? It's always going to be the high-profile kid. It's one of the reasons that the Chinese have gotten away with it for so long. They know that a lot of our efforts are directed at crime figures the public understands. That's why the Chinese don't want to be publicized or understood. If you are a DEA agent and make a case against a bunch of Italian hoods, then everyone congratulates you. They've all seen the *The Godfather,* and everyone knows about the Mafia. But you go home and tell your wife you've arrested a couple of five-foot-five Oriental guys whose names she's never heard of and can't even pronounce, and you get a big shrug of the shoulders. That's about the same response you get from your superiors."

The DEA is slowly starting to realize that its emphasis on cocaine, marijauna, and the Italian Mafia has been mistaken. The Chinese have quietly taken over half of the heroin market and the DEA is barely prepared for the rest of the Triad assault. With more than half a million hard-core addicts in the United States annually consuming eight tons of the narcotic, heroin has become the forgotten epidemic. Largely ignored by the press since 1980, heroin's international popularity has never been higher.

The chief agent for New York, Robert Stuttman, recognizes the problem: "These groups pose a major challenge to law enforcement. We are now dealing in languages and cultures we don't have real depth in. Chinese has a number of dialects that are very different, and agents with a knowledge of Chinese are few and far between." In 1983, Southeast Asian heroin made up

3 percent of the New York market. By 1987 it was 40 percent. By 1988 China White had jumped to almost 70 percent. "It's one of the most dramatic and significant turnarounds I have seen in law enforcement," said Stuttman.

The DEA is not the only federal agency with its hands full. The FBI has lagged far behind in pursuing the Triads and did not issue a report on the problem until 1985. In 1986, for the first time in its history, the FBI listed organized Chinese trafficking groups as a priority law-enforcement target. The customs service has few Chinese experts. The IRS cannot make a dent in U.S. money-laundering, much less crack the sophisticated Hong Kong banking system.

Even when they decide to target Triads and Southeast Asian heroin, law-enforcement agencies conduct operations that end in squabbles and disagreements. The criminals often go free. At times two separate agencies pursue investigations on the same person or network and refuse to share crucial information, each hoping to break the case first and take credit. Even when they cooperate the investigations are often pulled in different directions. The IRS may want to emphasize the money angle, while customs may be concerned only with narcotics arriving at a port. As a result they often spend their time pursuing different leads and duplicate many efforts. Occasionally arrests are made prematurely, allowing the "big fish" to get away. This is often because one agency has jumped the gun and tried to beat another in closing the case. Sometimes one DEA regional office even acts hastily to beat another regional office working on the same case. Different federal agencies take credit for their successes without acknowledging intelligence or cooperation from others.

The situation has deteriorated so that in some cases one agency actually investigates and arrests the undercover agents from another. This happens most frequently between DEA and Customs. As a rule the U.S. Customs Service conducts undercover work by selling narcotics and finding buyers. Customs wants to uncover importers. Meanwhile, DEA undercover work involves buying narcotics, because the DEA wants to discover significant wholesalers. Sometimes a DEA undercover agent will "buy" heroin from a customs "dope dealer," each group then trying to arrest the other.

While federal efforts are hampered by competition and fragmentation, the war on Triads is virtually nonexistent for state and local police. Officials at the state level have generally been uninterested in organized Chinese crime and heroin trafficking. An exception is California's Attorney General John Van de Kamp. He is the first state official to recognize the international nature of the problem and to try to gear his force to deal with it. But Van de Kamp's efforts stand alone. There is no cooperation between states on the movement of Chinese criminals or on the influx of Southeast Asian narcotics. There are no joint operations under way, and most state law-enforcement agencies do not even have a single person knowledgeable about the Triads.

As for the local police, they are concerned with crime in their own cities and not with what happens a hundred or a thousand miles away. It is hard to convince a New York City policeman that his Chinese gang problem is part of a nationwide network and that he should cooperate with investigations in other cities. If the local police are investigating a major criminal and he moves to another city, taking his illegal operation with him, that is as good as if he was arrested or died. Few local police have the energy or desire to continue an investigation once it becomes somebody else's problem. Certainly no Los Angeles police captain is going to commend his detectives for removing a major crime figure in Detroit. The police are worried about their own problems. Moreover, many police fear that if the investigation gets too large, then federal agents will step in and take over the case. In those instances the local police lose all control and serve as deputies to the federal agency.

One of the few local policemen who understood the seriousness of the Triad problem, and cooperated with police across the United States and in Canada, was San Francisco's John McKenna. Sergeant Barry Hill in Toronto, Detective Joe Carone in Chicago, and Detective John McVeety in New York are others who are working hard to stop a problem they realize stretches far beyond their municipal borders. But McKenna retired in 1986 and left a void on the West Coast. And the other police who are as savvy are, unfortunately, far and few between.

The underlying problem is that all local and state law-enforcement agencies have small jurisdictional viewpoints, while criminals think and operate internationally. The federal agencies that have the ability to approach the problem from a worldwide stance

254 WARLORDS OF CRIME

believe they are competing with one another for a limited piece
of the law-enforcement budget. In the view of most federal law-
enforcement officials, Congress allocates only a limited budget
for catching criminals and locking up narcotics traffickers. To
get the lion's share you have to be "better" than the other federal divisions. This competition between the DEA, FBI, IRS, Immigration and Naturalization, and the Customs Service works to
the criminals' advantage. There are few enough experts on Triads in the entire federal government; their effectiveness should
not be limited by placing them at odds with one another.

Eliminating the Triads and the heroin epidemic with a fragmented and sporadic police effort may not be possible. An effective law-enforcement battle will confront numerous obstacles
at many stages, but a number of significant improvements can
be made in the way in which the war is conducted. Initially there
is the issue of the source, the poppy fields that create 1,500 tons
of opium each year. They present the clearest chance to eliminate the heroin flow. When the chain of events is still at the opium
poppy, it is possible to see hundreds of thousands of acres and
to take action against them. Opium farmers make no attempt to
conceal their crops, and the locations of the poppy fields are
known to governments and law-enforcement agencies. But once
the poppy is converted into kilos of heroin and mixes in with
hundreds of thousands of tons of regular commerce and millions of international passengers, stopping the flow becomes too
costly and inefficient.

The United States should organize eradication efforts in the
Golden Triangle. It should also encourage crop substitution, together with education programs for the hill tribes, and an active
development program for presenting them with alternative crops
and markets in which to sell the new crops. For the hill tribes, it
is basically a matter of economics. They are the only persons in
the heroin chain who do not reap enormous profits. The kilo of
China White that sells for $2.5 million on the streets of America
is refined from only $900 of raw opium. If the farmers could
make more money by growing coffee or beans instead of culti-
vating opium, they would abandon the drug. The United States
should make a concerted effort to ensure that the hill tribes are
financially induced to grow crops other than opium. A viable alternative would be for the United States to pay the hill tribes not

to grow opium. It would cost only $75 million to pay the Golden Triangle farmers the going price not to grow poppies. That payment would annually eliminate 70 percent of the world's heroin. Considering that New York addicts steal a billion dollars a year to maintain their habits, it might not be such a bad investment.

To those countries that refuse to cooperate in an intensive effort to eliminate poppy cultivation, the United States should consider cutting off economic and military aid. The heroin flow is an epidemic. If producing countries need American aid, they should respond to efforts to stop the drug's flow at its source.

The United States should also stop any covert intelligence support to General Li's KMT army and to Kuhn Sa's Shan United Army. These two major trafficking groups always boast a current supply of the latest American weapons. If the CIA is not providing the weapons through front companies, then it certainly knows which country is sending part of their U.S. arms purchases to the Golden Triangle. If Taiwan is diverting U.S. weapons to the heroin armies, then a cutoff of military aid to Taiwan might be appropriate.

Effective international law enforcement would require a revamping of many disparate judicial codes. The United States has an excellent law, the RICO statute, which allows someone to be indicted and jailed for being part of a criminal enterprise. The key members of New York's Ghost Shadows, including gang leader Nicky Louie, were jailed under this law. The United States stands alone with this important law-enforcement tool. In addition to passing RICO-type codes, countries should strengthen and broaden their conspiracy statutes. Moreover, seizure of assets in drug cases should be used as a legal battering ram. The burden of proof in IRS-type cases should always be on the individual, not on the government.

Extradition treaties should be universal for drug trafficking. Countries such as Taiwan that afford sanctuary to corrupt policemen and to drug and crime kingpins should be international pariahs, as much as South Africa is for its apartheid policies. Sentencing laws should also be strengthened. While countries with the death penalty have noticed a sharp decline in trafficking, capital punishment may not be an acceptable moral choice for all nations. But certainly a maximum of twelve years, such as in the Netherlands, is too little for major drug dealers.

Even in those countries with strict laws and adequate sentences, the system must be capable of enforcing the statutes. For instance, in New York State, which has some of the harshest drug laws in America, the odds are that if you are arrested for a narcotics felony, three out of four times you will not go to jail. There has been an almost total breakdown in New York's criminal justice system. In 1985 there were 85,000 misdemeanor drug arrests, but only three judges available for trial. Only one-half of 1 percent of all cases ever get tried. Some traffickers are arrested eighteen and twenty times and are back on the street with a suspended sentence. The answer, therefore, is not only tough laws and long sentences for trafficking in narcotics but also a system large enough to handle the number of arrests and impose the maximum sentences. This assumes there is also an adequate jail system that can accommodate the new convicts. In the United States the prison system is already overcrowded and at the breaking point.

In addition to fighting drugs at the source and in the courts of different countries, it is also crucial to fight it among the addict populations. Public education must be expanded. Recent newspaper reports claim that "chasing the dragon" has grown in popularity with elite sets in Hollywood and New York. For $1,500 a gram, wealthy risk takers are moving beyond cocaine to a newer and more dangerous thrill. The DEA is also discovering that Chinese traffickers are mixing smokable forms of China White into vials of crack, thereby giving thousands of inner-city youths a taste for heroin. Education is crucial in showing the Hollywood starlet with too much money, as well as the unemployed teenager in the South Bronx, that heroin kills.

Aside from education that tries to keep heroin use from spreading, rehabilitation programs must be expanded. Only a fraction of New York City's addicts can be treated at government-subsidized methadone clinics. If methadone substitution was readily available, the profit in the heroin market could be kicked out from under the Chinese Triads. But governments do not want to spend that much money to help cure heroin addicts of their disease.

Suggestions for improving law enforcement and government efforts against the Triads may have little chance of being implemented. Hong Kong intelligence reports estimate the Triad's heroin profits as $80 billion and pinpoints another $20 to $25 billion from gambling, prostitution, and other organized crime enterprises. A $100 billion criminal syndicate can challenge law enforcement in untold ways. The money buys assistance from police officials, prosecutors, judges, and government officials. Pervasive corruption allows the Triads' illegal empire to thrive. Poppy eradication efforts will continue to be ineffective. The Golden Triangle opium armies will still carry the latest American weapons. Laws between countries will likely never be uniform. Police agencies will probably continue to fight one another as much as they fight the criminals.

It has been seventeen years since President Nixon first declared a war on "public enemy number one," heroin. Despite the full commitment of American law enforcement to crack the heroin syndicates, they remain largely unchallenged. A bad crop in the Golden Triangle does more to cut Triad profits than any single law-enforcement effort. Eventually, AIDS may also do what law enforcement has been unable to do. Officials estimate that more than 60 percent of U.S. intravenous addicts may be infected with the deadly virus. If current projections of near total fatality are borne out over the next two decades, AIDS will do more than anything in history to reduce the heroin market and take away the Triads' major business. It is a disgrace that a deadly disease may achieve what police agencies and governments cannot.

As for the other Triad organized crime enterprises, aside from drug trafficking, law enforcement must approach them the same way it approaches traditional organized crime. Triads must be targeted as a priority. The same operations that have worked against Italian organized crime, i.e., informants and undercover penetration of the syndicates, must be employed against organized Chinese criminals in America. An active effort to recruit Chinese agents and officers must be made. New York cannot effectively wage a war on Triads with just over thirty Chinese-speaking officers on a police force of almost 27,000. By 1985, Los Angeles had more than 500,000 Asian immigrants, but the Asian Task Force counted only fifteen members and only four Chinese. With numbers like this, U.S. law enforcement cannot expect to fight the current Chinese crime problem, much less the expected influx of Triads by 1997.

An effort must also be made within the Chinatowns to educate the public to report crimes. One hopes that law-enforcement agencies and local government administrations will be viewed as friends, not foes, by a new generation of Chinese. The citizens of the Chinatowns must stand unified and refuse to allow themselves to be victimized in silence any longer.

U.S. law enforcement should also make a concerted effort to take advantage of the forty years of modern-day experience the British and Hong Kong Chinese have had in fighting Triads. Although they have not always been successful, there is little question that the Hong Kong police know more about Triads than any other police agency in the world. By 1997 the police hierarchy will be different, and many current Triad experts will retire. Mainland China may limit access to files and records. Yet, even though the time to seek the assistance of the Hong Kong police is now, few American law-enforcement agencies have sought their help.

Tony Lee, a senior superintendent in the Hong Kong intelligence division, told me, "American law-enforcement agencies are terrible in coming to us for any help. And when they do come they generally have no understanding of Triads or how to approach them. For instance, in the United States the most important piece of identification you can have on a criminal is a fingerprint. If we were looking for an American criminal in Hong Kong, we would get a fingerprint from the States and match it to the person here. Well, for us, there is something as important as the fingerprint. It is the Chinese characters of someone's name. Since there is no standardized way of translating a Chinese character to English, the names in different police files look totally different. The Chinese character that represents the name pronounced 'Ing' is spelled by different people in different ways, including 'Eng,' most commonly 'Ng,' but I've also seen it as 'Ong,' as 'Eing,' and even as 'Enq.'

"So when a U.S. law-enforcement agency is seeking information on a Chinese criminal or Triad member, they must give us the person's Chinese name in Chinese characters. Even though we ask for this all the time, we always get requests in English and usually with the person's adopted American name. There's no way for us to find the information. We get requests, then we tell them you must give us the Chinese characters, and then we don't hear from them for six months until we get another request in English. It's crazy. In America they can't even ask us for the right name of a file on someone, much less work with us in catching the guys. It's the same with the Europeans. I don't know what they are going to do when the real Triads move in."

Although there are serious deficiencies in efforts to fight Triads, law enforcement is starting to realize there is a new and dangerous problem, and it is only going to get worse before 1997. At the end of 1986, Canada issued a Triad alert. Police intelligence identified eleven Chinese syndicates with connections to established organized crime, and the Canadian police highlighted their fear of the possible criminal exodus from Hong Kong. In 1985 the West German equivalent of the FBI issued a statement acknowledging that Turkish heroin, the traditional source of most of Germany's addiction problem, had been replaced by Southeast Asian heroin. The Chinese were recognized as a new criminal threat. In the autumn of 1986 a London police report listed Triads as "a network of fear and violence" and stated that the "law-abiding majority are afraid to speak." Scotland Yard identified the Wo Triad as the number one criminal syndicate in Britain, with the 14K, Sun Yee On, and Shui Fong close on its heels. The British concluded that the Triads were conducting a "campaign of terror" in London. By 1986 the Australian government officially complained that it had become a major Triad base as the exodus from Hong Kong increased. Members of the Australian Parliament criticized Hong Kong for not assisting in halting the flow of criminal talent out of the colony. In 1987 the Dutch released another report on the Triads, acknowledging that the Chinese still controlled organized crime and the heroin trade in the Netherlands.

United States law-enforcement agencies have begun to acknowledge the seriousness of the problem. In 1986 the FBI admitted Hong Kong Triads were a "grave problem" and that the United States faced "extremely dangerous consequences" if the Triads cooperated with traditional organized crime in America. John Van de Kamp, the California attorney general, issued a report in 1985 that stated, "Communist China will not tolerate the criminal activity of these organizations. Triad members are expected to migrate to California cities with large Asian populations." The attorney general highlighted major problems with the Wo Triad in Southern California, the Luen Kung Lok Triad in money-laundering in Los Angeles, the 14K in nightclubs around the state, and the United Bamboo in Los Angeles, San Francisco,

Monterey Park, and Daly City. By 1987, Van de Kamp heightened his warning. He said that Asian gangs had grown more powerful than La Cosa Nostra. He cited police fears of an "upsurge
in migration of Hong Kong's large, well-organized, and notoriously violent Triad gangs when the British colony reverts to
Chinese control in 1997.... There has not been a mass exodus
of criminals on this scale since 1980, when Fidel Castro opened
up his prisons and flushed the worst elements of Cuban society,
the 'Marielitos,' into Florida, and Miami is still struggling to recover from that catastrophe. Unless we send word across the Pacific that this is a dangerous and inhospitable place for gangs to
do business, the stage could be set for our own 'Marielito'-style
disaster in California."

America was slow in recognizing the Triad threat. Thomas
Kolaslu, chief of a federal Organized Crime Task Force, remem-
bered the delay in responding to the assault: "Since the fighters
of big-time organized crime were concentrating their efforts on
the Mafia, it was not until 1975 that U.S. crime-busters began
to realize that the Chinese Triads were possibly a far more formidable enemy than the infamous Sicilian brotherhood. Some
of the facets of the Tongs in San Francisco's Chinatown are
more effective, efficient, and sophisticated than the Mafia ever
dreamed of."

William Weld, the former chief of the Criminal Division for
the U.S. Department of Justice, echoed the fear that law enforcement has been caught unprepared: "With all the pressure on La
Cosa Nostra, we're looking down the road several years and won-
dering if the Asians may replace them. This concern is real."

By late 1986, U.S. law-enforcement agencies had joined those
of Britain, Australia, Canada, the Netherlands, and West Germany in being on a Triad alert. San Francisco's John McKenna
told a Senate investigating committee that "time is running out,
1997 is not that far away." Tom Sheer of the FBI told the sen-
ators, "They [Triads] can't operate under a totalitarian regime
as they can in a free democratic society. And that's why we'll have
an influx of organized crime gangs." The Manhattan district attorney declared in 1987 that New York's number one drug-
trafficking threat came from the Chinese.

"The Chinese have put together a criminal venture that is well-
defined, highly sophisticated and ruthless," said Detective James

Brady of Arlington, Virginia's, gang task force. "It has the potential of making the Mafia in America look like a fraternity of wimps."

A DEA agent summed it up: "Chinese criminals have hundreds of years of history and tradition behind them. They are willing to take risks, and they follow their leaders with blind obedience. It's just a matter of time before they take over. What we've seen so far is just the head of the dragon, you can be sure of that."

In 1985, Jon Elder, the police chief from Monterey Park, California, where Chinese Triads have invaded, had no doubts about what the future held: "Asian organized crime will end up being the number one organized crime problem in North America in the next five years. In my humble opinion, they'll make the Sicilian Mafia look like a bunch of Sunday-school kids." So far, his prediction is right on target.

Bibliography

BOOKS AND PAMPHLETS

Alexander, Garth. *The Invisible China: The Overseas Chinese and the Politics of Southeast Asia.* New York: Macmillan, 1973.

Ashman, Charles. *The CIA-Mafia Link.* New York: Manor Books, 1975.

Bastin, John, and Harry J. Benda. *A History of Modern Southeast Asia.* Englewood Cliffs, N.J.: Prentice-Hall, 1968.

Beeching, Jack. *The Chinese Opium Wars.* New York: Harcourt, Brace, Jovanovich, 1975.

Bianco, Lucien. *Origins of the Chinese Revolution: 1945–1949.* Stanford, Calif.: Stanford University Press, 1971.

Bloodworth, Dennis. *An Eye for the Dragon: Southeast Asia Observed.* New York: Farrar, Strauss & Giroux, 1970.

Blythe, Wilfred. *The Impact of Chinese Secret Societies in Malaya.* London: Oxford University Press, 1969.

Botjer, George. *A Short History of Nationalist China: 1919–1949.* New York: G. P. Putnam's Sons, 1979.

Bozan, Jian, et al. *A Concise History of China.* Peking: Foreign Languages Press, 1981.

Bresler, Fenton. *The Chinese Mafia.* Briarcliff Manor, N.Y.: Stein & Day, 1981.

Chesneaux, Jean, et al. *China from the 1911 Revolution to Liberation.* New York: Pantheon Books, 1977.

———. *China from the Opium Wars to the 1911 Revolution.* New York: Pantheon Books, 1976.

———, ed. *Popular Movements and Secret Societies in China, 1840–1950.* Stanford, Calif.: Stanford University Press, 1972.

Coye, Molly Joel, and Jon Livingston, eds. *China Yesterday and Today.* New York: Bantam Books, 1979.

Darling, Frank C. *Thailand and the United States.* Washington, D.C.: Public Affairs Press, 1965.

Embree, John F., and William L. Thomas, Jr. *Ethnic Groups of Northern Southeast Asia.* New Haven: Yale University Press, Southeast Asian Studies, 1950.

Epstein, Edward Jay. *Agency of Fear: Opiates and Political Power in America.* New York: G. P. Putnam's Sons, 1977.

Furuya, Keija. *Chiang Kai-shek: His Life and Times.* Annapolis, Md.: St. John's University Press, 1981.

Girling, John L. S. *Thailand: Society and Politics.* Ithaca, N.Y.: Cornell University Press, 1976.

Goldsmith, Margaret. *The Trail of Opium.* London: Robert Hale Unlimited, 1939.

Hahn, Emily. *Chiang Kai-shek: An Unauthorized Biography.* Garden City, N.Y.: Doubleday, 1955.

Hauser, Ernest. *Shanghai: City for Sale.* New York: Harcourt Brace, 1940.

Hill Tribes of Thailand. Chiang Mai, Thailand: Tribal Research Institute, 1986.

Hookham, Hilda. *A Short History of China.* New York: New American Library, 1972.

Isaacs, Arnold R. *Without Honor: Defeat in Vietnam and Cambodia.* Baltimore: Johns Hopkins University Press, 1983.

Kaplan, David E., and Alec Dubro. *Yakuza: The Explosive Account of Japan's Criminal Underworld.* Menlo Park, Calif.: Addison-Wesley, 1986.

Karnow, Stanley. *Vietnam: A History.* New York: Macmillan, 1982.

Keyes, Charles F. *The Golden Peninsula: Culture and Adaptation in Mainland Southeast Asia.* New York: Macmillan, 1977.

Koen, Ross Y. *The China Lobby in American Politics.* New York: Macmillan, 1960.

Lamour, Catherine, and Michel Lamberti. *The Second Opium War.* London: Penguin Books, 1974.

Leary, William M. *Perilous Missions: Civil Air Transport and CIA Covert Operations in Asia.* University, Ala.: University of Alabama Press, 1984.

Lebar, Frank M., Gerald C. Hickey and John K. Musgrave. *Ethnic Groups of Mainland Southeast Asia.* New Haven: Human Relations Area Files Press, 1964.

Loh, Pichon P. Y. *The Early Chiang Kai-shek.* New York: Columbia University Press, 1971.

Lyman, Stanford M. *Chinese Americans.* New York: Random House, 1974.

Mackenzie, Norman. *Secret Societies.* New York: Holt, Rinehart and Winston, 1971.

Marchetti, Victor, and John D. Marks. *The CIA and the Cult of Intelligence.* New York: Dell Publishing Co., 1974.

McCoy, Alfred W. *Drug Traffic: Narcotics and Organized Crime in Australia.* Sydney, Australia: Harper & Row, 1980.

———. *The Politics of Heroin in Southeast Asia.* New York: Harper & Row, 1972.

Moscow, Alvin. *Merchants of Heroin.* New York: Dial Press, 1968.

Musto, David M. *The American Disease: The Origins of Narcotics Control.* New Haven: Yale University Press, 1973.

Nees, Brett De Barry and Victor G. *Longtime Califorń.* Boston: Houghton Mifflin Co., 1974.

Nelli, Humbert S. *The Business of Crime.* Chicago: University of Chicago Press, 1976.

O'Callaghan, Sean. *The Triads.* London: W. H. Allen & Co., 1978.

The Opium War. Peking: Foreign Languages Press, 1976.

Owen, David Edward. *British Opium Policy in China and India.* New Haven: Yale University Press, 1934.

Punahitanond, S., C. Sitthi-Amorn, and Y. Onthuam. *An Interpretative Epidemiology of Drug Dependence in Thailand.* Bangkok: Institute of Health Research, Chulalongkorn University, 1978.

Purcell, Victor. *The Chinese in Southeast Asia*. London: Oxford University Press, 1951.

Ranelagh, John. *The Agency: The Rise and Decline of the CIA*. New York: Simon & Schuster, 1986.

Reid, Ed. *The Grim Reapers*. New York: Bantam Books, 1969.

Robertson, Frank. *Triangle of Death: The Inside Story of the Triads*. London: Routledge & Kegan Paul, Ltd., 1977.

Salisbury, Harrison E., ed. *Vietnam Reconsidered: Lessons from a War*. New York: Harper & Row, 1984.

Schriffrin, Harold Z. *Sun Yat-sen and the Origins of the Chinese Revolution*. Berkeley: University of California Press, 1970.

Scott, J. M. *The White Poppy*. London: William Heinemann, Ltd., 1969.

Seagrave, Sterling. *The Soong Dynasty*. New York: Harper & Row, 1985.

Siragusa, Charles. *The Trail of the Poppy*. Englewood Cliffs, N.J.: Prentice-Hall, 1966.

Skinner, G. William. *Chinese Society in Thailand: An Analytical History*. Ithaca, N.Y.: Cornell University Press, 1957.

———. *Leadership and Power in the Chinese Community in Thailand*. Ithaca, N.Y.: Cornell University Press, 1958.

Snepp, Frank. *Decent Interval: The American Debacle in Vietnam and the Fall of Saigon*. Harmondsworth, England: Penguin Books, 1980.

Spencer, C. P., and V. Navaratnum. *Drug Abuse in East Asia*. Kuala Lumpur, Malaysia: Oxford University Press, 1981.

Staunton, William. *The Triad Society or Heaven and Earth Association*. Hong Kong: Kelly and Walsh, Ltd., 1900.

Taylor, Robert H. *Foreign and Domestic Consequences of the KMT Intervention in Burma*. Data Paper No. 93. Southeast Asia Program, Cornell University, N.Y., 1973.

Trager, Frank N. *Burma: From Kingdom to Republic*. New York: Praeger, 1966.

Tuchman, Barbara W. *Stilwell and the American Experience in China: 1911–1945*. New York: Macmillan, 1970.

Waley, Arthur. *The Opium War Through Chinese Eyes*. New York: Macmillan, 1958.

Williams, Lea E. *The Future of the Overseas Chinese in Southeast Asia.* New York: McGraw-Hill, 1966.

Wise, David, and Thomas B. Ross. *The Invisible Government.* New York: Random House, 1964.

Young, Gordon. *The Hill Tribes of Northern Thailand.* Bangkok: Siam Society, 1969.

UNPUBLISHED DISSERTATION

Worobec, Stephen Francis. "International Narcotics Control in the Golden Triangle of Southeast Asia." Claremont University, 1984.

UNPUBLISHED OFFICIAL DOCUMENTS

"Analysis Report on the Central Registry for Drug Addicts, April 1972–March 1974." Hong Kong, 1974.

"Bureau of Narcotics and Dangerous Drugs. The World Opium Situation." Washington: undated.

Drug Enforcement Administration. "Heroin Source Identification for U.S. Heroin Market, 1972, 1973, 1974 and 1975." Washington: undated.

Royal Hong Kong Police. "Asian Crime/Gangs." Confidential document prepared for the Commissioner of Police by the Criminal Intelligence Bureau. May 12, 1986.

———. "The Chuk Luen Bong Triad Society." Criminal Intelligence Division, 1985.

———. "Discussion Document on Options for Changes in the Law and in the Administration of the Law to Counter the Triad Problem." April, 1986.

———. "Hong Kong Triads and Organized Crime: The 14K Triad Society." December 10, 1986.

———. "Organized Crime." Confidential document prepared for the Commissioner of Police by the Criminal Intelligence Bureau, May 2, 1986.

———. "Secret Societies." Confidential document prepared for the Commissioner of Police by the Criminal Intelligence Bureau, May 2, 1986.

San Francisco Police Department. "Asian Crime: Organized & Street Level." Intelligence—Gang Task Force, 1985.

United Nations Fund for Drug Abuse Control. "Crop Replacement and Community Development Project: Progress Report, September 1972–June 1973." Bangkok, 1973.

U.S. Department of Justice. Bureau of Narcotics and Dangerous Drugs, Strategic Intelligence Office. "Chemical Requirements for Opium Refining in Southeast Asia." 1972.

PUBLISHED OFFICIAL DOCUMENTS

Attorney General of California. Annual Report to the California Legislature. *Organized Crime in California.* 1982–1986.

——. *Triads—The Mafia of the Far East.* Criminal Intelligence Bulletin, 1973.

Brady, John J. *The U.S. Heroin Problem and Southeast Asia.* Report of a staff survey team of the Committee on Foreign Affairs, House of Representatives. Washington: U.S. Government Printing Office, 1973.

Bunge, Frederica M., ed. *Thailand: A Study Country.* Washington: U.S. Government Printing Office, 1981.

Cabinet Committee on International Narcotics Control. *World Opium Survey 1972.* .MDNM/Washington: U.S. Government Printing Office, 1972.

Department of Public Welfare. Ministry of Interior. *Hill Tribes and Welfare in Northern Thailand.* Bangkok, August 1971.

Federal Bureau of Investigation. Organized Crime Section, Criminal Investigative Division. *Oriental Organized Crime.* Washington: U.S. Department of Justice, January 1985.

Government of the Union of Burma. *Burma and the Insurrections.* Rangoon, 1949.

Hong Kong: First Report of the Commission of Inquiry Under Sir Alistair Blair-Kerr. Hong Kong Government Printer, 1973.

——. *White Paper on Triad Riots, 1956.* Hong Kong Government Printer, 1958.

——. *Narcotics Report.* Hong Kong: The Action Committee Against Narcotics, 1985.

——. *Second Report of the Commission of Inquiry Under Sir Alistair Blair-Kerr.* Hong Kong Government Printer, 1973.

Interpol. International Criminal Police Review. *Chinese Triad Societies.* October 1986.

Mansfield, Mike. *Postwar Southeast Asia.* Washington: U.S. Government Printing Office, 1971.

Morgan, W. P. *Triad Societies in Hong Kong.* Hong Kong Government Printer, 1964.

Murphy, Morgan F., and Robert H. Steele. *The World Heroin Problem.* Washington: U.S. Government Printing Office, 1971.

Report of the President's Commission on Organized Crime. *Organized Crime of Asian Origin.* Washington: U.S. Government Printing Office, October 1984.

Royal Hong Kong Police. *The Chuk Luen Bong Triad Society.* Hong Kong Government Printer, 1985.

——. *The Illicit Manufacture of Diacetylmorphine Hydrochloride. (No. 4 Grade),* undated.

——. *Triad Societies in Hong Kong.* Hong Kong Government Printer, 1974.

Singapore Police Force. *Chinese Secret Societies in Singapore.* Criminal Investigative Division, 1963.

The Strategy Council on Drug Abuse. *Federal Strategy for Drug Abuse and Drug Traffic Prevention, 1976.* Washington: U.S. Government Printing Office, 1976.

Thailand Narcotics Annual Report. Office of the Narcotics Control Board, Office of the Prime Minister, 1985.

Union of Burma. Ministry of Information. *Kuomintang Aggression Against Burma.* Rangoon, 1953.

United Nations. *Report of the International Narcotics Control Board. 1980– 1986.*

——. *Report of the United Nations Survey Team on the Economic and Social Needs of the Opium Producing Areas in Thailand.* Bangkok: Government Printing Office, 1968.

U.S. Central Intelligence Agency. Office of Current Intelligence. *Chinese Nationalist Irregulars in Southeast Asia.* Memorandum. OCI No. 3376-61. July 29, 1961. Declassified Document (77)162E.

U.S. Congress. *The Narcotics Situation in Southeast Asia: The Asian-Connection.* 94th Congress, 1st Session. Washington: U.S. Government Printing Office, 1975.

——. *Proposal to Control Opium from the Golden Triangle and Terminate the Shan Opium Trade.* 94th Congress, 1st Session. Washington: U.S. Government Printing Office, 1975.

——. *Review of Attorney General's Trip to Asia in Regard to the Narcotics Situation.* 97th Congress, 2nd Session. Washington: U.S. Government Printing Office, 1982.

U.S. Congress. House of Representatives. Select Committee on Narcotics Abuse and Control. *Southeast Asian Narcotics.* 95th Congress, 1st Session. Washington: U.S. Government Printing Office, 1978.

——. *The U.S. Heroin Problem and Southeast Asia.* 93rd Congress, 1st Session, Committee on Foreign Affairs. Washington: U.S. Government Printing Office, 1973.

——. *U.S. Aid Operations in Laos.* 86th Congress, 1st Session. Washington: U.S. Government Printing Office, 1959.

U.S. Department of the Army. *Minority Groups in Thailand: Ethnographic Study Series.* Washington: U.S. Government Printing Office, 1970.

U.S. Department of State, Bureau of International Narcotics Matters. *International Narcotics Control Strategy Report.* 1962–March 1987.

U.S. General Accounting Office. *If the U.S. is to Develop an Effective International Narcotics Control Program, Much More Must Be Done.* Washington: U.S. Government Printing Office, 1973.

Wolff, Lester. *The Narcotics Situation in Southeast Asia.* Washington: U.S. Government Printing Office, 1973.

ARTICLES

"America Targets the Asian Connection." *Asiaweek* (Hong Kong), March 22, 1985.

"Ask the CIA." *Asiaweek* (Hong Kong), November 18, 1977.

Bin, Lin. "Triad Heavies Don't Spare Snooker Cops." *The South China Morning Post* (Hong Kong), December 22, 1985.

——. "Triads Spread Their Wings Abroad." *The South China Morning Post* (Hong Kong), September 14, 1986.

Boucard, Louis and Andre. "On the Warlords Trail." *Far Eastern Economic Review* (Hong Kong), May 29, 1981.

Boyd, Alan. "In the Opium Den." *The South China Morning Post* (Hong Kong), March 13, 1987.

Browning, Frank, and Banning Garrett. "The New Opium War." *Ramparts,* Vol. 9, Issue 10, 1971.

Buruma, Ian, and John McBeth. "An East-side Story..." *Far Eastern Economic Review* (Hong Kong), December 27, 1984.

Butterfield, Fox. "Chinese Crime Network Reported Moving Into Areas of the U.S." *The New York Times,* November 30, 1986.

———. "Chinese Organized Crime Said to Rise in the U.S." *The New York Times,* January 13, 1985.

Cheung, Walter. "Influence of Triads 'Serious.'" *The South China Morning Post* (Hong Kong), June 10, 1985.

———. "Local Crime Syndicates Exuding Sophistication." *The South China Morning Post* (Hong Kong), September 24, 1986.

———. "Police 'Powerless' to Halt Triad Meets." *The South China Morning Post* (Hong Kong), April 16, 1986.

———. "Prisoner Triad Links 'Alarming.'" *The South China Morning Post* (Hong Kong), November 4, 1986.

Choi, Frank. "Tackle School Triad Problem." *The South China Morning Post* (Hong Kong), November 7, 1986.

———. "Triads 'Threat' to New Hawker Plan." *The South China Morning Post* (Hong Kong), October 9, 1985.

Chugani, Michael. "NY Aid Sought in Triad War." *The South China Morning Post* (Hong Kong), November 25, 1985.

"Cockpit of Anarchy." *Asiaweek* (Hong Kong), May 29, 1981.

Cohen, Paul T. "Opium and the Karen: A Study of Indebtedness in Northern Thailand." *Journal of Southeast Asian Studies,* Vol. 15, No. 1, March 1984.

Crossette, Barbara. "An Opium Warlord's News Conference Spurs Burma and Thailand to Battle Him." *The New York Times,* February 22, 1987.

———. "The War on Opium: More Than Just a Pipe Dream." *The New York Times,* October 18, 1984.

"DA Hits Chinese Connection." New York *Daily News,* January 29, 1987.

Daly, Michael. "The War for Chinatown." *New York* magazine, February 14, 1983.

Delaney, William P. "On Capturing an Opium King." *Society,* September/ October 1974.

Dessaint, Alain Y. "The Poppies Are Beautiful This Year." *Natural History,* Vol. LXXXI, No. 2, February 1972.

Dikkenberg, John. "Child Prostitution Racket Booming." *The South China Morning Post* (Hong Kong), July 6, 1986.

"Drug War Goes On." *Asiaweek* (Hong Kong), November 18, 1977.

Falco, Mathea. "The Big Business of Illicit Drugs." *The New York Times Magazine,* December 11, 1983.

Farnsworth, Clyde H. "'The Company' As Big Business." *The New York Times,* January 4, 1987.

Field, A., and P. A. Tararin. "Opium in China." *British Journal of Addiction,* Vol. 64, 1970.

Frank, Allan Dodds. "See No Evil." *Forbes,* October 6, 1986.

Gooi, Kim. "Getting Behind the Legend of Kuhn Sa, the Opium King." *New Straits Times* (Hong Kong), January 27, 1986.

Grandstaff, T. B. "The Hmong, Opium and the Haw: Speculations on the Origins of Their Association." *Journal of the Siam Society,* July 1979.

Hugh, A. Y. "Significance of Secret Societies in Chinese Life." *China Weekly Review,* September 10, 1927.

Ignatius, Adi. "Casino Boss Keeps Hong Kong Waiting." *The Asian Wall Street Journal* (Hong Kong), March 26, 1987.

Janssen, Peter. "Narcotics Trade Up for Grabs in Golden Triangle." *The Island* (Sri Lanka), November 25, 1986.

Johnson, Marguerite. "The Great Opium War." *Time,* March 1, 1982.

Kaplan, David E., Donald Goldberg, and Linda Jue. "Enter the Dragon." *San Francisco Focus,* December 1986.

Kaylor, Robert. "How Bustling Hong Kong Copes With Uncertainty." *U.S. News & World Report,* June 27, 1983.

Kerr, Peter. "Chasing the Heroin From Plush Hotel to Mean Streets." *The New York Times,* August 11, 1987.

———. "Chinese Now Dominate New York Heroin Trade." *The New York Times,* August 9, 1987.

———. "On the Heroin Battlefield, Half a World Away in Asia." *The New York Times,* August 10, 1987.

"KMT Affair." *Far Eastern Economic Review* (Hong Kong), July 9, 1973.

Kristof, Nicholas D. "Hong Kong Program: Addicts Without AIDS." *The New York Times,* June 17, 1987.

Landon, Kenneth. "The Politics of Opium in Thailand," in Luiz R. S. Simmons and Abdul Said, eds., *Drugs, Politics, and Diplomacy: The International Connection.* Beverly Hills: Sage Publications, 1974.

Leung, Matthew. "Tougher Fines to Curb Triads." *The South China Morning Post* (Hong Kong), January 23, 1987.

Leung, Stanley. "Triad Tactics in the DB Elections Feared." *The South China Morning Post* (Hong Kong), January 7, 1985.

Lewis, Tommy. "Massive Hunt for Kingpins." *Hong Kong Standard,* May 18, 1985.

——. "War Looms for Triad Rivals," *The South China Morning Post* (Hong Kong), January 23, 1987.

Light, Ivan. "From Vice District to Tourist Attraction: The Moral Career of American Chinatowns, 1800–1940." *Pacific Historical Review,* August 1974.

Lindsey, Robert. "Californian Sees Rise in Asian Gangs." *The New York Times,* July 9, 1987.

Lintner, Bertil. "Alliances of Convenience." *Far Eastern Economic Review* (Hong Kong), April 14, 1983.

Liu, Melinda. "The Triangle's Pecking Order." *Far Eastern Economic Review* (Hong Kong), September 14, 1979.

May, Clifford D., Holger Jensen, and Melinda Liu. "No More Refuge?" *Newsweek,* January 31, 1977.

McBeth, John. "A Heroin King Is Dethroned." *Far Eastern Economic Review* (Hong Kong), February 17, 1982.

——. "Drugs: The New Connections," *Far Eastern Economic Review* (Hong Kong), September 14, 1979.

——. "Heroin: The Vientiane Connection." *Far Eastern Economic Review* (Hong Kong), April 25, 1980.

——. "New Force in the Opium Trade." *Far Eastern Economic Review* (Hong Kong), July 25, 1980.

McCoy, Alfred W. "The New Politics of Heroin in Southeast Asia." *Oui,* December 1976.

Meyer, Michael R., and Melinda Liu. "The Gangs of Asia." *Newsweek,* April 1, 1985.

Nellis, Joseph L. "Lunch With an Opium Warlord." *Regardie's* (Washington, D.C.), January 1987.

"Next, a $35 Million Opium Deal." *Asiaweek* (Hong Kong), May 20, 1977.

"On the Asian Beat, Los Angeles." *Asiaweek* (Hong Kong), December 13, 1985.

Paul, Anthony. "Secrets of the Lost Army," *Asiaweek* (Hong Kong), September 4, 1981.

Pileggi, Nicholas. "Money Laundering: How Crooks Recycle $80 Billion a Year in Dirty Money." *New York* magazine, October 31, 1983.

Porter D. Gareth. "Saigon National Assembly Racked by Corruption and Smuggling." *Dispatch News Service International,* April 19, 1971.

"Prince of Darkness." *Asiaweek* (Hong Kong), February 8, 1987.

Pye, Lucian W. "The China Trade: Making the Deal." *Harvard Business Review,* July–August 1986.

Raab, Selwyn. "New York Sets Up Special Courts to Deal With Rise in Drug Cases." *The New York Times,* June 7, 1987.

Roberts, Sam. "A Chinatown Merchant Portrayed as Crime Boss." *The New York Times,* October 25, 1984.

Russell, George. "Battle of the Warlords." *Time,* January 17, 1983.

Saul, John Ralston. "The Route of Evil." *Asia Magazine* (Hong Kong), October 5, 1986.

Scardino, Albert. "Commercial Rents in Chinatown Soar as Hong Kong Exodus Grows." *The New York Times,* December 25, 1986.

Schram, Stuart R. "Mao Tse-tung and Secret Societies." *China Quarterly,* July–September 1966.

Schultheis, Rob. "My Search for the Red Tiger General." *Mother Jones Magazine,* February–March, 1982.

Solomon, Robert. "The Burmese Opiate Trade and the Struggle for Political Power in the Golden Triangle." *Journal of Psychedelic Drugs,* Vol. 10, No. 3, July–September 1978.

Sumondis, Pummarie. "Government Tightens the Screw on Drug Dealers." *Bangkok Post,* September 17, 1979.

Sun, James. "Mainland Gangs 'Infiltrating HK.'" *The South China Morning Post* (Hong Kong), July 1, 1986.

———. "More Police Drafted for Anti-Triad Fight." *The South China Morning Post* (Hong Kong), July 25, 1986.

Suwanewela, Charas, and Vichai Poshyachinda. "Drug Abuse in Asia." Drug Dependence Research Center of Bangkok, *Bulletin of Narcotics*, June 1986.

Tai, Corrina. "Triad Terminology Explained." *The South China Morning Post* (Hong Kong), September 10, 1986.

Tanser, Andrew. "Little Taipei." *Forbes*, May 6, 1985.

"Tidal Wave of Heroin." *Asiaweek* (Hong Kong), August 5, 1983.

"The Triads: How Great a Menace?" *Asiaweek* (Hong Kong), February 23, 1986.

"Triads—an Evil Right at the Heart of Society." *The South China Morning Post* (Hong Kong), April 18, 1986.

"Triads Making a Killing in Protection." *Hong Kong Standard*, January 11, 1985.

Tun, H. C. "Surprise Catch on the Border." *Far Eastern Economic Review* (Hong Kong), April 5, 1977.

Wai, S. Y. "Triads 'May Have Infiltrated Police.'" *The South China Morning Post* (Hong Kong), November 18, 1985.

"Warlord on the Run," *Asiaweek* (Hong Kong), February 19, 1982.

Whalen, Bill. "Drugs on the Market." *Insight*, March 30, 1987.

Wu, John. "The Chinese Connection." *Asian Outlook*, Vol. 8, Issue 2, 1973.

Zelfden, Alan Van. "Gangs Import Terror Campaigns to Asian Neighborhoods." *Dallas Times Herald*, March 9, 1987.

ARCHIVE SOURCES

The Asian Wall Street Journal, Hong Kong; *Asiaweek*, Hong Kong; *Bangkok Post*, Bangkok; British Library, London; Drug Enforcement Administration Library, Washington, D.C.; *Far Eastern Economic Review*, Hong Kong; *The Guardian*, Rangoon; Hoover Institution of War, Revolution and Peace, Stanford, California; Interpol, Paris, Amsterdam and Hong Kong; *The New York Times*, New York; Royal Hong Kong Police; San

Francisco Police Gang Task Force; *The South China Morning Post*, Hong Kong.

FREEDOM OF INFORMATION ACT

Requests were made to United States government agencies for documents relating to Triads, Tongs, or Chinese organized crime and/or heroin trafficking. Documents were received from: Central Intelligence Agency, Washington, D.C.; Defense Intelligence Agency, Washington, D.C.; Department of the Army, Washington, D.C.; Department of Justice, Criminal Division, Washington, D.C.; Department of State, Washington, D.C.; Department of the Treasury, Alcohol, Tobacco and Firearms Division, Washington, D.C.; Department of the Treasury, Customs Service, Washington, D.C.; Drug Enforcement Administration, Washington, D.C.; Federal Bureau of Investigation, Washington, D.C., and field offices in San Francisco, Los Angeles, New York, and Chicago; Federal Reserve Board, Washington, D.C.; Immigration and Naturalization Service, Washington, D.C.; Internal Revenue Service, Washington, D.C.; National Archives, Washington, D.C.

Index

Addiction, and addicts,
  characteristics of, 13–20, 29
Addicts, fighting drugs among,
  256
Afghanistan, 26
Agencies, anti-narcotic, 252–254,
  257
  (*See also* U.S. Drug
    Enforcement
    Administration and
    agents)
Agent Orange, 145, 146
Ah Kong Triad, 192, 194–195
AIDS, 20, 101, 134, 199, 257
Air America, 70, 71
Air Opium, 73
Alsop, Joe, 71
American Medical Association,
  (AMA), 13
Amsterdam, 154, 182–184,
  198–200, 233, 236
  cannabis cafes, 183–184
  Chinatown, 185–188, 192
  police, 183, 191–193
Anderson, Geoffrey, 228

Asian Task Force, Los Angeles,
  257
Atkinson, Leslie, ("Ike"), 143–144
Aung San, 85
Australia, 259, 260

Bahamas, 8, 222, 230
Ban Hin Taek, 90, 91, 94–96
Bangkok, 69, 74, 75, 78, 81, 92,
  93, 95, 101–103, 126, 127,
  131, 138, 139, 141, 143–145,
  148, 149, 162, 163, 168,
  200, 206, 224, 236, 248
  history and character of,
    133–135
Bangkok Narcotics Suppression
  Office, 131
Bangkok Post, 92
Bank of America, 232
Bank of Bangkok, 142
Bank of China, 37
Banks and banking, 8, 126, 142,
  144, 220, 221, 230, 252
  Chinese underground system
    234–235

Banks and banking (*Cont.*):
and computer analysis, 225, 227
(*See also* Money laundering)
Bansmere, Mike, 115–117, 119, 121–123, 129
Bax, Arie, 154, 195, 196, 199
Bayer company, 13
Benny (informant), 14–17, 29, 43–60, 168–174, 176, 177, 180, 182
Big Circle Gang, 43, 195
Black Eagles, 219
Black Masonic Club, 143
Blood Angle, New York Chinatown, 237
Body bag connection, 144
Boxers and Boxer Rebellion, 32
Brady, James, 260–261
British drug trafficking, 62–64
Brokerage houses and money laundering, 234
Bulldog cafe (Amsterdam), 182–184
Burma, 8, 22, 63, 65–67, 70–73, 75–77, 83–97, 104–110, 114, 118–119, 122, 128, 137, 143, 145–148
(*See also entries beginning with the word* Shan)
Burmese Communist party, 86, 91, 95

California, 202–220, 244, 247, 253, 259–260
and anti-Chinese laws, 207
and money laundering, 226–230, 232
(*See also* Los Angeles; San Francisco and money laundering)
Cambodia, 63, 65
Canada, 244–246, 253, 259, 260

Canada–Asia Finance Group of North America, 221, 223
Cannabis cafes, Amsterdam, 183–184
Canton Disco, Hong Kong, 28–29, 44–60, 109, 182
Capone, Al, 33
Carone, Joe, 253
Carter, Jimmy, 100
Casinos and money laundering, 233–234
Castro, Fidel, 174, 260
Center for Disease Control, 20
Chan, Eddie, 179, 238–244, 247
Chan, Jackie, 246
Chan (guide), 83, 98, 100–103, 105–106, 108, 110, 115, 116, 119, 121, 122
Chan Tse-Chiu ("Fast Eddie"), 179, 238–244, 247
Chan Wai-man, 176
Chan Yuen-muk, 193–194
Chang Chi-Fu, 87, 93
(*See also* Kuhn Sa)
Chang Tse-chuan, 90, 94
Chase Manhattan Bank, 232
Chasing the dragon, 256
Chavolit Yodmanee, 146
Chemical Bank, 232
Chen Chi-Li ("Dry Duck"), 215
Cheng Ah Kai, 162
Chiang Ching-kuo, 160, 215
Chiang Inn, 115–116
Chiang Kai-shek, 32–34, 36, 40, 41, 71–72, 156, 160, 207, 211, 215
Chiang Kai-shek, Madame, 71
Chiang Mai, 78–82, 92, 93, 96, 97, 105–106, 110–112, 114, 116, 117, 120, 126, 128–130, 145, 149, 163, 237, 250
Chiang Rai, 83, 100–102, 115, 116, 118–121, 149

Chicken coop, 101–102, 119, 120
Child pornography, 155
Chin, Peter, 245
China Lobby, 71–72
China White, 10, 26, 70, 82, 158,
    168, 182, 187, 201, 252,
    254, 256
Chinatowns, 169, 196, 207–208,
    210–212, 215, 257–258
    (*See also* Amsterdam,
        Chinatown; New York
        Chinatown; San Francisco
        Chinatown; Tongs)
Chinese connection, 200–201,
    250
Chinese Crime Task Force,
    236
Chinese Exclusion Act, 206–207
Chinese Freemasons Tong, 214,
    241–242, 245
Chinese narcotics traffickers,
    113, 116–118, 137–139,
    141–142, 149, 184, 185,
    218–219, 250, 251
    (*See also* Triads)
Chinese Nationalists (*see*
    Kuomintang; Taiwan)
Chinese people, culture,
    traditions, and history,
    xvi-xviii, 50, 169, 177, 208
Chinese secret societies (*see*
    Triads)
Chinese underground banking
    system, 234–235
Chiu Chau, 37, 40, 42, 156, 195
Cholon Triad, 69, 70
Chung Mon (*see* Unicorn, the)
CIA, 10, 85, 87, 107, 110, 115,
    132, 146, 234, 255
    and support of narcotics trade,
        8, 20, 67–77, 88, 91n.
Civil Air Transport, 71
Cline, Ray, 71

Cocaine, xv, 9, 21, 81, 184,
    216–219, 221–222, 228, 245,
    250, 251, 256
Codeine, 12, 13
Colombia and Colombians, 6,
    218–219, 250, 251
Columbus, Christopher, 61
Commodity companies and
    money laundering, 233–234
Computer analysis in banking,
    225, 227
Conspiracy statutes, 255
Corsicans, xv, 6, 8, 25, 68–69,
    73, 138, 139, 159
Cosa Nostra, La (*see* Mafia)
Counterfeiting, 171, 173
Couriers, drug, 139–140, 144,
    149, 154, 155, 166–167, 172,
    176, 185, 190–192, 198, 222
Coward, Noel, 135
Crack, 256
Crocker Bank, 232
Crop substitution, 145, 254–255
Cuba, 174, 260

D-24, 145–146
DEA (*see* Drug Enforcement
    Administration and agents)
Diem, Ngo Dinh, 69
Dien Bien Phu, 68, 70
Dirzulaitis, Michael, 229
Dominican Republic, 8, 222, 230,
    233
Dragons and Dragon Heads,
    179, 193, 215, 239–247
    Ma brothers, 156–168
    New York Chinatown,
        239–243
    young turks, 238, 244–247
Drug Enforcement
    Administration (*see* U.S.
    Drug Enforcement
    Administration and agents)

Dry Duck, *(see* Chen Chi-Li)
Dunning corporations and
    money laundering, 230–231
Dutch, the *(see* Netherlands, the)
Dyer, Fran, 221–225

East India Company, London,
    62
Eight Trigrams Sect, 32
Elder, Jon, 226–227, 261
Eradication of crops, 145–147,
    248, 254, 257
European Economic Community,
    198
Extradition treaties, 255

Fast Eddie *(see* Chan, Tse-Chiu)
FBI, 10, 71, 102, 132, 215, 246,
    252, 254, 259, 260
    report on organized Chinese
        crime, 213–214
Federal agencies, anti-narcotic,
    252–254
    (See also U.S. Drug Enforce-
        ment Administration and
        agents)
Federal Reserve system, 228, 230
Ferraro, Geraldine, 240
First National Bank of Boston,
    232
Fists of Harmony and Justice,
    32
Five Dragons Corporation,
    178–182, 194, 215, 238–240,
    248
Flower power, 184
Flying Dragons, 214, 239, 242
Foochow monastery, 29–30
Fort Bragg, 144
14K Triad, 5, 37–41, 43, 70,
    138, 156, 159, 173, 176,
    178, 188–195, 214, 240, 246,
    259

Freemasons Tong, 214, 241–242,
    245
French connection, the, xv, 25,
    191
French Indochina, 63–64, 67–69,
    71, 76
Frogmen, 219
Fu family, 175
Fung Sui-may, 176
Furama Hotel, Hong Kong, 175

Gambling, 68, 169–170, 177,
    188, 190, 194, 200, 208,
    209, 212, 214, 228–230, 256
    and money laundering, 233
    (See also Macao)
Ghost Shadows, 214, 239–241,
    245, 255
Godber, Peter, 178
Godfather, The, 251
Godfathers, New York
    Chinatown, 239–245
Golden Blow Guide, 184
Golden Crescent, 26
Golden Dragon (San Francisco),
    202–205, 214
Golden Ma, 158
    (See also Ma Sik-chun)
Golden Star (New York
    Chinatown), 242
Golden Triangle, xvi, 8, 9,
    22–26, 40, 42, 67–73, 77–97,
    100, 102–129, 133, 135, 137,
    140, 143, 147–149, 156, 157,
    162, 163, 165–166, 168, 177,
    182, 191, 198, 215, 216,
    248, 249, 254–255, 257
    chemists and laboratories *(see*
        Heroin)
    routes out of, 148
    (See also Burma; Laos;
        Thailand)
Grand Caymans, banks in, 144

Green Gang Triad, 33–34, 36–39
Group 41, 236–237

Hagler, Marvin, 131, 132
Hague, The, 194, 195, 198, 200
Hall of Mirrors, Saigon, 68
Hashish, 183–184
Hatchet boys, 210
Hatchet wars, 211
Havana casinos, 174
Herbicides, 145–147
Heroin, xv–xvi, xviii, 5, 7–11,
    60, 184–187, 191, 251–252
  addiction among American
      servicemen, 70, 76, 87, 89,
      91n., 143–144, 187, 196,
      199
  chemists, laboratories, and
      refineries, 24–26, 37, 70,
      72–73, 107–110, 112–114,
      125, 147–149, 159,
      162–163, 165–166, 168,
      197, 199–200
  and CIA, 8, 20, 67–77, 88, 91n.
  discovery and early history,
      12–13
  establishment in Hong Kong,
      38–40, 43, 55
  in Europe, 183–201, 259
  and European colonial
      empires, 61–66, 77
  fight against, prospects,
      248–261
  numbers 3 and 4, 25–26, 70,
      199–200
  production of, 21–26
  servicemen dealing in, 143–145
  shooting gallery, 17–20
  in U.S., 20–21, 60, 71–72, 191,
      193, 199–201, 226, 248,
      251–252
    California, 202–220, 244,
        247

Heroin: in U.S. (*Cont.*):
    New York, 17–20, 208–210,
        212, 214, 236–245
Hill, Barry, 253
Hip Sing Tong, 202–205, 212,
    214, 239–243, 245
Hippocrates, 12
Ho, Stanley, 175–177, 182, 233
Ho Chi Minh, 67
Holland (*see* Netherlands, the)
Hong Kong, xvi, xviii, 6, 8, 10,
    31, 75, 93, 108, 124, 135,
    140, 148, 155–156, 169, 181,
    193, 199, 206, 212, 213,
    250, 256–259
  banking system, 227
  Canton Disco, 28–29, 44–60,
      109, 182
  and counterfeiting, 171, 173
  customs service, 163–168, 182,
      197
  Dragons and Dragon Heads,
      156–168
  financial center, xvii, 27–29,
      226, 252
  Golden Mile, 44
  as a hub, 163–168, 182, 197
  jewelry store robbery, 1–7
  Ladder Street, 14–18, 20, 29,
      182
  Ma brothers, 156–163, 168,
      179–180, 182
  and money laundering,
      221–235
  and Opium War, 63
  and People's Republic,
      27–28
  police corruption, 177–182
  and reversion to mainland
      China, xvi, 6, 27–28, 153,
      170, 201, 219–220,
      225–226, 229–230, 235,
      237, 247, 258–261

Hong Kong (*Cont.*):
   Triads in (*see* Triads, Hong
      Kong, control in)
   Walled City, xvi, 150–156, 182
   World War II and after,
      35–43, 152
Hong Kong–Shanghai Bank, 232
Hoover, J. Edgar, 71
Hop Sing Tong, 213, 216
"Hot dog" Michael Louie, 203–205
Hu, (guide), 83, 98, 100–108,
   110, 115, 116, 119, 121, 122
Hung Mun, 54, 214

ICAC (*see* Independent
   Commission Against
   Corruption)
Immigration and Naturalization,
   229, 254
Immigration laws, American,
   anti-Chinese, 206–207
Import–export companies and
   money laundering, 234
Independent Commission
   Against Corruption (ICAC),
   178–180
India, 148
Indonesia, 148
International Herald Tribune, 221
International law enforcement,
   255, 257
Interpol, 159, 160, 184,
   195–198, 200, 248, 249
Investment houses and money
   laundering, 234
Iran, 26
IRS undercover agents, 225,
   227, 229, 252, 254, 255
Irving Trust, 232

J.J. (informant), 17–20
Jack's American Style Bar
   (Bangkok), 143–144

Japan, 159
Jew, Vincent, 244–247
Joe Boys, 203–205
Joint Declaration, 27
   (*See also* 1997 deadline)

Ka Kwei Yei (KKY), 86–88, 93, 95
Karin United Revolutionary
   Army, 85
King Lung Commodities
   Limited, 233, 241
Kipling, Rudyard, 211
KKY (*see* Ka Kwei Yei)
Klink, Rollin, 228
KMT (*see* Kuomintang)
Knowland, William, 71
Kolaslu, Thomas, 260
Kon, Yu-leung ("Johnny"), xviii
Kuhn Sa, 87–97, 104, 105, 107,
   109, 110, 112–113, 121, 122,
   124, 130, 162, 248, 255
Kung fu, 30, 46, 176
Kung Lok Triad, 244
   (*See also* Luen Kung Lok Triad)
Kuomintang (KMT), 33–34, 40,
   71–73, 76, 77, 81, 85–89,
   91, 96, 97, 109, 110, 113,
   156–157, 163, 191, 207, 211,
   215, 216, 255
Kwong, Benny, 28
Kwong Luen Shing Triad, 228

Ladder Street (Hong Kong),
   14–18, 20, 29, 182
Lansdale, Colonel, 69
Lansky, Meyer, 159
Laos, 8, 21, 22, 63, 65, 68–70,
   73–74, 76, 77, 88, 90, 96,
   115, 137, 148
Lau Wing-kuei, 175, 244
Law enforcement, 256–261
   and cooperation with Hong
      Kong police, 258–259

Lee, Aaron, 221, 223, 224
Lee, Charlie, 176
Lee, Tony, 227–228, 258
Lee Wai Man, 228–229
Leonard, Sugar Ray, 131, 132
Li, General, 71–73, 75, 76, 81,
    85, 87–89, 91, 96, 97, 113,
    121, 156–157, 191, 248, 255
Li Choi Fat, 38–39
Li Ka-shing, 176
"Limpy," (see Ng Sik-ho)
Lisboa Casino, Macao, 174–177
Liu, Henry, 33n., 215, 216
Liu, Herbert, 241–243, 245
Liu Chong Hing Bank, 223–225
Lo Hsing-Han, 87, 89–91, 93,
    95–97
Lo Hsing-Min, 87, 89
Loan sharking, 55, 172, 173,
    176, 190, 200, 208, 230
London as transit center, 197
Los Angeles, 210, 211, 213, 245,
    253, 259
  Asian Task Force, 257
Louie, Michael ("Hot Dog"),
    203–205
Louie, Nicky, 214, 240, 245, 255
Lu Hsu-shui, 126
Lucas, Frank, 222
Luce, Henry, 71
Luen Kung Lok Triad, 214, 244,
    245, 259
Lui Lok, 178, 180, 182, 194, 239
Lung Tin, 244–245

Ma Sik-chun, 156–163, 180, 188,
    194
Ma Sik-yu (White Powder Ma),
    155–163, 168, 179–180, 182,
    188, 191, 194, 215, 241, 248
Ma Woon-yin, 157–158, 160, 180
Macao, 49, 157, 158, 167,
    169–177, 233

Macao Tourism and
    Entertainment Company,
    175–176
Macao Trotting, 176
McKenna, John, 203, 213, 246,
    253, 260
McVeety, John, 253
Madonna, 46
Mae Sai, 125–126
Mafia, xvi, 6, 9, 10, 33, 37, 40,
    42, 43, 50, 58, 59, 139, 178,
    190, 217, 251, 257, 260, 261
Mak, K. L., 163–168, 197
Malaysia, 148, 243
Man, Peter, 244, 245
Manchus, 29–32, 206
Manes, Donald, 240
Manufacturer's Hanover Bank,
    232
Mao Tse-tung, 32, 36, 66, 71,
    72, 193
  Cultural Revolution, 43
Marielitos, 260
Marijuana, 183–184, 245, 251
Marseilles (see French
    connection, the)
Maugham, W. Somerset,
    135
Mazzini, Giuseppe, 50
Meo hill tribes, 68
Merritt, Brian, 227
Methadone, 256
Mexico and Mexicans, 10, 113,
    118, 145, 249, 250
Miami Herald, 221
Mo, Danny, 241–245
Money laundering, 8–9, 57, 60,
    108, 176, 180, 221–235, 241,
    252
  and banks in U.S., 226–228,
    230–233, 241
  and Chinese underground
    banking system, 234–235

Money laundering (*Cont.*):
and dunning corporations,
230–231
Monroe, Marilyn, 99
Monterey Park, California, 226,
244, 260, 261
Morphine, 12, 13, 24–25, 63–64,
108
Myrick, Jasper, 141–145

Nat Sa'Kui, 107
National Chinese Welfare
Council, 240
National Intelligence Council,
234
National Security Agency, 234
National United Front for the
Liberation of Vietnam, 219
NATO, 196
Ne Win, 85, 86, 88, 93
Netherlands, the (Dutch), 154,
183–201, 255, 259, 260
anti-narcotic laws and
enforcement, 184–186,
189–190, 192, 200–201
approach to drugs, 183–184,
200–201
and business climate, 199
customs service, 198–199
14K Triad in, 188–195
heroin laboratories, 199–200
immigration laws, 186
prisons, 186, 192
Triad European base, 186–188
(*See also* Amsterdam;
Rotterdam)
New World Group, 175
New York Chinatown, 8, 117,
179, 208–210, 212, 214, 236,
238–245
godfathers in, 239–245
money flood and commercial
rents, 229–230

New York Chinatown (*Cont.*):
and money laundering, 230
and police, 240–241
New York City, Division of Real
Property for, 229
New York criminal justice
system, 256
New York Times, The, 10, 75
Ng Sik-ho ("Limpy"), 156, 159,
162, 188
Nguyen Cao Ky, 69, 219
1997 deadline, xvi, 6, 27–28,
153, 170, 201, 219–220,
225–226, 229–230, 235, 237,
247, 258–261
Nixon, Richard M., 20–21, 60,
71–72, 191, 257
Nussbaum, Michael, 240

On Leong Tong, 212, 214,
239–243
Ong, Benny, 239–243, 245
Ong, Sam, 239
Operation X, 67–68, 76
Opium, 8, 9, 12–17, 20–24, 26,
29, 31, 34–36, 40, 60, 137,
149, 153, 163, 182, 184,
188, 191, 208–210, 248,
254–255
eradication, 145–147, 248,
254, 257
and European colonial
empires, 61–66, 76, 77,
208
after World War II, 67–77
(*See also* Chiang Mai; Golden
Triangle: Heroin)
Opium Wars, 62–63, 88–89,
95–97, 152
Order of the White Elephant
(Thailand), 126
Organized Crime Task Force,
228, 243, 260

Oriental Daily News, 157, 161
Overseas Chinese Association,
188, 190

Pakistan, 26
Panamanian freighters, 160, 162
Paris, 236–237
People's Republic of China, 95
and Hong Kong, 27–28
(See also 1997 deadline)
Pep, 115, 117, 119, 121, 123
Phao Sriyanonda, 75
Phoumi Nosavan, 74
Ping On gang, 244
Ping Pai Shing, 244–245
Pink Knights, 219
Pockmarked Huang, 34
Poppies *(see* Opium)
Pornography, 173
child, 155
Powers, Joyce, 92, 112
Powers, Mike, 92, 112
Prem, Prime Minister, 94
President's Commission on
Organized Crime, 242–243,
246–247
Prostitution, 34, 55, 68, 80,
99–102, 119–120, 134, 139,
144, 153–155, 173, 188, 200,
208, 209, 212, 230, 256

Rangoon, 84–87, 90, 93, 95–97,
105, 110, 146–147
Rats' Piss (street), 151–152
Rattikone, Ouane, 88–89
Reagan, Ronald (Reagan
administration), 21, 94
Real estate, New York City,
229–230
Red Gang, 32, 34, 36
Red Guards, 42–43
Red Pole, 29*n.*, 44–60, 182
Red Turban Uprisings, 31

Refineries *(see* Heroin, chemists,
laboratories, and refineries)
Rehabilitation programs, 256
Richard (undercover DEA
agent), 236–237
RICO statute, 255
Ricord, Auguste Joseph, xv, 159
Roosevelt, Franklin D., 207
Rotterdam, 140, 167, 186–187,
189, 192–194, 198–199
Royal Canadian Mounted Police
(RCMP), 246
Royal Hong Kong Customs and
Excise Service, 163, 166
Royal Hong Kong Jockey Club,
157, 228
Royal Hong Kong Police, 5, 14,
36, 40, 59, 60, 138, 159,
172, 227–228, 234, 244–246
and corruption, 178–182

Saigon, 68–70, 73, 138
Saigon Cowboys, 159
San Aung, 85
San Francisco and money
laundering, 229, 230, 232
San Francisco Chinatown,
202–206, 208, 210, 212,
216–220, 245–247, 260
and opium, 208, 209
street gangs, 202–206, 210,
214
Tongs, 207
tourists, 212
Savani, Antoine, 69
SDECE (French intelligence),
67–69
Sea Supply, Inc., 71
Secret societies, Chinese *(see*
Triads)
Security companies and money
laundering, 233
Sergeant Smack, 143–144

Servicemen, American: heroin
   addicts, 70, 76, 87, 89, 91n.,
   143–144, 187, 196, 199
   heroin dealers, 143–145
Seymour–Johnson Air Force
   Base, 144
Shan Revolutionary Army, 85
Shan State Volunteer Force,
   93
Shan States, 65–66, 71–73,
   83–97, 105–109
Shan United Army (SUA), 87,
   88, 90, 91, 93–96, 105–107,
   109, 110, 113, 122, 124, 255
Shanghai, 34, 64, 66
Sheer, Tom, 260
Shoaf, George, 112
Shoaf, Sheryl, 112
Shui Fong Triad, 259
Singapore, 159, 192, 194, 233
Smedley, James Warren, 144
Smuggling methods, 139–141,
   144, 165–168, 198–199
So Kwong Shing, 223–224
Soong, Charlie, 32, 71, 207
Southeast Asia, 8–10, 21, 64–66,
   75–77, 159, 162, 197, 199,
   226, 241, 249–253, 259
   (See also Golden Triangle;
      specific countries and cities)
Spectrum computer analysis, 225
Spraying with herbicides, 145–147
State law-enforcement agencies,
   253
STDM, 175–176
Stuttman, Robert, 251–252
SUA (see Shan United Army)
Suey Sing Tong, 213
Sukree Sukreepirom, 136–137
Sun Yat-sen, 32
Sun Yee On Triad, 29, 43, 45,
   147, 156, 159, 195, 259
Swiss banks, 144, 226

Tachilek, 89
Tai Lo, 178
Taiping Rebellion, 31, 206
Taiwan, 33n., 41–43, 71–73, 86,
   87, 89, 156–157, 160–163,
   176, 179–180, 188, 215–216,
   219, 224, 229, 239, 243,
   244, 248, 255
Tang Sang, 179
Thai Border Police, 94, 125,
   128, 130
Thai people, character of, 135
Thailand, 8, 22, 63, 65, 66, 69,
   70, 72–83, 90–97, 100–105,
   108–130, 155, 156, 160, 162,
   165, 167, 168, 182, 189,
   198, 237–238, 249
   Chinese in, 138–139, 141–142
   GI dealers in, 143–145
   heroin refineries, 147–148
   institutionalized corruption,
      125–126
   laws and narcotics traffickers,
      121–128, 147
   Mae Sai, 125–126
   prostitution, 80, 99–102,
      119–120, 134, 139, 144
   provincial police, 102, 125–127
   transit country for narcotics,
      143–145, 147–149
   (See also Bangkok; Chiang Mai;
      Chiang Rai; Viraj
      Juttimita)
Thailand Narcotics Control
   Board, 146
Thunder Tigers, 219
Time magazine, 71
Tin Lung, 244–245
Ting, Lee Yoo, 244–245
Tongs, 207–220, 239–248, 250
   commission, ruling council, 217
   initiation ceremonies, 213, 218
   and Triads, 213–214, 218

Tongs (*Cont.*):
  and Vietnamese gangs, 219
  wars, 211, 214, 239, 242, 245
Toorenaar, Gerard, 191–192
Toronto, 245, 246, 253
Trafficante, Santo Jro, 159
Travel agencies and money
  laundering, 235
Travis Air Force Base, 144
Triad Society Bureau, 41
Triads, xvi, xviii, 5–8, 66–68, 71,
    72, 108, 143, 206, 225, 236,
    237
  Big Circle Gang, 43, 195
  Boxers, 32
  and Chiang Kai-shek, 33–34,
    36, 40–41
    (*See also* Kuomintang;
    Taiwan)
  Chiu Chau, 37, 40, 42, 156, 195
  Cholon, 69, 70
  computerization, 173, 182
  criminalization, 31–43
  in Europe, 90, 194–195
    (*See also* Netherlands, the)
  executions and executioners,
    45–46
  founding, meaning, history,
    and organization of, 29,
    45, 47, 49–53
  14K, 5, 37–41, 43, 70, 138, 156,
    159, 173, 176, 178, 188–
    195, 214, 240, 246, 259
  Green Gang, 33–34, 36–39
  high-tech, 173–174, 182
  Hong Kong, control in, 35–44,
    55–61, 69, 73–74, 82, 90,
    110, 130, 137–139,
    147–149, 162–163,
    169–182, 188–191, 194,
    240, 242, 244–247
  and police, 35–36, 38–41,
    43, 55, 169, 177–182

Triads (*Cont.*):
  initiation, oaths, ceremonies,
    and rituals in, 30, 48–53,
    118, 170
  and KMT (*see* Kuomintang)
  Kung Lik, 214
  Kung Lok, 244
  Kwong Luen Shing, 228
  and legitimate business, 43,
    54–55, 157–158, 162, 173,
    188, 193, 240–242
  Luen Kung Lok, 244, 245, 259
  Macao, 169, 170, 172–173
  and Manchus, 29–32
  membership, selection and
    probation, 54–55
  and money laundering,
    221–235
  and Nationalist Chinese (*see*
    Kuomintang; Taiwan)
  officials, character of, 59–60
  and protection money, 171–173
  Red Gang, 32, 34, 36
  Saigon, Vietnam, 69, 70,
    76–77
  and shipping invoices, 165,
    166
  Shui Fong, 259
  and Sun Yat-sen's republic,
    32–33
  Sun Yee On, 29, 43, 45, 147,
    156, 159, 195, 259
  and Taiwan (*see* Taiwan)
  Thailand, Bangkok, 74–75, 77,
    81, 91
  United Bamboo, 33*n.*, 41–43,
    215–216, 239, 244,
    259–260
  in the U.S., 57, 60, 90, 159,
    162, 168, 202–220,
    225–227, 237–247
  war against, prospects,
    248–261

Triads (*Cont.*):
  Wo syndicate, 37–39, 43, 159,
    192, 195, 214, 240, 259
  Yee Kwan, 156
  (*See also* Hong Kong; Tongs)
Truman, Harry, 71
Trump Tower, 231
Tse, Stephen, 117, 189–190, 245
Tse, William, 245
Tu, Yueh Sheng ("Big-eared
  Tu"), 33–34, 36–38
Tuan, General, 72, 73, 85
Turano, Anthony, 159
Turkey, 21, 70, 191, 249, 259

U Nu, 85
"Uncle 7," 239, 242, 243
Unicorn, the (Chung Mon),
  188–195, 199–201, 248
United Bamboo Triad, 33n.,
  41–43, 215–216, 239, 244,
  259–260
United Nations, 248–249
United Orient Bank, 241, 242
United Press International, 92
U.S. Attorney's Office in New
  York City, 245
U.S. Customs Service, 229, 252,
  254
U.S. Department of Justice, 260
U.S. Drug Enforcement
  Administration (DEA) and
  agents, xviii, 8, 10, 60, 78,
  79, 81, 83, 92, 93, 97, 102,
  107, 144, 145, 147, 148,
  159–160, 163–166, 176, 181,
  182, 185, 189–190, 194–195,
  198–199, 229, 234, 235–237,
  241–243, 247, 249–252, 256,
  261
  Chinese Crime Task Force,
    236
  and Congress, 250–251, 254

U.S. Drug enforcement
  Administration (DEA) and
  agents (*Cont.*):
  foreign offices and efforts,
    249–250
  Mexico, 249
  and press relations, 250
  promotion system, 250
  Thailand, 110–130, 132, 135,
    237–238, 249
United States Organized Crime
  Strike Force, 229
U.S. State Department, 93, 110,
  127, 147
U.S. Strategic Materials
  Stockpile, 13n.
U.S. Treasury Department, 226,
  228, 232

Vancouver, 221, 223, 233
Van de Kamp, John, 253, 259,
  260
Viet Ching, 218
Vietnam, 20, 25, 63–65, 67–71,
  76, 87, 89, 90, 91n., 115,
  137, 138, 143, 148, 159,
  191, 196, 199
  and GI heroin addicts, 70, 76,
    87, 89, 91n., 142–143,
    186, 195, 198
Vietnamese gangs in U.S.,
  219
Viraj Juttimita, 92, 95, 96,
  131–149, 163
  birth and training, 131–133
  honesty and dangerous life,
    135–137

Wa National Army, 85, 91, 95,
  110
Wah Ching boys, 202–205,
  244–246
Wall Street Journal, The, 221

Walled City, Hong Kong, xvi,
    150–156, 182
Wan A Ti, 123–124
Weijenburg, Richard, 187, 195,
    197–198
Weld, William, 260
Weng, Hsi-Ling, 215
West Germany, 259, 260
White Powder Ma, 157–163,
    168, 179–180, 182, 188, 191,
    194, 215, 241, 248
White Tigers, 214
Whitehead, Darryl, 221–225
Wipon, Captain, 128–231,
    237–238
Wo On Lok Triad, 214
Wo Shing Wo Triad, 70, 159,
    214
Wo Syndicate, 37–39, 43, 159,
    192, 195, 214, 240, 259

Wolff, Lester, 92
Wong, Kot Siu, 39
Worobec, Steve, 114
Wright, C. R., 12–13

Yakuza, 159
Yamaguchi, Mike, 216–220, 225,
    226
Yarbrough, Ben, 110–131, 145,
    147, 189–190, 249
Year of the Dragon, The (film),
    246
Yee Kwan Triad, 156
Ying On Tong, 213
Yip Hon, 175–176
Young, Tony, 244, 245
Young Turks, 159
Yu, "Crazy" Melvin, 204–205

Zwart, Koos, 184